A WOMAN'S WORK: CHIARA LUBICH

A WOMAN'S WORK:
CHIARA LUBICH

JIM GALLAGHER

New City Press

Published in the United States by New City Press
202 Cardinal Rd., Hyde Park, NY 12538
©1997 Jim Gallagher

Originally published in English by
HarperCollinsPublishers Ltd. under the title:
A WOMAN'S WORK: CHIARA LUBICH;
A Biography of the Focolare Movement and Its Founder

Cover design by Miguel Tejerina

Library of Congress Cataloging-in-Publication Data:
A catalog record for this book is available
from the Library of Congress.
ISBN 1-56548-099-6

1st printing: April 1997
3d printing: February 2003

Printed in the United States of America

To Anne-Marie, Maureen and Nicky.
And, of course, Chiara.

CONTENTS

LIST OF ILLUSTRATIONS

Plate 1
Above right: Baby Silvia Lubich. Born in Trent in January 1920, she would come to be known to popes and bishops, princes and kings, ordinary men and women the world over, simply as 'Chiara'.
Above left: Chiara on the right with elder brother Gino and younger sister Carla.
Below: Chiara with her parents in their native Dolomites near Trent.

Plate 2
Above left: This medieval image of Mary, with her mantle covering all vocations, inspired Chiara in the development of the Work of Mary.
Above right: The young schoolteacher with some of her charges at the Capuchin Primary School, where she taught from 1940 to 1943.
Below: A district of Trent after the bombing of 13 May 1944.

Plate 3
Above: Two Foundresses, Chiara and Mother Teresa.
Below: Receiving the Templeton Prize from HRH the Duke of Edinburgh.

Plate 4
Above: With Patriarch Athenagoras of Constantinople. 'You have two spiritual fathers,' he told her. 'One in Rome, and a second one here.' He considered himself a Focolarino.
Below: The Archbishop of Canterbury, Dr Robert Runcie, welcomes Chiara to Lambeth Palace. She is accompanied by interpreter and fellow Focolarino, Dr Dimitri Bregant.

Plate 5
Above: Public life – Chiara salutes a 'Genfest' Focolare Youth Gathering in a sports stadium in Rome.
Below: Getting to grips with the lawn around the house left to her in Switzerland in 1978. This photo was taken in September 1979 and Chiara has spent some of the summer in the pure air of the Alps every year since then. As with every aspect of the Movement, Chiara does not just sit at her desk and direct operations – she rolls up her sleeves and gets down to work wherever it needs to be done.

Plate 6
Chiara was first received by Pope John Paul II just days after his election in October 1978. His esteem for Chiara is evident here, during a warm embrace in front of hundreds of thousands in St Peter's Square, Rome.

Plate 7
Above: Chiara exchanges a word with England's Cardinal Basil Hume outside the Synod Hall in 1995.
Middle: Pope John Paul listens attentively as Chiara addresses the extraordinary world Synod of Bishops on the Laity.
Below: This Buddhist monk said Chiara was his 'spiritual mother' and asked her to give him a new name. She called him 'Luce Ardente', Burning Light.

Plate 8
Above: Celebrating 50 years of the Focolare, Chiara is surrounded by some of her 'first companions'. (Standing centre right is Father Pasquale Foresi, whom Chiara describes as 'co-founder'. Kneeling, bottom right, with checked suit, is Dori Zamboni, whom Chiara tutored to pass her university entry exams. Standing, second row, left, between two priests, is Natalia Dallapiccola, the first to follow Chiara's footsteps in a vow of total consecration to God. Second row, far left, is Giulia Folonari, Chiara's secretary. Immediately behind her is Enzo Fondi, who inherited the land on which the Centre of the Work was built at Rocca di Papa. With Natalia Dallapiccola, he is responsible for the Movement's relations with members of other religions.)

Below left: Chiara and the author in her office at the Centre of the Work at Rocca di Papa.
Below right: A modern sculpture entitled 'Mary Mother of the Church' at the chapel of the Focolare Centre at Castelgandolfo. The centre is in the grounds of the Papal summer residence.

ACKNOWLEDGEMENTS

I acknowledge the work of all those who have already written of Chiara and the Focolare. In particular, I would like to thank the following who gave generously of their time, and all those who helped in any way: Enzo Fondi; Giulia Folonari; Marguerite de Marie; Mari Ponticaccio; Murray White, my editor; Dr Anna Fratta; Michel Pochet; Fr Tom Norris; Pontifical University of Maynooth; Cardinal Eduardo Pironio; Cardinal Francis Arinze; Archbishop John Foley; Brother Roger of Taizé; Dimitri Bregant; Veronica Towers; Sally McArdle; Patrycja Milkulska; Maureen and Mike Doughty; Vera Al-Mutawa; Mr and Mrs S. P. Colonetti; Natalia Dallapiccola; Graziella de Luca; Giuseppe Zanghi; Anne Devine; Nadine de Kerchove; Don Silvano Cola; Giorgio Marchetti; Don Antonio; Sister Loretto Maes; Mr and Mrs D. Zanzucchi; Tomasso Sorgi; Claretta and Arnaldo; Cecile d'Ermitanis; Nunzi Cilento and team at Mariapolis Castelgandolfo; Centre for Unity, Welwyn Garden City; Palmira Frizzera, Helmut Sievers and everyone at Mariapolis Foco, Montet; Kim and Mary Frances of the St Clare Media Centre; New City Publishing, Rome, for photographs.

PREFACE

Time Management
– or Strategy of the Present Moment?

A behind-the-scenes look at the gruelling schedule of the head of a multi-national organization

Monday

5 a.m. Work on talks and speeches until 7 a.m. This morning prepare acceptance speech for the reception of Honorary Doctorate being awarded next month. Likewise for the Freedom of City which will be granted next week.

7.30. Breakfast. Big decision: which jam to choose today from the array of little jars laid before me? An English colleague always brings me these as a gift.

7.55. Leave for the office. Short walk through garden of my house, and I reach our international HQ. The last stretch is now a covered walkway, so I can reach the office privately.

8.00. Enter HQ building and take lift to my top-floor office suite. Staff are waiting to run through the diary of the day.

8.05. New paintings arrive for the walls of the adjoining sitting-room where I receive visitors. I don't like always having the same decor, so we frequently change paintings, light-shades etc., or I'll throw drapes over the sofas to change colour and style.

8.10. Begin to tackle the mountain of mail. I like to read every letter addressed to me. If I can't answer them all personally, I at least write a remark on them to indicate to my secretary what she should write for me. Then I'll sign them later.

8.20. Interrupted by an SOS from Algeria. Following the murder of seven Trappist monks by Islamic fundamentalists, they want to know if they should evacuate or remain. They will act on my decision. Their fate could be in my hands. What to advise?

8.40. Return to mail. Over 1,000 letters to get through today.

9.00. Twice-weekly meeting with an academic group set up to study my 'thought'. It consists of sociologists, psychologists, philosophers, medical doctors, theologians etc. We had to set up an office to deal with this study group – plus the increasing amount of requests that come for information and research from people doing theses and doctorates on various aspects of my thought, systems, writings.

11.00. Five-minute coffee break where I relax with the study group before returning to my office.

11.05. Ready to continue with reading and answering correspondence. While I've been downstairs there were 18 telephone calls from around the world from people wanting to speak to me. Faxes even outnumber the phone calls.

11.30. Time for a break. With private secretary go for a spin in the car and a chance to listen to my favourite rock music.

12.15. Mass.

13.00. Lunch with men's group. They are a group of men responsible for our organization in 15 different countries who have gathered here for a meeting. This lunch is the only chance I'll have to be alone with them without various assistants and secretaries and paperwork. Good to see how things are developing, and I appreciate how the men get straight to the point – no long preambles or beating about the bush.

14.15. Back to the office. Work through some 'boxes'. Every month I receive full detailed reports from our 74 zones covering 198 countries world-wide. I scatter them so that I do a few every day. I have to draw conclusions for my reports to the Board. Where there are any ambiguities, I mark this on the report so that it can be followed up and full info. can be obtained. Likewise any suggestions for further action.

16.00. Receive the President of the Republic for afternoon tea.

17.10. Back to desk, and one last effort to complete today's 1,000-plus letters. Can't afford to put off until tomorrow, when at least several hundred others will arrive.

18.30. Last half hour in office. Deal with the more personal side of my affairs. Choose a present from a selection and wrap it for my niece. who's graduating from university tomorrow. I can't attend, or all the media would focus on me. I'll see her when she comes for the family gathering on Sunday.

Likewise choose and wrap a present and write a quick note for the Queen of the Bangwa tribe in Cameroon. Have known her since she was a young girl on my first visit there, when her father was on the throne. We keep in touch, and since a couple of our men leave for Cameroon tomorrow, I take the opportunity to send this with them.

Also I do a note to a European Prince and Princess who kindly sent me a gift and a nice note. My private secretary addresses this and ensures that it will arrive discreetly.

19.00. Take time out for a quick swim – doctor's orders following two spinal operations.

19.40. Arrive at house. The group of men I lunched with have had a large bouquet of flowers delivered. The scent fills the hallway.

20.00. Watch the evening news. Make notes if there is anything I need to address or act on tomorrow as a result.

20.30. Light supper with my three companions who share the house with me. Catch up on each other's news.

21.00. Sometimes we watch a video. I love detective stories. Sometimes a movie, but it has to be beautiful – no gratuitous violence or sex scenes.

22.00 (or thereabouts) Retire to my room. Take a little flask of warm milk and honey with me. Often, if I still haven't slept by one or two in the morning, I have a glass of warm milk. Usually does the trick. Before retiring, if it's a clear night, I might look at the stars for a while.

Before sleeping, examination of conscience. It's always the same question: Have I really lived today? Ah, sleep!

Tuesday
4 a.m. Rise slightly earlier than usual, as I have to leave at six to reach Rome before seven. Don't want to arrive late.

6.50. Arrive at the St Anne's Gate. Swiss guards salute and wave us through. They know us by now and don't need to ask for ID.

6.55. Have parked in the San Damaso courtyard and am mounting the great staircase. The Prefect of the Household is an old friend now and greets us warmly before leading us to the doors of the chapel. There the Private Secretary takes over and leads us to our seats.

7.00. On the dot, the Pope, vested and ready to offer Mass, comes out of the sacristy and approaches the altar. He will know I am there in his private chapel, but at this stage he gives no sign. He is totally concentrated on what he is about to do.

7.40. Mass finishes. Knowing the routine, I remain in my seat to continue prayer of thanksgiving. After removing his vestments, the Pope returns to his seat and prie-dieu at the front of the chapel. Profound silence.

7.55. His Holiness seems to display an extra paternal tenderness today as we take our leave. He holds my face in his hands and kisses my forehead.

9.35. Arrive at the office. Take the private driveway so I can gain the covered walkway and avoid being detained by well-wishers.

9.40. Greet all the staff of my office suite. Tackle today's mail.

11.00. Recording session for video message to be played to 60,000 who will attend next week's laity congress for the whole of Italy.

11.20. Back at desk. Reply to Cardinal Ratzinger's query on our on-going work together of developing statutes.

11.35. Two more offers of honorary degrees have arrived. After consultation, decide to accept one of them.

11.40. Telephone call from our publishing house. Sales of my latest collected writings have just passed 90,000 in Italy and have been published in eight different languages in the past month.

11.45. Drop quick note to His Holiness to thank him for his hospitality. Accept invitation to visit Thailand next year from renowned Buddhist leader there. He wants me to speak to his several hundred local leaders at one mass gathering in Bangkok.

11.55. Escape with private secretary for our run in the car. No phones ringing, no decisions to be made. Beautiful Italian countryside around Lake Albano to inspire the spirit. And a chance to listen to a great new tape of 'rap' music.

After lunch change into comfy slacks and spend the afternoon with 2,000 children (as many as we can cope with in our gardens around HQ). They are all part of our children's movement. The games we had planned turned out well. Their joyful enthusiasm makes me feel I'm about the same age as them again!

17.00. Back to the office. Go through the boxes. Detailed reports from Russia, Argentina and Burundi today.

18.00. Meeting with our financial people to discuss the economic progress of the industrial zone attached to our little town in Brazil. Over 60 businesses are now taking part there. The shanty town where our people are working (once known as 'Hell's Island') is now completely transformed. As the locals have decided to rename their quarter 'St Teresa's', they ask me for a message which will be read out at the renaming ceremony tomorrow. We send it by fax.

19.00. Make a few phone calls to heads of zones around the world. Try not to phone those for whom it is the middle of the night!

19.40. Home. Watch the news and sit down to supper with my three housemates. Missed my swim today. Must make an effort tomorrow. Back feeling pretty stiff, which affects my legs.

21.00. We watch a video of the youth rock concert which was put on last weekend during a 'Day for Peace' held at our little town in New York State.

22.30. To bed. Have I really lived today?...

Where does she draw her indefatigable energy from? What is the secret of her serenity? Is it her time management or her strategy of living the present moment to the full? How come her staff have to work on a rota basis just to keep up with her? A 76-year-old woman just shouldn't have so much energy!

ONE

NIGHT OF STARS AND TEARS

'I can't remember how long I cried that night, lying out in the open, gazing up at the stars overhead. But I do remember that at one point a quotation from Virgil, which I'd read at school, suddenly came to mind. It was "Love conquers all", and it seemed an answer from God. "All, all, all?" I asked myself. Could love resolve even this? That's when I said my "Yes".'

The Italian city of Trent suffered one of its heaviest bombings of the War that day, 13 May 1944. The Lubich family had taken to a hillside overlooking the city, carrying only a few blankets and some food. Their second child and first daughter, Chiara, now 24 and still the bread-winner of the family, was faced with a dilemma. Her response to that dilemma and the choice she was about to make would change her life for ever – and would have an effect on millions of people in the years to come.

'The first stirrings of the movement had already begun, so I felt I ought to stay behind in Trent. Yet how could I leave my family without even a roof over their heads?'

The dilemma was no small one. From the age of 13, Chiara had been the one to earn some money to keep the family. Her father, Luigi Lubich, had been one of the victims of the severe economic crisis which hit Italy following the 1929 Wall Street Crash. The Depression struck Italy with all its force. He, a fervent anti-Fascist, refused to take the party card which would have opened the doors to work, money and the means to put food on the family table.

The dilemma turned around and around in Chiara's head. She had always been docile and done what was best for the family. Yet now something was calling her to leave them behind, to go back down to the city – the city which was being pounded to a pulp and was no longer a safe place to live. There were few air-raid shelters, and even these offered little protection – save that of being with the others. If they were going to die, at least they would die together.

She made up her mind, said her 'Fiat', and the tears finally ceased. From the hillside they could see that their house had been hit. The next morning, they went down together to see if there was anything they could salvage. It was then that Chiara announced her decision. While the rest of the family would quit Trent, she had decided to stay.

'My Dad understood,' she says today. 'He was classed as a Communist, but was really just a Socialist and, more than anything, anti-Fascist. Somehow he understood what I had to do and gave me his blessing. Mum, on the other hand, never really understood. Even though she would spend her final years living with us at the Movement's headquarters, she never quite grasped what we were all about. But she was a great Christian and we really loved and respected each other. But that day in May 1944, it was her turn to shed tears.'

The 'first stirrings of the movement' which Chiara referred to were the beginnings of what would become known as the Focolare Movement, the largest organized lay movement in the Church today. But then, in 1943, she had no idea of a 'movement', let alone a name for one.

She had simply begun to share the Gospel life with some friends. But something about her drew other people. Young people in particular seemed to be almost irresistibly attracted towards her and what she had to say. So much so that they too would leave family, home, work, careers and friends to follow Chiara and her 'Way'.

The young, dynamic woman with a mane of thick, shining hair, which she preferred to keep short, possessed a certain natural beauty. She never wore make-up, having instead a clear and delicate skin and shining eyes. Only five feet two inches tall, she carried imperceptibly an air of natural authority and self-possession which ensured that people around her naturally looked to her to take the lead. Despite the austerities of the War and her own family's poverty, she always turned out well, her dress sense being admired by all the other girls. She dressed simply but always with an air of dignity and harmony. Her clothes, usually a mid-calf skirt and a blouse or sweater, seemed to accentuate her tiny waist and adorn her body with an elegance which was attractively modest.

The young men noticed her too. She was not short of male admirers. But Chiara was far too single-minded even to notice. Her heart was elsewhere and the many men she eventually attracted around her saw her as a sister and, even though still young herself, a spiritual mother. While small in stature, she had a boundless energy, which seemed to propel her even as she walked. She was someone who didn't just walk, but appeared always to be thrusting ahead, someone who knew where she was going.

When Trent started to suffer the aerial bombardments, she and her friends would run to the air-raid shelters. Many people didn't make it and were killed. There was no time to waste once the warning siren sounded. The only possession Chiara would grab to bring with her was her little book of the Gospels.

In the midst of war, with death and destruction all around them, those few young girls questioned everything. What was it all about? What was the meaning of life, which could be here one moment, and snuffed out the next?

'As the war continued, many things were destroyed. Many ideals which had occupied our young minds collapsed. One of us loved her home – and it was destroyed. Another loved her fiancé – and the boy never returned from the front. I was studying at a university in another city – the war prevented me from continuing. Another who loved art saw valuable works shattered in an instant. We used to meet together every day, as much as eleven times in one day, in the air-raid shelter, which itself wasn't even safe. We could have died from one moment to the next. One question weighed on our minds. Surely there must be an ideal which doesn't die. An ideal which is worth being followed and which no bomb can destroy. The answer came immediately: *Yes – God*. "So," I said, "Let's make God our life's ideal, then." '

And they did. Within a few months they numbered over 500 people in and around Trent, all following this 'Ideal'.

TWO

'JUST AN ORDINARY GIRL'?

Who was that young woman who attracted so many people to live for an ideal which was God? Who is she who continues to do so today and has an outreach that touches millions of people all around the globe? When I asked Chiara Lubich this question, sitting in her office, the very heart at the heart of the Movement's international headquarters outside Rome, we fell out!

'I'm just an ordinary person like anyone else!' is how she described herself. I told her that we didn't agree and that on the first question of our first meeting, there we were, 'falling out'! It was said in jest, of course, but it helped to break the ice and push Chiara Lubich into speaking about herself. It's not something she likes to do. She always brings the focus back to the Movement, to God and what He has done.

'The pen doesn't know what it's going to write, any more than the paintbrush knows what it's going to paint – until the writer or the painter takes it up and begins to use it.' It's like that with her, she says. She is just an instrument which God has chosen to use.

Yes, but hasn't God given His human creatures a free will? Unlike a pen or a paintbrush, they can choose what to do or not do, whether and up to what point to co-operate with these plans of God.

She agrees. And in order to allow the story of God's action in and through her to be told, she submits to being questioned about herself. She admits that it isn't easy, and by force of habit, reflecting her own way of thinking, she still tends to answer most questions with a story about how God has done this or that. It's understandable, you see. The two of them are so linked: God and Chiara. Who chose whom? While she made a radical choice to have God as her Ideal, the Christian religion tells us that God Himself comes to seek us out.

Chiara was born in Trent on 22 January 1920, the second of four children born to Luigi and Luigia Lubich. The next day she was baptized as Silvia in the city's church of St Mary Major. The city is still proud that it was the site of the great Church Council of 1545–63.

The Lubichs had married on 15 August 1916, after Luigi returned wounded from the front in the First World War. Luigi Lubich and Luigia Marinconz had met when they both worked in the print-works of the *Il Popolo* newspaper, the voice of the Trentine Social-ists, run by Cesare Battisti. Chiara points out that Battisti was a national hero. Once a Deputy for Trent in the Vienna Parliament, he had been executed by the Austrians for having defended Trent as being part of Italy.

While her father, a foreman at the print-works, was a Socialist, Chiara's mother, Luigia, a typesetter, was a traditional practising Catholic. She went to Mass and Holy Communion every morning before work. She often told her children later, that even though Bat-tisti was a Socialist, he never made any snide remarks about her keeping her Mass book, her daily Missal, beside her on her desk at work. It seems that everyone respected the young Luigia for her in-tegrity in practising her faith.

Their first child, Gino, was born in 1918, Chiara's younger sister Lilliana in 1922 and the youngest, Carla, in 1925. They were a close-knit family and were pretty much self-contained.

With the rise of Mussolini and his Fascists, Chiara's father was fer-vently anti-Fascist. Because of this, he came to be classed by some people as a 'Communist'. Chiara points out that her father was never a Communist, but was a true Socialist. He had long since given up the practice of his religion. Until, that is, some years later his two children, Gino and Chiara, asked him to go to Confession and Mass so that they could all share the sacraments together as a family. Luigi was touched by this appeal from his young children and complied with their request. In fact, he would die in the centre of the Foco-lare in Rome in the 1960s. At that time, the centre was wherever Chiara lived.

A little over two years after the birth of Chiara, in October 1922, the King of Italy asked Benito Mussolini to form a government, and Italy entered its Fascist period. At first, in order not to frighten off the world of finance, Mussolini drew only four members of his thir-teen-member government from his own party. The elections of 1924, though, saw the Fascists win three-quarters of the seats in Par-liament, and the following year saw the introduction of the 'Fascis-tissime Laws' which would create a real Fascist dictatorship.

With these, Mussolini, the Leader – Il Duce – could create laws by decree and was answerable only to the King. The unions and non-Fascist political organizations, as well as Catholic organizations such as the Scouts, were banned. Political opponents, such as the Communist leader Gramsci, were either imprisoned or exiled. State institutions, especially the army and the world of education, were severely 'cleansed'. The media became subject to censorship, and to ensure that the party line was followed, a political police force was formed – the OVRA.

The *Il Popolo* newspaper was suppressed. With a wife and young family to provide for, Luigi had to find other work quickly. He soon set himself up as a wine merchant, and in this way managed to sup-port his family in relative comfort. During this period, the Lubichs were able to spend some time in the mountains in the summer months. In fact, Chiara's first memory is of one of those visits. She remembers as a four-year-old the contrast between the atmosphere in town and the wide open space, the lack of restrictions and the complete feeling of freedom in the mountains. Especially, she can still recall the child's joy of getting up in the morning and going out-side to wash in a running stream. And then – the joy of it! – sliding down the hillside with her big brother Gino on a home-made wooden sled. That feeling of freedom and of a lack of day-to-day cares would remain in her memory for the rest of her life.

But across the Atlantic Ocean, the events of October 1929 were to have a devastating effect on the Lubichs as well as millions of oth-ers. It was the Wall Street Crash. The following year its effects began to be felt in Italy, and by 1932 there were over a million men unem-ployed in Italy. Less than a quarter of them received any social assis-tance. (Three million people, on the other hand, had joined the Fascist Party.)

Luigi Lubich was one of those unemployed. His flourishing little business had collapsed. In the dire economic situation, the last thing people thought of buying was wine. He was also one of the majority who received no dole. Neither could he find any kind of paid employment. True to his principles, he remained fervently anti-Fascist and refused to take the party card, which would have no doubt led to employment in one of the State institutions or on a Government-approved newspaper.

Many were the people who urged him to use his previous acquaintance with Mussolini to resolve his situation. He flatly refused. Before his marriage to Luigia, and as he came from outside the city of Trent, Luigi rented a room not far from his newspaper works. As he worked at night on the production side of the newspaper, he slept in his room during the day. His landlord asked if he could let his room to someone else during the night. Thus it came about that Luigi slept in his bed in the daytime and another used it at night! That other was Benito Mussolini, who was at that time a writer on Battisti's newspaper. And in any case, the locals would say to Luigi, surely Mussolini owed him a return favour. At one time, while Trent was still governed by the Austrians, the Austrian Police came to arrest Mussolini. Luigi Lubich warned Mussolini, and he fled in time to escape arrest.

This was long before Mussolini founded his Party in 1919, but in the Great Depression of the 1930s friends and neighbours urged Luigi to remind Mussolini of their earlier association. Surely Il Duce would find some work for him? Luigi would have none of it. He would have no voluntary contact whatsoever with the Fascist Party, nor its leader – even if he had to starve.

Both Lubich parents often went hungry in order to provide for their children. And even then, the children still sometimes went hungry. They lived in poverty but, Chiara remembers, they always managed to keep their dignity.

For Luigia Lubich the most cherished possession of all was her Catholic Faith. This she communicated to her children, even if later her only son, Gino, would reject it. Chiara, on the other hand, has remained ever true to what she considers this most precious gift. She has no hesitation at all in saying that it was her mother who taught her to pray. She professes to always having had an interest in religion and anything to do with God.

So much so that some, at first sight, might have thought her a rather serious child. She says of herself that while she never knowingly got into trouble, her mother did once have to tell her off for not doing her household chores on time. But, even then, in early childhood, she says that for her it was simply a question of making a choice:

'It seemed to me that every action was a choice, and very often my thinking about God or praying to Him seemed more important than doing chores. So on one occasion I was scolded by Mummy.'

This contemplation seems to have been part of her life from a very early age. She remembers quite clearly that from the age of six she was attracted to adoring the presence of Jesus in the Eucharist reserved in Catholic churches. For sure, the Sisters of the Child Mary who taught the catechism had often spoken to the girls in the parish about this presence and told them that they must never neglect such a gift. Chiara, studious and conscientious, took them at their word. She developed a desire to spend time with Jesus present in the Eucharist.

'I remember when I was a little girl, from the age of six onwards, that I would look at Jesus in the Eucharist and I would pray to him. I would say, "You who are light and warmth, enter me through my eyes." I would repeat this over and over, and quite insistently. So much so that once I sort of blacked out when I was doing this, because I was only a little girl. And sometimes I would gaze so intently at that sacred host that it seemed that the host would become dark and everything else surrounding it light, instead of the other way around. But I was only a little girl.'

'Only a little girl.' In this way she dismisses whatever it was that she experienced during those times spent alone in front of the monstrance. But it set her on a path, one which she continues to tread to this day, and which would affect millions of people, not only in the Movement she would lead, but throughout the whole of the Catholic Church – and beyond.

Chiara was ten when her father's wine business collapsed. At that time she also fell seriously ill with appendicitis and resulting peritonitis. 'It was a very formative experience for me,' she says now. 'The doctor who operated on me said that only about one person in a thousand came through it at that time. Anyway, I came through and recovered completely, thanks to the prayers of the Sisters and of my parents. I think that it was from that moment that I began to know the presence of suffering in my life, and the possibility of bearing it through love.'

In spite of their poor circumstances, the Lubichs placed great importance on the education of their children – and they, in turn, were open and receptive to this, especially Chiara and her elder brother Gino.

The teachers at the school were aware that they were dealing with a child of above-average intelligence in Chiara Lubich, or Silvia as she was still known then. Already at the age of 13, Chiara began to tutor other children privately in order to earn the family's keep. She taught Italian, maths and geography above all. She obviously enjoyed it and was much appreciated by her young pupils and their parents. It developed in her, too, a passion for education, and she would eventually train to become a primary school teacher.

While still at school, Chiara was used to getting high marks, usually at the top of the class. But she insists that her brother Gino was even more intelligent than she. 'He was a little genius,' she recalls.

On Saturdays the Lubich children, like others, were obliged to take part in the exercises of the 'Italian Youth', part of Il Duce's experiment to make the 'New Man'. This infuriated Luigi Lubich. Chiara remembers that her mother would dress Gino in his uniform in the bathroom and get him out of the house before their father returned.

Did this compulsory youth activity organized by the Fascists have any influence on Chiara? Did it even propel her towards her later involvement in Catholic activities? About this she is quite certain: 'Oh no, it had no influence on me whatever. In fact, I had no interest at all in their activities. So much so, that at school I used to always get ten out of ten in philosophy. But I remember one particular year, when the final exam came and the external examiners arrived, one of the questions they asked was about 'Fascist mysticism'. Well, I didn't know anything about that! I had never bothered about the Fascist stuff we were supposed to learn, so they gave me a seven. My marks went down because that was the one thing I didn't know about.'

Another year, though, she remembers that she got top marks, despite the fact that she had interrupted or argued with the philosophy teacher in every single lesson. She explains, 'The teacher was a nonbeliever and sometimes spoke ill of religion. This hurt and annoyed me, especially because I was afraid that my classmates would accept what he was saying. So, never a class passed but I didn't ask to speak so that I could put over my point of view, or that I didn't at least pipe up, "That's not true!" I was surprised, then, when at the annual assessments, he gave me the top mark. A few years later he told me, "I've begun to pray to that God you believe in." '

Chiara continued giving her private lessons, and every one of her students did well, passing their exams with flying colours. An abiding memory of this time is that she was always just very, very busy. As well as continuing her own education, she was working at full stretch to support her family.

Life continued in a round of school, her private tutoring and household chores – which she had learned to master by now! She says quite candidly today that she was 'a good child and always obedient'. That is part of the nature of Chiara Lubich; once she is told to do something, or has learned something, it remains.

Today she remembers one other spiritual 'high point' of her teenage years. At about the age of 15 she felt a call within herself to be a martyr. Over 60 years later she laughs as she says, 'I don't know how that will be confirmed, but I distinctly remember feeling that call. It was as if Heaven asked me, and I said "Yes." '

A couple of years later, on the feast day of St Thomas Aquinas, Chiara felt a powerful attraction to sanctity. She told a friend, 'I want to be a saint.' The friend said, 'Me too,' and they both ran right away to the Catholic Youth centre and told the leaders there that they wanted to be saints! She laughs again as she remembers now that the director was impressed and invited them to come to their meetings.

At that time the only form of Catholic apostolate in Italy for lay people was through the highly organized form of Catholic Action. Thus Chiara became part of Catholic Action's youth branch and later joined its student arm.

Chiara passed all her final school exams at the Magisterum (teacher training school) in 1939 with high grades. Her dream was to go to the Catholic University of Milan, the only Catholic university in the country, believing that there they would speak about God and the truth. She entered the exam for one of the 30 places that were available. Out of hundreds of candidates, she came thirty-third. She was sorely disappointed. Since she couldn't get into Milan, she enrolled at the University of Venice. She received her diploma and became a State Registered Teacher at Trent.

Her brother Gino, meanwhile, had been accepted to study medicine, to the joy of his parents and his younger sister.

While happy for Gino, Chiara had been saddened by her failure to gain a free place at university herself. She had set her heart on getting to university, where she thought that there must be so much wisdom that she would find the truth. The dream had been snatched away. But then she had a spiritual experience that remains engraved on her memory to this day. She was sitting with her mother on the sofa, crying uncontrollably because she couldn't go to the Catholic University, when suddenly she perceived an 'interior voice'. 'I Myself will be your teacher,' said the voice. While not knowing what it meant, she accepted it, and peace reigned in her spirit once more.

In 1939, at the age of 19, Chiara was to set out on the longest journey of her young life. It would have ramifications that would change her life for ever.

THREE

AN 'UNEXPECTED THOUGHT'
– THE BRIDE OF GOD

Loreto, in the central Italian region of the Marche, is about 350 kilo-metres from Trent. At the age of 19, it was the longest journey Chiara had ever made, the furthest she had ever been from home. She went because the Catholic Action student group in Trent was sending some members (paying their fare and all the costs) to take part in a student congress at Loreto.

A house, reputed to be the house of the Holy Family of Nazareth, came to be venerated there. Legend has it that it was transported from the Holy Land by angels. In any case, it has been venerated as the House of the Holy Family since the fifteenth century.

'The first time that I entered the little house, which is inside the fortress-church, I was filled with emotion,' says Chiara. 'I just wanted to go there to pray. I was just a normal teenage girl, and I didn't worry my-self about finding "my way" in life – that thought had never occurred to me. I certainly didn't have the time to ask myself whether or not this was the actual historical house that the Holy Family had lived in.

'I found myself alone, plunged into this great mystery. And, what was most unusual for me, I shed copious tears. I wasn't normally given to displays of emotion, but the tears flowed and flowed. I began to meditate on everything that might have happened within these walls: the annunciation of the Angel to Mary, the family life of Jesus, Mary and Joseph.

'I touched with great veneration the stones and the beams. In my mind's eye I was seeing and imagining the house built by Joseph. I seemed to hear the voice of the child Jesus. I imagined him crossing the room. I was looking at those walls which had had the fortune to hear the voice and the songs of Mary.

'Whenever there was free time from the congress, while my com-panions stayed at the school where we were being put up, I wouldn't miss a chance every day to run back to the "little house". And each time it had the same effect on me, the same deep emotion. It was as if a particular grace of God was enveloping me completely, almost as if the Divine was overwhelming me.

'It was all contemplation, prayer, as if in some way I was living with the three persons of the Holy Family.'

At the end of the congress there was a High Mass in the fortress-church in which the 'little house' stood. What she experienced there during that Mass was to be the culmination and crowning point of those mysterious, mystical hours spent alone inside the House of Loreto.

'The church was full to bursting point with all these Catholic students. There were some boys there, but the majority were girls – all wearing their white mantillas. And somehow during that High Mass, while everyone was attentively following the proceedings in their missals, I knew that I had found my "way". It was a "fourth way". Then I had an image of a whole host of white-clad virgins following after me on this way. I didn't know what it meant, but that's what I experienced.'

On her return to life and work back at her first teaching post in Castello d'Ossana, the parish priest asked Chiara how it had gone at Loreto. When she told him she had found her 'way', he asked her if she meant she was going to get married. No. Was she going to lead a consecrated life in the world, then? No. So, she was going to enter a convent, then? 'No,' she replied, meeting total incomprehension from the priest. 'Anyway,' she says, 'I didn't need any encouragement or support. My life was to continue in just the same way until 1943.'

And life did carry on as before. Chiara continued her work at Castello d'Ossano in her first teaching post. It was a little village in the mountains around Trent. Parents and children as well as the parish priest all remembered later that she was a brilliant teacher, and loved by all the children. There was something about her. Her manner showed that she really loved the children, but there was more than that. Her whole demeanour; her dress, her 'style' somehow communicated peace and harmony. And when she was in church, her whole manner seemed to radiate prayer and love of God – so much so that it inspired those who saw her to a deeper belief and more fervent prayer.

As a junior teacher, she had assignments in different villages for the first two or three years. At Castello d'Ossana in the Val di Sole she got the older children involved and set up a branch of Catholic Action, to the delight of the parish priest. In addition to the few elderly matrons who attended his early-morning daily Mass, now there was their new young schoolteacher. Her presence among them, in fact, seemed to spark a whole new spiritual dynamic and joy in their Faith. 1939–40 saw Chiara serve as a supply teacher at Verollo di Livo State School.

When I once asked Chiara about the existence of Guardian Angels, she was emphatic that they exist. Not only was it a matter of faith, because they are several times mentioned in the Scriptures, and the Church teaches it, but she remembers one personal experience while she was stationed in one of her mountain teaching posts.

'Once I came down the mountain at night to visit someone who was sick down in the valley. When I came out from that person's house, I had to take the train to go to Trent. It was already dark and I got mixed up. I started walking in the wrong direction. I was going further into the countryside towards the vineyards instead of towards Trent. At a certain moment, I felt that something was warning me, saying, "Turn around, turn around, go the other way!" And I got back in time to catch my train for Trent. I was 18 at the time, and so I could have been in danger. I've always had the impression that it was my Guardian Angel who made me turn around and go back. So the Guardian Angel does intervene, just as we ask him to in our traditional daily prayer, "to light and guard, to rule and guide".'

At the age of 20, Chiara obtained a teaching appointment at a school in Trent city which was run by the Capuchin Fathers, a reformed branch of the Franciscans. She worked there for the next three years. The Fathers there recognized a young woman of deep faith and spirituality who was also dedicated to helping others and was active in Catholic Action. In 1943 one of them invited Chiara to join the Third Order of Franciscans, a branch of the Order for lay-people living and working in the world. While they continued to live their normal day-to-day lives, and followed their 'state of life' (i.e. either as single people or married), and went on with their jobs and other activities, they retained a special link with the Franciscan Order and took part in spiritual exercises at the Franciscan Capuchin church.

Chiara says that while the Capuchins were known for their austerity and ascetic lifestyle, she was not attracted to this. Probably the best-known Capuchin priest is Padre Pio, a stigmatist who died in 1968. But that type of spirituality never appealed to her. In fact, she says that stories of stigmatists such as St Gemma Galgani and others left her cold. The idea of 'victims' didn't appeal to her at all. That was not her way.

So why did she join the Third Order of Franciscans? 'Well, that's what other girls in our neighbourhood did, and I did the same thing.'

Part of the tradition for people entering this branch of the Order was to take a 'new name in religion', signifying their 'putting off of the old man' and their new religious identity – just as monks and nuns did on their entering religious orders. Silvia Lubich chose the name Chiara – the Italian form of Clare.

'I was a great admirer of St Francis of Assisi, and so I chose the name Chiara. I liked Clare of Assisi because, when she consecrated herself to God and St Francis cut off her hair, he asked her, "Daughter, what do you desire?" and she replied, "God." Afterwards, when I read the Bull of Canonization, which was wonderful, it was all "light, charity; charity, light". And I also read her biography. I really liked it, above all because it said that she left behind her a "whole trail of light". This attracted me.'

And so Silvia Lubich began to use the name Chiara – but she hadn't said anything about this to her parents. To them she was always their Silvia, until towards the end of their lives; when they saw everyone else calling her Chiara, they did so too.

Obviously, as she continued in a life of prayer and service to others, Chiara became ever more sensitive to that 'interior voice', to spiritual insights. This was to lead her to take that decisive step that would eventually release a whole new powerful wave of Christian commitment and mission for countless people who would follow her 'fourth way'.

She remembers that it all began one morning in December 1943, when her mother asked her to run an errand for her. 'I was to go to the dairy in a hamlet called Madonna Bianca, about a mile or so from our house. So to please my Mum, I set off on the errand. On the way to Madonna Bianca I suddenly felt a call. It was as if God were saying to me, "Give yourself to me." I was so struck by this unexpected thought that I stood stock still, right there in the middle of the road.'

Once she had accomplished her errand and returned home, she immediately wrote to her confessor. A few days later he would give her permission to consecrate herself to God for life. But arriving at that point was not quite so painless or easy. Normally the Church demands long periods of preparation before allowing someone to pronounce vows for life. For Chiara, however, such procedures were unknown. All she knew was that God had asked her to dedicate her life completely to Him. She knew nothing of postulancies or novitiates or training to answer such a request.

'I didn't know that such complicated things existed in the Church. I went to see my confessor to discuss this call I felt, sure that everything would go smoothly. But at one point the priest began to ask me a series of questions: Had I thought it over properly, had I thought about this or that aspect? I replied that I had, and he continued, 'Do you realize that your brother and your sisters will get married and have children, your parents will die and you will end up all alone in an old folks' home, and you'll have nobody?'

Chiara then said, 'As long as there is a tabernacle on this earth, as long as the Eucharistic presence is in the world, I will never be alone.'

Her confessor was won over. He recognized that what was going on in the interior life of Chiara Lubich was not a fantasy, not some sort of wish to escape 'the world'. There was a genuine desire to cement this intimate relationship with God which she so obviously experienced. Chiara was overjoyed. She was, as she describes it, about to 'marry God'.

She told no one. Yet her friends knew something had happened. She didn't want to tell anyone; not yet. She was only aware of a bubbling joy within her, 'like a fire which had been suddenly lit'. But it showed on her face; her joy was contagious and attracted others. She herself says, 'Despite the fact that I kept everything secret, when my friends met me they were touched by that flame that had been lit in me, and they wanted to follow me.'

For the moment, she did not even tell her parents. When the priest had set a date, 7 December, for her ceremony of consecration, she only told her mother that she was attending a special service at the church that morning which would take a little longer than the normal daily Mass.

Her confessor had suggested she keep a vigil of prayer the night before. Despite her best efforts, she only managed to stay awake for a couple of hours. Besides, as she says today, even then she 'wasn't convinced of the value of certain pious practices which turned out not to be in conformity with my vocation.'

So she fell asleep. Not, though, before noticing that the crucifix she knelt in front of had become covered with condensation from her breath. The body of the Christ figure appeared to be covered in a fine mist. She perceived a sign in this: 'The Crucified One whom I was to follow would not be so much the Christ of the physical wounds which many spiritualities emphasize, but rather the Christ of spiritual sufferings.' Her way, too, would be one of spiritual, rather than physical suffering. Over half a century later, she says this has been consistently confirmed.

Before five o'clock on 7 December 1943 Chiara got up and put on her best dress, and set off towards the little friary where the private ceremony was to take place.

A storm was raging. A biting wind drove freezing rain against her. She had to struggle to hold the umbrella in front of her as she fought through the storm. But she was at peace within herself. She thought that having to fight the elements to reach the little chapel where she would 'marry God' was not without meaning:

'It seemed to me to signify that what I was about to do would encounter obstacles. In fact, it even seemed to remind me of a sign of a hostile power which would fight against me on the way I would follow.

'On my arrival at the friary, the scene changed. An enormous outer gate opened before me as I approached – of its own accord, automatically. I had a great feeling of relief and welcome, like the wide-open arms of God, who was awaiting me.'

Of course, no doubt there had been someone in the gatehouse who had seen her approaching and had released the lock on the portal. Chiara laughs at the memory. It was not some sort of miracle, like the parting of the Red Sea. 'But as a young girl, and in a state of anticipation of what I was about to do, this was the spiritual meaning it seemed to suggest to me.'

Inside, the little friary chapel had been decorated and looked ready for a wedding. At the back of the chapel a statue of the Blessed Virgin was prominent. In front of the altar, on the sanctuary, someone had placed a prie-dieu.

The priest who had advised Chiara to make her vigil of prayer before the ceremony also told her to ask for a particular favour from God, which He in His goodness would surely not refuse on such a day. She duly wrote down her request on a piece of paper folded small, as the priest had told her. Her request was that God would grant the gift of faith to someone who was very dear to her. The priest placed it under the chalice, and the Mass began.

'Before Communion,' says Chiara, 'I saw in a flash what I was doing: in consecrating myself to God I had crossed a bridge. The bridge was crumbling away behind me – never again would I be able to return to the world. Because my consecration was not just a formula like that which I had read out before the Sacred Host held up before me – "I make the vow of perfect and perpetual chastity" – it was something else; I was being married to God. That meant not only celibacy – renouncing human marriage. It meant leaving all: parents, studies, school, entertainment, everything in my little universe that I had loved up until then. This sudden insight into what I was doing was momentary, but so powerful that a great big tear fell onto the open page of my Missal.'

The Mass ended in silence. Chiara came down from the sanctuary and took a place in the pews. The priest, after removing his Mass vestments, came and knelt a few rows behind her. A long period of silence followed. Then the priest came up to her and said, 'You will be a bride of blood.' However, this did not fit into any spirituality that Chiara felt she could adopt.

'While I was grateful for anything that might be said to me, those words just did not connect with what I felt deep within me. The expression "Bride of blood" struck me as being anachronistic. It wasn't for me. And without saying so to the priest, in my heart I rebelled against it and said, "No. I am the bride of God." And it was this God who was later to reveal himself as the Forsaken One. Blood indeed, but blood of the soul.'

The new 'bride of God' ran all the way home, stopping only to buy three red carnations to adorn the crucifix which was waiting for her in her room. Still she told no one about her secret alliance with God. She had no plans to form any sort of movement. All that mattered was that she had formally committed her life to God. Her work in the Capuchin school for orphans, the Opera Serafica, continued, as did her life of study. For by now the young teacher had managed to enrol in the University of Venice to study philosophy.

Attendance was only required a certain number of days per term. Chiara could continue her teaching while still doing what she loved best of all. She was filled with a passion to learn, to reach the truth. As it happened, the roads were closed because of the War, but Chiara continued her study at home in Trent. People who first met her in those years and who would become 'followers' remember that she would sometimes study before the Blessed Sacrament in the Cathedral of Trent.

Around this time, one of the pupils whom Chiara was tutoring was Dori Zamboni. Her parents had asked Chiara to prepare their child for university entrance exams. Dori didn't think that she could do it, but Chiara told her that she would and that the two of them would go to university together. Dori passed the exams with top marks. She says that studying with Chiara made it no longer a chore but something she really enjoyed. The young teacher gave her even younger pupil an overview of philosophy. Their encounter with the work of the German philosopher Immanuel Kant was to be a turning point in both their lives.

They were not to know that twice in the previous century certain attempts to put the ideas of Kant at the service of the Church had been roundly condemned by the Church. (The leading ideas of the philosopher-theologians Georg Hermes and Anton Gunther were condemned by the Holy Office in 1835 and in 1857.)

One morning in the Spring of 1944, Chiara was tutoring Dori. Her enthusiasm for Kant's ideas was contagious and her pupil was fascinated. Some years later, at the request of fellow Focolarine, Dori wrote an account of that event:

'As well as giving lessons, Chiara was preparing for university: she would enrol for the philosophy course. She already had the study notes from her course professors and sometimes she would read them to me. The papers were covered with the professor's notes and exclamation marks. She explained that if we were to learn really well, we had to absorb the ideas, those of the professor and the philosopher whom the professor was trying to explain, and that this was how we would get inside their thinking, into their method, so as to understand them from the inside.

'In this way we would sometimes discover the point at which each of the philosophers substituted his "own" truth for *the* Truth. You could see where he deviated and how there might be a crack in the thinking just like a vase which looks perfect but when you tap it, it makes a cracked sort of sound. Chiara also told me that we could have written our own book and it would be a book on the history of philosophy. On one side of the page we could write the truth about things, historical fact, the discovery of genuine truth, and on the other side of the page, we could write up the various philosophies. A comparison of the two reports would perhaps reveal the reason for the apparent deviations, the incompleteness and the inconsistencies, she said.

'She drew me into her plans, into her abilities just as if I were as capable as herself. This fascinated me and lifted me above my own narrow thoughts to a more vast way of of thinking.

'One morning, I arrived at Chiara's and found a bouquet of flowers at the entrance which I picked up and took in with me. Chiara was delighted and even more so when I explained that I hadn't brought them but that someome else must have left them on the doorstep. She said, "I was just thinking how nice it would be to have some flowers to brighten up the room today and I told Jesus this. This is his answer."

'We went into her parents' bedroom because they had a visitor in the house and they had given him the best bedroom. In this other room they had set up a little table. Just above it, on the wall, there was a picture of the Sacred Heart of Jesus.

'That day we were studying philosophy and those were the best hours for us! Chiara was explaining Kant to me and she was talking with such enthusiasm about his philosophy, about his concepts...that I was really loving it. It was all so clear, obvious, reasonable and explainable: the universe and the spirit.

'Suddenly my teacher stopped abruptly. "Our Christianity," she said, with feeling, "our faith, can't be reduced to science and physics. We are also citizens, in the early stages, of a world which is unknown to the empirical world of mechanical necessity and we are part of that world not only with our souls but also with our bodies. And what of the resurrection? In what we've just been reading the resurrection of the body doesn't fit in!"

'After a short pause in which she reflected intently, she announced, "Come on, let's recite the Creed."

'That "Come on" made me act like her and with her. We said the Creed, pronouncing deliberately that phrase, "the resurrection of the body".

'We had risen to our feet to say the prayer and when we sat down again, she began to explain the resurrection of the body to me. She explained it not only in a way that I had never heard before but in such an irrefutable, actual and logical manner that I instinctively pinched both my arms to see if I was still in my body or whether I had left it. We both had the impression that a ray of light had descended on us from somewhere. The image of the Sacred Heart was above us on the wall. It was a light that Chiara had translated into words and which she summed up when she said, "this is the Ideal."

'From that day on, the flame which animated us, the light which was lit within us, the life which it produced in us and around us, we would call "Ideal".'

This episode typifies Chiara's desire even in those early days to 'gather all things together in Christ'. With the grace of God, it seems, she would cut through all that was not the Truth and shed this 'light' (Chiara means light) wherever she went and to whomever she was with. Thus, as Dori hinted, the Ideal was to build unity; or perhaps a better way to describe it would be a 'harmony' – a harmony of thought, will, lifestyle and, above all, of heart and soul. This explains in some way why those other girls were seemingly so irresistably attracted to the person of this young teacher from Trent. It would explain why, half a century later, a whole team of theologians, philosophers, sociologists, psychologists and other academics would gather around Chiara to explore this harmony of thought transcending all the disciplines.

It is clear that in those early days, Chiara's overriding concern was to build unity among all who followed Christ and to urge them onto a greater realization of God's tremendous love for them. In this sense her 'charism' was evident to all whom it touched.

A letter she wrote sometime in 1943 illustrates the driving force in Chiara – and what she would wish for the other girls who were 'following her'. It echoes the prayer of St Paul writing to the Ephesians: 'I ask that your minds may be opened to see his light, so that you will know how great is the hope to which he has called you…' (Ephesians 1:18). In that letter she wrote:

My dearest sisters,

I would like to be close to each one of you and to speak to you from the bottom of my heart with the tenderness of God.

The Almighty has a design of Love on you, too.

You, too, can give your life for something great.

Believe me: God is in you!

Your soul in grace is the home of the Holy Spirit: the God who sanctifies.

Enter within yourself: Seek God, your God who lives within you!

If you knew who it is you have within you!

If only you were to leave everything for Him…

This brief life ebbs away a little more each day. If only it was turned towards God.

Oh! If only God was the King and master of your soul and, at His Divine Service, all that you do could be for Him!

Oh! If only you were to love Him with all your heart, mind and strength!

Then…you would 'fall in love' with God and you would go through the world announcing the Good News!

God exists. Live for Him.

God will judge you. Live for Him.

In a short time when this life is over, God will be everything for you. Give yourself to Him now!

Love Him.

Listen to what He wants of you in every moment of your life. Follow Him with all your heart, giving all of yourself to God's service.

'Fall in love' with God!

There are many things in this world! The most beautiful of all is God! Do not waste your youth and find yourself full of regrets like St Augustine, saying; 'Late have I loved thee, Oh beauty so ancient and so new: late have I loved thee!'

No!

Life's blood still courses through your veins and mine!

Our hearts still beat and can still love!

We can still prove our love, overcoming all difficulties.

No! I love you now, my God and my all.

Command now and I will follow! Your will is mine! I want what you want.

To be in love with God on earth means to be in love with his will, so that our soul, having lived at his divine service, may see Him and be with Him for eternity.

Chiara

FOUR

THE 'FIRST COMPANIONS' – 'FROM THAT MOMENT I NEVER LEFT HER'

On the 3 September 1939 France and Britain had declared war on Hitler's Germany. Benito Mussolini of Italy remained neutral. He had already annexed Albania on 7 April of the same year. He would wait for the defeat of France before entering the Second World War.

When he did, the city of Trent suffered heavily from aerial bombardments from both the Allies and the Germans at different stages in the War. Between 1943 and 1945 an ever-growing number of girls gathered around Chiara Lubich. They wanted to follow her in her commitment and consecration to God, and thus they became the foundation-stones of what would eventually grow into an organized movement. Today they are called 'the first companions' of Chiara. Younger generations of the Movement respect them for the role they have played in the development of a new spirituality and for their early recognition of the charism and leadership role of Chiara.

Dori Zamboni, the 15-year-old schoolgirl whom Chiara prepared for university, is one of those first companions and now lives and works at the Focolare Movement's world-wide headquarters outside Rome. Another 'first companion' is Natalia Dallapiccola. Now aged 72 and also based at the international centre of Focolare, she remembers precisely her first meeting with Chiara:

'In 1943, at the age of 19, I was going to one of the Capuchin priests in Trent for confession. He felt that here was a soul searching for something, and once he asked me if I would like to take part in a day retreat he was organizing. I said "Yes" immediately, for I knew I was indeed searching for something. Like many young girls, I had briefly flirted with the idea of becoming a nun when I was younger. But I didn't, and in 1943 I was working as a secretary in the Chamber of Commerce.

'My dad had died a couple of years previously, so I was still in half-mourning and I lived at home in a village outside Trent with my Mum and my three younger sisters, my brother already having married.

'So this priest invited me to his day retreat at the Capuchin church and school the following Sunday. When I arrived I found the place rather dull, a feeling of sadness around it – but then maybe that was just me, because I was sad inside. I sat there criticizing the sombre decor and the dullness of the place to myself. About five minutes later I noticed this young woman come in. I realized that her whole demeanour was in fact the complete opposite of mine. Who was she? I was struck by a harmony about her which was even reflected in her dress. As people were arriving and we were waiting for the start of the day, I sat and watched her.

'Then the church opened for us to go to Mass. Again, in the church, I kept looking at her. Something was touching me deeply. I felt there was some sort of mystical reality present in that young woman. Her whole manner of being at the Mass fascinated me. I wanted to know her.

'After the Mass we went back into a room in the Capuchin school where the priest was going to speak. He introduced the day and then he called on this young girl to speak. I was delighted. She spoke about love. And that was my own problem. The situation in my family, things inside myself, all had led me to conclude, as a perhaps slightly romantic teenager, that you couldn't really, fully, love on this earth.

'Over 53 years later, I can still feel it as if I was there again at that talk. I can see her as she described this love. She began, "There are many beautiful things on this earth...but the most beautiful is love."

' "Well," I thought to myself, "so she believes in love?" She went on to speak so beautifully about love. She spoke of all the different expressions of love. Then she told us that if we can know and experience this here on earth, what then would the love of God in Heaven be like?

'I was transported. I felt as if I was being lifted up – right into the Heart of God. Everything in my life was being turned upside down and a great love of God was being awakened in me. This certainty that I was loved by God was becoming stronger and stronger. It seemed that all the barriers in me were falling away. I realized that everything that had happened to me until then had been permitted by God's love. Everything in my life seemed to fall into place.

'I'm sure that this wasn't just a feeling of great joy, it was really a divine experience. I knew there and then that this was my 'way'. And I knew it wouldn't just be a "flash in the pan" but would be lasting, the path of my life.

'At the end I felt a completely different person. I was normally so timid and mouse-like, but I felt I had been transformed. I felt like a queen. I tried to speak to Chiara at the end, but everyone else was crowding around her and I just said "Thank you" and left for home.

'Back at work the next day, the priest called me on the phone and asked what I had thought of the day. I told him I wanted to meet this Chiara Lubich again. He gave me her address and suggested I get in touch with her.

'So I wrote, and Chiara replied, suggesting that I call in to see her at the Capuchin school where she worked. Although I felt completely different about life and about myself since I had heard her speak the previous Sunday, I was still shy. I thought to myself that she was a teacher, an important, educated person, and that I would probably be wasting her time. My heart was pounding as I rang the doorbell – and Chiara opened the door with such an expression of love, and greeted me as if she had always known me, that all my fears melted away. She was wearing the pinafore that teachers of the time used to wear.

'It was playtime for the children, and Chiara told me to stay with her for a while to have a chat. Although she was completely available to me, I could see that she was still attentive to the children running around. And as different children would come up to her to show her something, or ask a question, or just for a hug, you could see that she loved each one of them equally.

'She asked me about my life and told me about hers. She gave me her testimony – God is love. I could see that she lived that. She was indeed what she spoke of. I told her that her talk the previous Sunday had changed my life. Chiara replied, "Yes, of course. God is love."

'I asked her why she could not teach this to the whole world. "Yes," she said, "the world is waiting. We won't preach it – we have to witness to it. If we can live this moment by moment, if we can live like Jesus would live, the world will believe." '

As Natalia recounts this over half a century later, it still brings a lump to her throat and tears of emotion to her eyes. 'Since then,' she says, 'my path has been to follow Chiara unreservedly.'

On 2 September of that same year, 1943, another young girl in the Trent region was caught in an air-raid. Nineteen-year-old Graziella De Luca was working as a civil servant in Trent when the siren went off. She quickly ran alongside the river to the agreed spot where her family used to meet up during air-raids. The shelters which would later be dug out under the rocks by the river had not yet been made.

She had just made it there when the planes arrived overhead. The family threw themselves down on the ground, knowing that the bombardment was about to begin and that they had no time to run elsewhere.

Graziella recalls that 'Each bomb seemed more tremendous than the last. And there in that moment I shouted out with all my strength, "God, don't let me die now, because now I've understood that you exist. And I've got nothing to give you if I die now. I understand what it means to live now." I had told nobody at home what was going on inside me.'

Graziella, like Natalia, had been someone looking for a purpose and meaning to life. She grew up in Sicily in a comfortable middle-class family. She was bright and talented and wanted for nothing. Her father was an avowed Marxist and Theosophist and tried to pass his values on to his daughter. Her mother was a practising Catholic. Graziella says she went to Mass on Sundays just to keep her mother happy. She didn't like it, or rather she says that she didn't like the clericalism of the Church in that place at that time. She came to hate all that she describes as 'smelling of the sacristy'.

The sort of problems which Graziella had when growing up were whether to play the piano or the harp, for she was gifted in music. Likewise in sports, where she was selected to join a regional basketball team to go on a national tour. When she decided not to pursue music as a career she had to decide what to study at university. Should she choose philosophy or literature, or why not medicine? She wanted to study everything, just as she excelled at all the sports she played. The teenage Graziella had to come to terms with the fact that there was only one life and she couldn't do everything.

While being interested in all other subjects, the one she didn't care for was religion. She says that when there were catechism classes at school she used to play games like noughts and crosses at the back of the class.

As a teenager she had no lack of suitors – which is not hard to understand, because even today she still looks like a model! When you meet her you think she must have been an actress or a ballet dancer. Her looks, her figure, her elegance and her perfect couture convince you that she must be a star of the old school. When she was a young woman she had even been offered a part in a film.

But by the time of that air raid in 1943 Graziella was almost despairing. Her question then was, 'Is it worthwhile being alive? What's life all about?'

She remembers two chance encounters that made a deep impression on her life. When she was twelve years old a Paulist priest came to give a mission in her parish. During it she felt the need to speak to a priest in confession – this was unusual for her, because normally she went just out of a sense of duty or to keep her mother happy.

She says that as soon the old priest heard her first words in that confession, he told her that she should really have a spiritual director. This didn't go down well with Graziella, who thought the old priest was suggesting that he himself should carry out that task. He asked her name, her age and the details of her life. She says, 'It really got on my nerves, because it seemed to me he was taking my freedom away in wanting to know all these things about me.'

But the priest also added that he would pray every day for Graziella and that at his Masses he would pray that she might find the right spiritual director for her. By the time she left the confessional there was a new hope in her heart. The fact that this old priest, whom she didn't even know, was going pray for her encouraged her to believe that she would find an answer for her life. She had understood something new – in her own words, 'That the priest is a bridge between our soul and God.'

When in 1943 the family moved back up to Trent from Sicily, Graziella was transferred to the University of Venice, but very soon the roads were closed and, as Chiara and Dori had discovered, it was not possible to get to the university. Graziella began working in the civil service. Once, on a free day, she went out for a walk in the hills around Trent. As she was silently mulling over her existential questions, she met a beggar who asked her for money. She had no money on her but took out her packed lunch from her bag and gave it to him. The man was filled with gratitude and kissed her hand. As she continued on her hike she felt good. That little act of kindness had shown her another way of living, and she said to herself, 'Your life must change.'

Yes, but how could her life change? It seemed she was being tormented with all these questions and the search for another way of life, but where were the answers? On her path she came across a little wayside shrine and stopped. She looked up at the little statue of St Francis. 'If you are really a saint, show me somehow that God exists,' she demanded. 'I've got to find an answer!'

And so on that day in September 1943, as the bombs fell around her and her family, she made her act of faith when she screamed out, 'God, I know you exist!'

As soon as the bombs had all been dropped and the planes were gone, soldiers came running up to the De Luca family. 'Don't you realize that a bomb has exploded just three metres away from you?!' they said. 'Three other bombs have fallen beside you, and they could explode at any moment! Run! Get out of here!'

On 1 March the following year, a colleague in her office invited Graziella to go along to a meeting. It wasn't a colleague whom Graziella liked or felt any affinity with, because she was 'a pious, religious sort of person'. So she decided to take a rise out of this fuddy-duddy by going to her meeting dressed up in the trendiest way possible, since she thought all religious people had poor taste in clothing.

When she arrived at the meeting place, she found that it was gloomy and had a low ceiling – in fact it was a bit too much like a sacristy for Graziella's liking! But there in a corner of the room stood a statue of St Francis with his arms outstretched. 'How strange,' she thought. 'Are you now going to answer that question I asked you?'

She remembers that just then three girls came over to speak to her. It was Chiara and her two 'first companions', Dori and Natalia. 'It was as if they had always known me,' says Graziella, 'and I felt that they loved me, even though they had never seen me before.

'Then Chiara started talking, and we were all sitting in a circle around her. I had always hated religious conferences in church halls or classrooms, but here we were, just sitting around like friends. Chiara was just chatting to us as if she hadn't prepared a talk or anything like that. It seemed she was just saying what came from her heart.

'She was speaking about the love of St Francis and the love of St Catherine for the poor. And then, I have to tell you, I had a difficult moment. When Chiara spoke like that, when she spoke with her soul, it was my "Road to Damascus".

'I realized she was speaking about God, who is infinite love – and I was experiencing this love. I realized that God had already done ninety-nine per cent, and I only had to do the remaining one per cent. I had to say my "Yes". At that meeting I understood that we all have to become saints.

'I understood other important things that evening too – that my life was linked to the whole of the Mystical Body of Christ, to the whole of humanity. If I said "Yes" to Him, I would be helping to build up the Body throughout the world. But if I said, "No", that would be damaging the Body. So I understood that my role would be important, whichever decision I made.

'I had never cried in my life, because I had always wanted to be a young lady, to appear grown up and strong. But that evening, as Chiara was speaking, I said my "Yes", and the floodgates opened. I poured out all my tears that evening.

'At the end of the meeting I asked Chiara if she had a spiritual director. She said she had, and she would give me his name if I liked. At that moment I felt I had to make a general confession, as if to do a whole laundry and start my life anew.

'Then I emptied my pockets and gave everything I had to Chiara – not because she needed it or had asked for anything, but because it seemed logical to me to do so, regardless of what she herself had or didn't have. And from that moment I never left her.'

FIVE

ALL AROUND THE HEARTH
– THE FOCOLARE

From an early stage other girls began to gather around Chiara. They were inspired by her and wanted to live as she did. This became even more pronounced after she had made her secret consecration to God on 7 December 1943. Her young pupil Dori was already committed to her. Natalia met her at the end of that year and decided to follow Chiara and her way to God unconditionally. In March 1944 Graziella had her first encounter with Chiara, which immediately prompted her to rush to make a general confession.

Of course, there were other girls who followed Chiara, came to her talks and tried to live the same life of charity and service to the poor. Not all, though, were called to the same radical commitment and lifelong celibacy that would mark Chiara and her 'first companions'.

They had no intention of starting a 'movement'. All they knew was that the Gospel and Christian message had come alive for them. Since meeting Chiara Lubich their lives had changed. They loved to spend any time they could with this young woman who seemed to communicate the Divine. When they were with her it seemed to them that Heaven was very close.

Subsequently, they held no formal meetings and had no rules or structures. They were just a group of friends who tried to live the Gospel and to help each other to live it. During 1943 and 1944, the aerial bombardments of Trent seemed to be unceasing. The friends made a pact to meet in the air-raid shelter whenever the siren sounded. The only possession they brought to these meetings was Chiara's little book of the Gospels.

One thing on which they had all agreed was that in this life everything would pass. Only God endured, only God was eternal. Everything else was vanity.

After one air raid Chiara was passing the Hospital of St Clare in Trent. Her brother Gino was working there, soon to qualify as a doctor. He saw his sister passing and called her in. The hospital's venereal diseases unit had been hit by a bomb. It was utterly devastated. Chiara remembers looking at the broken and charred bodies of the women who had been receiving treatment there.

'It was terrible! These poor women still had on all their make-up and jewellery, but they were dead. Their lives had been wiped out in an instant. My brother Gino pointed to them and said, "You see – all is vanity." The only person in that unit who survived was the nurse in charge, a religious sister.'

Chiara appreciated every day her privilege of living for God alone. Her personal consecration had really forged her relationship with her Creator. 'I was married to God,' she says.

Today it is more widely recognized that lay people in the Church can live out consecration to God, a commitment they share by their common baptism. But in those days people still had to fit into one or another 'category' or 'state of life' in the Church. Chiara had entered on what would become known as the 'fourth way'.

Soon others also wanted to go through a similar rite or ceremony. Natalia was the first to express this desire. She too wanted to give her whole life to God in a formal commitment. Chiara advised her to speak to her confessor, and eventually a date was set.

Graziella, by then another of the 'first companions', remembers clearly that night in April 1944. She still giggles as she remembers Natalia's consecration. 'Just a month after I had first met Chiara and had been spending as much time as possible with her and the other girls, she invited me to join them on a retreat they were having. It was being held in the guest-house of a Sisters' convent in Trent. I arranged to take some days off work.

'My father, who was a Marxist and a Theosophist, didn't hold with all this religion, so I played out a charade. I would get up and go out every morning as if I were going to work. Of course, I was going to the retreat! But then there was the weekend. I couldn't pretend to go out to work on the days when he knew the office was closed. So I asked him if I could stay the weekend in the city to attend a philosophy course I was interested in.

'My Dad was no fool and wasn't taken in by my story. However, perhaps because he had seen a change in me, as all our parents had, he eventually allowed me to stay the weekend in Trent for my "course".

'At the convent where we were staying, they put me in a room with Natalia. She was very quiet and pious – not my type of person at all. On the Saturday night when I got into bed, I looked and saw Natalia. She was wearing this long flowing night-dress, with all its little ribbons and bows and so on. And then, as if that weren't bad enough, she got down on her knees to pray beside her bed. Whatever next!

'Well, I pretended to be asleep, but with one eye I was watching her, and it seemed as if she was never going to get up off her knees. Those prayers were going on and on! Now, I knew that in the Gospel it said, "When you pray, pray with few words." So what was going on? Had we changed a page of the Gospel or something?

'Eventually, I couldn't keep my mouth shut any more, and I opened the other eye and asked her, "Natalia, what on earth are you doing?"

'She replied, "I'm preparing for something, but it's a secret."

'Well, if there was a secret, I wanted to know it, so I sat up and quizzed her until I found out what it was.

' "Tomorrow I'm going to make my flight for always – an eternal flight," said Natalia. In Italian this was a play on words: *voto* means 'vow' and *volo* means 'flight'.

'So I said, "What? Are you going on a plane somewhere, then?"

' "Of course not," said Natalia. "It's another sort of flight. If you want to bring many souls to God, you have to renounce the possibility of having your own family. Then you'll be the mother of many."

' "All right, then," I said. "I'll do that as well. I'll make that little flight tomorrow too."

' "No, no, no!" retorted Natalia. "It's not as easy as that. You can't just do it like that. You'll have to speak to Chiara about it. And she'll make you see a priest. I'm sure she will because, you see, it's not easy to do this." '

And that's what happened. Graziella went to see Chiara, who sent her right away to see a priest. When she spoke to the Capuchin priest and told him what she wanted to do, he was completely opposed. This was something she might consider when she was 40, but not now at the age of 19.

Graziella reckoned that Natalia was going to do it, so why couldn't she? The priest explained that Natalia was making a life-long consecration – a vow. Dori, the other 'first companion', was only making a temporary vow for three months. That was the opening which Graziella needed. Okay, so surely she could do it for three months too, then?

After a long conversation, it was finally agreed that she could make a temporary vow for three months. This satisfied Graziella, who thought, 'A bird in the hand is better than two in the bush.'

She takes up the story of that night in April 1944 when the first members of what would become the Focolare Movement followed the example of Chiara in dedicating their lives to God through a vow of chastity.

'I had obtained permission to make my temporary vow. Even though I couldn't stand clericalism, "churchiness", convents, or anything like that, if Chiara had entered a convent I would have followed.

'This priest used to make us get up at midnight to recite the offices and so on – we were all in the Third Order at that time. I could accept all that, so long as I could follow Chiara.

'So we went to this church at night. The tabernacle was surrounded with beautiful scented flowers. And I thought, "When I make my flight for ever, I'll do it at midnight with lots of flowers around."

'Dori and I sat in the front row. Then, of course, Natalia made her entrance. She had a veil on – which was just awful in my opinion! And worse – she was carrying a lily in her hand. Yuk! Let's just say it wasn't my taste!'

'She was accompanied by Chiara and made her vow. Then Dori and I were called forward and we made our temporary vow or promise. That was it – I'd made the first step.'

When, over 50 years later, Natalia heard Graziella's recollections of that night, she was horrified. What had happened was that the good sisters of the convent where they were staying were so excited that these young girls were about to make a vow that, just before the private ceremony began, they whisked Natalia off to the sacristy. She only remembers that her heart was full of the step she was about to make, and she found herself being led down the aisle after the sisters had stuck a veil on her head and an artificial lily in her hand! She was keen to point out to me that she wasn't a person given to religiosity or shows of piety, but had just gone along with whatever was done to her while her heart was preparing to make her vow.

This was how life continued for Chiara and her first companions through 1943 to 1944. Then came the night of 13 May 1944. That was the night when Chiara and her family saw their home destroyed from the hillside where they had gone for safety. That was the night when Chiara took the decision, through her tears, to leave her family, who had decided to quit the city, and go back down to stay with her companions.

While the decision itself had been painful to make, it was even harder to tell her parents the next morning when they went down to inspect the damage to their house.

Chiara recalls, 'The house had been badly damaged and rooms had collapsed. We had to clamber over the debris to recover a few objects and put them into rucksacks. I had to speak to my parents, to tell them of my decision. I went to find my father in the kitchen, knelt down and said, "Dad, I belong to God, and others are following me; I can't leave!" My father must have been granted a special grace, for he gave me his blessing with perfect calm and allowed me to stay.

'The most harrowing moment was the parting, when I had to put the rucksack I was to have carried on to my mother's tired shoulders. I wondered what would become of my family. Much later they told me that they had scarcely turned their backs on Trent to go away when they suddenly felt a great joy. They began to joke and laugh. They walked for a few miles and soon found shelter with two ladies in the village of Centa.

'But I was disconsolate. I just knew I had to stick to my decision. I headed towards the town. The destruction was total: trees had been uprooted, houses were in ruins, roads were covered with debris. Tears came to my eyes…and I let them flow.

'Suddenly a woman appeared at the corner of a street. She grabbed hold of me and began to shout in a frenzy, "They're dead – all four of them! Do you hear? All four of them!"

'I comforted her and realized that I had to silence my own grief in order to take on that of others.

'It was six o'clock in the morning, and the streets were deserted. I began to look for my friends. Thank God, they were all alive. At that time we were a little group of six or seven girls aged between 15 and 24.'

As well as having left her family, Chiara was now homeless. She needed somewhere to stay, and was offered a little flat adjoining the Capuchin church. Its address was 2 Piazza Cappuccini. It had two rooms and became known to the girls as 'the little house', with its connotations of the little house of Loreto.

More of the first companions came to live with Chiara. She was now seeing lived out what she had only seen intuitively in the little house at Loreto: a group of virgins imitating the life of the three virgins who composed the Holy Family in Nazareth.

By this time, due to the frequency of the air raids on Trent and the destruction of the city, the Capuchin school had been closed, and Chiara no longer had to teach classes every day. She therefore kept house while the other girls went out to work. Natalia's mother had reached the stage where she saw such a change in her daughter that, despite the unconventionality of it for the time and place, she readily gave her permission for Natalia to leave the family home in the countryside and move into the 'little house'. Graziella's parents had moved back to Sicily, and when the time came for her and her brother to follow, she kept stalling her parents, saying she would come later. She never did. Her brother never forgave her. Her parents did eventually. Other girls joined the group and some took up residence in the 'little house' – but not Dori, who was still too young at that stage.

Of course, some tongues began to wag, especially in the small, traditional villages from which some of the girls came. Young girls just didn't up and leave their families to set up home together. When Natalia's mother began to hear some of the gossip, she went personally to every one of her neighbours and told them that her family had never been so united and content as they had now become since Natalia began following Chiara Lubich. The mother eventually joined the movement which had attracted her daughter.

In the 'little house' the girls lived a life of evangelical poverty. They desired to live in unity at every moment, for that was another one of Jesus' words that they had discovered: 'That they may all be one, Father, as you are in me and I am in you' (John 17:21).

They made a pact with one another. Before setting off from the little house every day, they would look at one another and promise,

'I am ready to die for you.' Jesus Himself had said, 'A man can have no greater love than to lay down his life for his friends' (John 15:13), and they wanted to live that sort of love.

Chiara remembers life in that first community as being 'Beautiful, wonderful! It was very poor accommodation because we had reduced it to a strict minimum. We had got rid of the few pieces of furniture which we possessed by giving them to the poor. In our bedroom (they only had one bedroom for all of them) we kept only our mattresses and bed-frames, which we laid of top of tins of the powdered milk which was issued to us during the war.' The only other item in that bedroom was a picture of the suffering Jesus on the wall.

In January 1944 Dori, the youngest of Chiara's companions, was taken ill. One day (and Chiara still remembers the precise date – 24 January) a priest called to visit the patient while Chiara was there. As they chatted by Dori's bedside, he asked them if they knew when Jesus suffered the most. Chiara replied that it must have been during his agony in the garden of Gethsemane. No, the priest said, it was when he cried out, 'My God, my God, why have you forsaken me?' (Matthew 27:47). He, the very Son of God, had been, or felt, completely abandoned, forsaken even by His Father.

From then on, the girls decided to follow the forsaken Jesus. When they woke in the morning their first act would be to look at that picture on their bedroom wall and say, 'Because you are forsaken.' That is, He would be their motivation for everything. Not that they would offer their day 'to' Him, or do things 'for' Him, but they would see Him in every person and situation, and it was He Himself whom they would serve in those persons and situations.

Thus, another founding characteristic of the little band that was Chiara and her companions was defined. They were living their lives for an ideal – which was God – and it was all for Jesus who was forsaken.

Despite the constant running to the air-raid shelters, often spending the whole night there before going to work the next day, despite living in poverty, since those girls who were working had to support their families as well, Chiara refers to that time with great fondness. She says, 'They were unforgettable days, among the best of my life. The air-raid shelter where we took refuge was not very safe. It was an excavation under a rock – solid enough, but it had no door. If a bomb had fallen in front of it we would all have been killed.

'The air-raid warnings came one after another, night and day, up to eleven in a single day. People only went back to their houses long enough to fetch absolute necessities, and then scurried away again as fast as they could. My companions already made up a fine group; they had the courage to run right across the city when the sirens sounded in order to assemble in the shelter where I was, and if need be, to die together.

'As there was no question of doing anything else, I used to take the Gospels, which we would read in a corner of the shelter with the people who were taking refuge there. And the Gospel was opened up to us, in the sense that all its words were illuminated. I saw them light up one after another as if they were completely new and as if I were reading them for the very first time.

'At the same time as the Lord was giving me this light, He was encouraging me to live for Him. He enlightened my spirit and encouraged my will. I attribute this fact to the presence of Jesus amongst us – just as at Emmaus he had explained the Scriptures to his disciples. One after another we took up those words which had touched us as if we were hearing them for the first time, even though we had already heard them often on the lips of excellent preachers. We were able, without delay, to put them into practice, because our neighbour was always there. Those who were suffering were right there beside us. The mother with her children was there a few feet away. One of my companions would take a child in her arms and look after it, another would help the old people or get them something to eat. We would hurry home to make an enormous pot of soup, and then we would run to distribute it to the hungry. The poor were our brothers. They also came to our house. And all around the table you would see little groups of two – one of us and someone in need.'

As Chiara has many times explained since those days, 'One day in the shelter we felt a strong desire: Was there a word of Christ which particularly pleased Him? If we were shortly to find ourselves before Jesus, we would want to have lived whatever He had most at heart. We recalled His last farewell, when He gave His apostles a command which He called both 'my' and 'new': "This is my commandment:

that you love one another as I have loved you. No one has a greater love than this: to give his life for his own friends" [John 15:12–13].

'We felt those sacred words burn through us like fire. We looked at one another and declared to one another, "I am ready to die for you – I for you, I for you, all for each of us."

'Since we were ready to die, it wasn't difficult then to share each day our sufferings and our joys, our new spiritual experiences, and our poor possessions. Mutual love was the foundation for everything.

'And because of this, God was present among those few girls – He who had said, "Where two or three are gathered together in my name, I am there among them" [Matthew 18:20]. Now, when God is present and you allow God to act, things don't remain as they were before. The terrible situations which surrounded us were like a training field which brought love into action, not only among us but among those whom we encountered. The Gospel continued to guide our behaviour, and we realized that with it a revolution was born. "Love your neighbour *as* yourself" [Matthew 19:19]. As yourself – this was something new. "Love your enemies" [Matthew 5:44]. Who had considered this? "May they all be one" [John 17:21]. All.'

SIX

MOVEMENT FOR UNITY
– 'LET'S SEE WHO GETS THERE FIRST'

At the flat at Piazza Cappuccini a revolution had indeed been born. For Chiara and her first companions a life of simplicity and poverty was not enough on its own. They had to reach out to serve and console the One whom they followed and whom they loved as the Forsaken One. He it was whom they saw, or determined to see, in the poor of Trent, in those who were bereaved by the War, in anyone who was lonely or suffering.

They had put together their poor belongings and had given them away to those who needed them more than they. But then they discovered another word of Scripture: 'Give and it will be given unto you.' People who knew them in Trent saw what the girls from the 'little house' were doing, and soon goods of all sorts began arriving at 2 Piazza Cappuccini. The little house became a warehouse, or rather a clearing house, as clothes, furnishings, utensils – anything, in fact, that the owners didn't need – arrived there, only to be passed on and distributed to those who did need them.

They began to live what would become known in the future Movement's shorthand as 'the hundredfold'. Just as they had discovered the Lord's promise, 'Ask and it shall be given unto you' (Matthew 7:7), so also they began to experience something of what He meant when He said, 'Anyone who has left father or mother for my sake...will be repaid a hundredfold, even in this life' (Matthew 19:29).

Chiara and her companions laugh today when they remember how they became bolder in taking the Lord at His word! 'One day,' says Chiara, 'a man confided to me that he needed a pair of shoes. He took a size 42. With that completely new faith which God had given us, I went into a church and I said to Jesus, "Jesus, you need a pair of shoes, size 42, and I am praying for them now." I left the church and bumped into a lady, who handed me a parcel – a pair of size 42 shoes!' 'Give and it will be given unto you': they gave all they had, and the Lord would never be outdone in generosity!

Another illustration of this that Chiara remembers was when someone brought some apples to the focolare. 'You should have seen our little house at that time,' she says. 'Goods were piled up and then distributed, only for more to arrive shortly. So with the apples. As soon as we received them we went off to distribute them to the poor. On our return there were some more apples! This sequence of events was repeated three times in succession, until, in the evening, a suitcase filled with apples arrived!'

This trust in Providence became an essential element of the first statutes of the budding movement. Chiara and her companions still insist that they never had any intention of starting a movement. They only wanted to live fully the Christian Gospel.

Within months of the establishment of that first little community at Piazza Cappuccini, over 500 other people became associated with the little group. They were scattered in 158 towns and villages in the region of Trent. People had come to call Chiara and her companions the *Focolarine* – a term which is difficult to translate into English. The Italian word *Focolare* is normally translated as 'hearth' or 'fireside'. The *Focolarine*, then, were seen as 'fire-bearers'. The people could see that these young girls were aflame with their Ideal, the love of God, and seemed to communicate this wherever they went.

Soon they were being invited to share their experience with others. Hence the rapid expansion of the Ideal to all those surrounding towns and villages. Chiara did her share of speaking to people, but she couldn't be everywhere, and so she delegated her companions, who were sent out to witness to what they had 'seen and heard' in their lives with Chiara as they had lived the Gospel.

Natalia, who was as quiet as a mouse, found herself speaking without fear to congregations in village halls. Graziella, with her long golden hair and her elegant style – definitely what the Italians call *un bel figurino* – found herself in many sacristies, convents and churches as well as village and parish halls, speaking to capacity audiences.

Within months they were known all over the region of Trent. But not all was sweetness and light. Not everybody was filled with admiration for these young girls, who had left home and family to follow the Lord. Word went around that they were Communists. Chiara and her companions had discovered the last prayer of Christ in St John's Gospel: 'that they be one, Father, as you are in me and I am in you' (John 17:21). They were being called to live in unity. They had discovered that this was the thing which was closest to the Lord's heart, as he had prayed this during his last evening with his apostles. In those days, remembers Chiara, only the Communists spoke about 'unity'. It was not something that you heard preached about in Sunday sermons. So were they Communists, then? Either that or Protestants! All this reading of Scripture and living of Gospel phrases! Perhaps they had embraced Protestantism and were leading the good people of Trent astray!

Chiara points out that such accusations were always made by people who did not know them, who hadn't even met Chiara or her companions. To those who had met them or had benefited from their care and compassion, they were simply 'the Focolarine'.

But such radical living of the Gospel, simple as it was, couldn't just go along without any rules or recognition. Especially not now that other young women were leaving their families to throw in their lot with the young leader, Chiara Lubich. Pressure grew on Chiara to formalize her Ideal, to somehow register the young community with the Church authorities.

'I didn't realize things had to be so complicated,' says Chiara today. 'All I knew was that we had heard the call of the Lord and wanted to live out His Word.' When a local priest pressed her to provide a name for this 'movement' she protested that they didn't want any name, saying, 'We're Christians, that's all. Christians!' But it wasn't enough. She had to come up with a name. 'If we have to have a name, then,' said Chiara, 'let us be known as the Movement for Unity.'

In a short time Chiara drew up some statutes for her 'Movement for Unity' which were to be presented to the local Archbishop for approval. They encapsulated, as best she could, the spirit and ideal of herself and her companions. They were to work for their keep as well as relying on Divine Providence (hadn't God promised them 'the hundredfold'?). They were to endeavour to realize among themselves that unity for which Christ had prayed. They were to hold all things in common...and so on and so forth.

Chiara did her best in drawing up the statutes and handed them in to the Archbishop's house.

After the hospital had been bombed and as the end of the War drew near, Chiara's brother Gino joined the partisans who were fighting to overthrow Mussolini and his Fascists. At that time the partisans included Communists, Socialists and Christian Democrats, all working together against the Fascists. Gino was still a Communist. He and his party looked for a new tomorrow where all Italians would be equal, and above all, where there would be no poverty. All land and goods would belong to everyone. This was his ideal.

The work of Chiara and the Focolarine did not go unnoticed by the Communists of Trent. Chiara explains: 'My friends and I lived what we found in the Gospel. In the air-raid shelter we would come across the phrase, "Love your neighbour as yourself." I would tell my friends how I understood these words. I'd say, "Look, we have to love our neighbour – we have to love them as we love ourselves. So let's put this into practice – let's start right now!' And so we would split up and go out to all the other people present in the shelter and see how we could love them.

'Another time we would open the Gospels and find the phrase, "Whatever you did to the least of my brethren, you did it to me" (Matthew 25:40). And we would live those words. Each phrase, one after the other, provoked what we call "the Christian Revolution". If everybody lived this, the world could be different. And we were all linked by the Gospel. We lived it to the letter. Once, for example, we decided to work to transform Trent. So we went into the poorest districts of the town to help the poorest of the poor. When we saw what someone needed, we'd write down the person's name and needs, because we wanted to help that particular person. We discovered that the poor person belonged to us – they were like our own family, and so we would give them whatever we had.

'Now people knew that we were going to the poorest, so they would bring us whatever they had: potatoes, flour, jam, firewood, everything. One day in May 1945, two Communists came into our little focolare and said to me, 'Look, we've been watching you. We've seen the way you girls share everything and how you give it all away to those in need.'

Chiara remembers the meeting very clearly because the two Communists asked her, 'What's going on? Why on earth are you doing this? Tell us the secret of your success.'

She says, 'I pointed to the crucifix on the wall, because He is the one who is love and who taught us to love. They lowered their eyes.'

One of them said to her, 'What you're doing on a small scale, we will do all over the world.'

Chiara challenged them: 'We are few, we're young, we're poor. But God is with us. Let's see who gets there first, shall we?'

The reason why she remembers the incident so vividly is that one of the Communists was her brother Gino. She continued to have a great respect for him because 'his greatest concern was for the poor.' She also says that she has always had a great love for Communists and they for her movement because they shared this common concern for the poor and for unity. But the means to achieve their respective ends were very different. Chiara would eventually penetrate behind the Iron Curtain and would bring her Movement there in spite of the Communist authorities' attempts to create a 'state without God'.

In 1945 Chiara already had the conversion of Communists at heart. Those first statutes of the Movement defined the central aim of promoting unity – the unity of all people – as the central idea of the Gospel.

As the War approached its end Gino Lubich served on the Liberation Committee for Trent. His specific remit was the area of the Press, and he eventually worked as a journalist on the Communist newspaper *Unity*, based at their Milan bureau.

In the same family, then, there was Gino working to promote the Communist ideal and Chiara, his younger sister, living a life of evangelical poverty in order to achieve the unity of all.

SEVEN

GROWING NETWORK
– A CHARISMATIC FOUNDRESS

When they were called to speak in the outlying villages and towns, Chiara would give her companions written notes, the fruit of her contemplation – but always with the instruction that they were to read them and then destroy them. She was adamant that she did not want the other girls to be reliant on her. They were to understand Scripture for themselves and then get rid of the intermediary, as it were. Besides, they had made a commitment to evangelical poverty and so should have no collections of Chiara's thoughts – the book of the Gospels was enough.

People who had met her in Trent or at one of the meetings elsewhere, or who had heard about her from her companions, also wrote to Chiara. In the grace of those first months and years, as well as in the heady excitement of living a radical message, the other girls automatically referred people back to Chiara. She was the centre of their community, she was the cause of their finding this new life. As Natalia had discovered during her first visit to see Chiara the schoolteacher, she was completely available to everyone. So the companions had no hesitation in constantly putting others in touch with her.

Chiara would respond to the many letters which arrived addressed to her at 2 Piazza Cappuccini. She believed, as she still does, that she and the community should use every means at their disposal to keep in touch with those who shared their spirit. This was also part of creating unity.

And so she was constantly writing letters, using every spare moment, so that none of these people who were in contact with her would feel abandoned. But as with the outlines of talks which she gave to the first companions, Chiara insisted that these letters should be destroyed once they had been read. She certainly did not want people leaning on her words instead of building their own spiritual base and developing their own understanding of their own vocation. And she certainly did not want to encourage any cult of personality.

Natalia remembers that in the first focolare they had made a pact not to hold on to anything that was not God. That is, they would let go of everything except the Ideal that they had chosen – God himself.

She says, 'We were so fired up by what we had discovered through Chiara that we would invite other people along to meet her. They in turn would invite their friends, and so the whole network of people following the Ideal grew.

'Of course, once the War ended we still felt somehow responsible for all these people. We had read in Scripture how Jesus loved His friends: "He loved them until the end." So Chiara would sometimes write a circular letter or a meditation and we would go out, in a way like the apostles, to take it to other groups of friends, to other towns and villages. But we knew we then had to destroy the letter.

'Some years after the War and once the Movement had become established, a Focolarina called Dina Fedrizzi sent back a whole packet of letters that she had received from Chiara. She had been in a sanatorium and didn't know that she was supposed to destroy them. When she learned that she shouldn't have kept them, she sent them back with a letter to Chiara, thanking her for her faithfulness in writing to her and saying, "I can only give back to you the gift you gave to me."

'Now Chiara can see with hindsight that those letters still have a certain value, and sometimes she uses them in her teaching and writing. Also, I think it was useful to have those letters returned because it reassures us, and Chiara, that her charism was there even in those early days.'

That Chiara Lubich was the possessor of a charism seemed to be confirmed already in 1945. A charism, as outlined by St Paul, is a spiritual gift given to someone, not for their own benefit but for the up-building of the Body of Christ, the Church.

Another of those 'words' of the Gospel discovered by Chiara and her companions was 'He who hears you, hears me' (Luke 10:16). Our Lord had told his apostles that those who listened to them would, in effect, be listening to Him. So to be sure that they were doing what the Lord wanted, they had to listen to the successors of the apostles, the bishops.

Chiara wasted no time in seeking an audience with the local archbishop. Monsignor Carlo De Ferrari was a large and rotund man. In the clerical Italy of that time he was perhaps a rather formidable figure to a young single laywoman. But the Lord had said, 'He who hears you, hears me.'

Chiara went in total confidence to her first meeting with Archbishop De Ferrari and responded calmly to his questioning, outlining simply what she and her companions were living. The Archbishop's response was equally simple, and perfectly clear: '*Digitus Dei hic est*' ('The finger of God is here').

Chiara remembers the importance of that meeting in 1945. 'If the Archbishop had told us to disband or stop what we were doing, we would have done so immediately,' she says.

But he didn't. What he did do over the next two years was constantly to encourage Chiara to write some sort of Rule for her budding Movement. In those days, perhaps more than today, it was deemed necessary to give legal form to groups and associations within the Church.

Chiara and her companions didn't understand this at first. As Natalia remembers it, 'We wanted our only Rule to be the Gospel, the pure Gospel.'

Chiara herself said that if they had to express a rule for their life it would be love. 'Our life will be all love,' she said.

But, of course, in line with her own understanding (which was exactly the Catholic understanding) of the voice of Christ being discerned in the voice of the Bishop on matters of faith and morals, she submitted. In 1947 the Archbishop granted the first official diocesan approval for the Movement, still widely known informally as the Focolare, but officially called the Movement for Unity.

Despite her protestations that she is 'just an ordinary person', it seems likely that Chiara Lubich was beginning to understand that she had been given a special role as the foundress of such a movement. As she says today, 'At that time we didn't speak about "charism". That only came later, and through our submission at every turn to the appropriate ecclesiastical authority. Although it is a matter of faith that the Lord speaks through the ordained successors to His apostles, we know that this is true not only by faith but also by our own experience of it.'

When I questioned Chiara about her understanding of her role and charism as a modern-day 'foundress', she was quite clear. When asked if God used the War – the fact that the first members daily faced death as they reached out to the injured and impoverished – she says that this is not the most significant element in the birth of the Focolare. So was a more deciding factor, then, that God wanted to use this young woman, Chiara Lubich?

'Yes, that is the more important element. But the War was also used in that it made us focus our lives on God and choose Him as our Ideal.'

So the most important element must have been God's choice of person, then, because many other cities in Europe were also being bombed during the War.

'Yes, that's it. The War was secondary, like a framework for it.' (By 'it' I believe she means God's choice of her as an instrument.)

Did she know that she was somehow chosen? Is she conscious of having been prepared from childhood to undertake this work and mission? 'Yes, I knew it. But I was just a young girl. This had to be confirmed by the Church. I wasn't a priest, I wasn't a bishop, so I needed the confirmation of the hierarchy. The Archbishop always did this for me – this job of assuring me that I was doing what God wanted me to do.'

While the Archbishop of Trent recognized the charism of Chiara and she herself was beginning to understand that she had somehow been 'chosen' by God to accomplish a particular work which she was just beginning to see unfold, not everyone else did. 'The prophet is not accepted in his own land' (Luke 4:24). In Chiara's case, at least, while her family accepted it, they didn't all recognize or understand the greatness and uniqueness of her calling.

Naturally, this made Chiara suffer. Her father seemed to accept her mission much more readily than her devout, traditionally Catholic mother, who was a daily communicant. Chiara puts this down to her father's social concerns and his seeing the social or charitable side of Chiara's and her companions' activities. Although both parents eventually moved to be with Chiara, and lived and died in the heart of the Focolare, some say that her mother never really understood the greatness of Chiara's calling. In those first months after Chiara left her family to dedicate herself to her companions and their living of the Gospel, Luigia Lubich was inconsolable as Christmas was approaching and she thought of her family not spending it together. This bore heavily on the daughter, who knew she was doing what God wanted of her but who had always been available and at the service of her mother, who perhaps relied on her more than on the others.

A heart-rending appeal for understanding was addressed by Chiara to her mother near the end of 1944, in which she writes: 'I am sure that He will give a special blessing to the mother of a girl who may be worthless and mediocre, but whom He has chosen as His spouse so that the greatness of His work might stand out more clearly in the light of her littleness.'

The full text of that letter written just before Christmas (and given to the Focolare by Luigia Lubich 20 years later) illustrates the ardent desire which Chiara felt to have her own mother share in this work, in this new understanding of the Christian message which had begun in and through her.

The Lubich parents, with their two younger daughters, were living up in the mountains in the region of Trent where the two elderly ladies had taken them in on the day when they had quit Trent and Chiara had decided to stay. She wrote:

Dearest Mum,

For some days now I have had a terrible suffering within me. Dad came and found that I have a touch of flu. The air-raid shelter is really draughty and the sirens never stop. The lorry journeys are bitterly cold and I would never survive it. Thinking it over, Dad felt it would be impossible for me to come home for Christmas, and I feel the same way.

I see Him there on that cross; He too is suffering from homesickness, from the abandonment of his Father. Then I realize that He is granting the request that I ask Him so often: 'Let me experience something of Your sufferings, especially a share in Your terrible abandonment, so that I might be close to You and resemble You more who, in Your infinite love, have chosen me and taken me to spend my life with You.'

Then He comforts me and tells me that if, when He called me, I left father, mother and home to live where there was danger and need, for love of Him alone, He will be my consolation. And He lights that fire within me that makes me cry out, 'Love is not loved!' This is my first cry to you, Mum. You at least must listen to me. In the name of your love for me, for Gino, Dad, Carla and Liliana, I beg you to listen.

Don't think that what I am asking you is just a whim or mere imagination. No; you must believe me. In this life, which passes in a flash, only one thing matters, and this is what we must ask God for: to love Him. Believe me. You will see in Heaven, where I want you beside me forever; then you will say I was right. Your life has been to love and marry Dad, and to love your children. You have loved God, too. But now the Lord is using me, as bad as you know me to be, to tell you that what matters is to love God!

Believe me, Mum, Jesus died for you. He would have died for you alone if your salvation alone had been necessary. Look at Him, there on the cross, and just think: how would you have felt if He had been your son? Listen to Him cry out, 'My God, my God, why have you forsaken me?' This cry is constantly repeated in my heart. Imagine Him dying there almost in despair and nailed like a lamb. Poor Jesus. Go on, Mum: say that you love Him too and that you want to make others love Him. Say that if your Silvia were to die before you, you would continue to burn with the fire that burns in me. I have met all kinds of people in my life, but I have never found anyone who loves me as much as He does. One day you will find out how much He has given me; you will know of the wonders He works in me and the girls who follow my way, the way of Love. Keep this to yourself, Mum.

As a leader and spiritual mother to thousands, for each one of whom she feels a personal love, she often feels the pain of a mother. Her reaction, she says today, is to embrace this, like Jesus embracing his cross, and to go forward. That is, she never lingers on the pain, but, accepting it, she seeks a way ahead, a positive response to the situation which is causing her or others suffering. In the paragraph which follows, Chiara, probably unwittingly, gives an explanation of her spirituality which has remained a fitting description right up until today:

I have married Him, and for His sake I have tried to shut off every other desire. He is my life, my greatest love. I have been swept away by Him and His cry, and they have enabled me to overcome everything, even though it makes my heart bleed. He alone could do this. He doesn't *make us ignore our affections but makes them more deeply felt than ever and then lets us go beyond them, because he is almighty; he is God.*

Now Christmas is approaching, and my heart breaks because I will probably be away from you. If only you could come down from the mountains. But it is too dangerous, because the sirens never stop and we are constantly going to the air-raid shelters. I couldn't bear the thought of you in the shelters all the time.

Today Dad has gone to see Gino, and when he comes back we'll make the final decision. In any case, it is better if Carla and Liliana spend Christmas with you, and it will be a new chance for Gino and me to offer a new sacrifice to Love.

Yes, everything, even death itself, as long as Jesus who has loved us to the point of dying for us might be loved by men. May this consolation be His and may ours be the peace which comes from only wanting to love Love.

You will see, Mum, how everything else comes as a consequence when we only seek His Kingdom. And His Kingdom means to tell everyone to love God and each other. Share my passion of love and spread it to everyone, since you are so good with words. Be sure that Jesus expects you to love Him as St Rita did, for she was a mother too.

Write to me about this. Nothing else matters. May the child Jesus bring this passion of mine into your heart. I am sure that He will give a special blessing to the mother of a girl who may be worthless and mediocre, but whom He has chosen as His spouse so that the greatness of His work might stand out more clearly in the light of her smallness.

With a heart which perhaps you do not yet know.
All my love,

Chiara.

EIGHT

THE 'SECRET' OF UNITY
– JESUS IN THE MIDST

While Chiara may describe the early days of that first Focolare as among the most beautiful of her life, the letter to her mother illustrates that she was not understood by everyone. And how much it pained her that those who were dear to her could not see the greatness of the call which God also addressed to them. Again there are echoes of St Paul: 'If only you knew what hope his call holds for you' (Ephesians 1:18).

She admits that life in the 'little house' was not always easy either, but as is her wont, she attributes value even to that, in as much as it allowed her to grow in her vocation of unity and the abandonment of Jesus Forsaken.

If, due to tiredness – which is perfectly understandable, considering the pace at which they were living – the girls parted company in the morning without having renewed their pact of unity in Jesus Forsaken, they would all sense a loss. As soon as they were together again they would renew their commitment.

While her companions went out to work, Chiara stayed at home to run the house. She had lost her job when the Capuchin school was forced to close because of the bombings. She had been prevented from continuing her university course when the roads to Venice became blocked. But she accepted that and embraced her new role as the leader of the burgeoning movement (although 'leader' is not a word she would ever use about herself – she prefers to call herself a 'focus'). So she packed away her beloved books in the attic at 2 Piazza Cappuccini.

Chiara admits that 'Unity among us was not always perfect, of course. Unity has to be earned: it demands mortification of the ego so that Jesus may live in us.

'One morning the other girls had parted a little brusquely to go to work, and I had stayed at home feeling that Jesus was no longer in our midst. It was as if everything was crumbling away. I couldn't understand any more why I had left my parents whom I loved so much, nor why I had given up my studies. Nothing made sense to me any more. I went up to the attic to fetch wood for the stove to prepare the meal for the other girls. There I saw my beloved books again, and I wept over those old volumes. As they fell, my tears disturbed the dust. At that moment I remembered my reason for living: unity, Jesus. If I was feeling all these things, it was because our bond as brethren had disappeared with the departure of our Brother – that is, Jesus in our midst. So as soon as my companions came back, the first thing to be done was to call our Brother into our midst. In that way everything would become clear again.

'I went back downstairs, put the finishing touches to the meal, and when the others arrived I said to them, "One of us is guilty of a fault; if it's me, I ask you to forgive me." We all asked each other's forgiveness, and Jesus returned among us. I saw afresh that it was worth having left everything – studies, parents, a future family, everything – and that was the end of the matter.'

The unity that Chiara and her companions wanted to live was an expression of Jesus present among them. In the movement's shorthand this has come to be expressed simply as 'Jesus in the midst'.

But for people who are not in the Focolare Movement, what does this mean? How do you 'call our Brother into our midst', as Chiara did after that little rupture in the unity of the first focolare? I asked her how this was done. Was there some technique, or was it some sort of psychological manipulation?

'Well,' she responded, 'Jesus says in the Gospel, "Where two or more are united in my name, I am there in their midst" [Matthew 18:20]. Studying the Fathers of the Church, you realize that this "in my name" means two or three who are united in "my love", in reciprocal love. Two people, or three or four, *who love one another in Jesus*, have Jesus in their midst. They have the presence of Jesus; there is the presence of Jesus in the midst of them.

'This is what we do: we try to love the other person, making ourselves one with him, with his situation, his way of thinking. He, in turn, tries to love you, practically, trying to understand you, to understand your way of thinking. This brings the presence of Jesus in our midst.'

But isn't this something like the Kantian hypothesis that truth may be your perception of it, and 'my truth' is my perception of it? Is she saying that we just mix up the two together to reach some sort of synthesis which she calls unity, or 'Jesus in the midst'?

'No. This unity we are talking of is not a human unity. It's the practical application of Jesus' promise.'

So is it possible to have 'Jesus in the midst' with someone of completely different thought and belief from yourself?

'Yes, if we love one another as I described, and if we are in grace, of course. People of other religions and non-believers of goodwill can also be in the grace of God.'

There is a certain *kind* of unity which is possible, then?

'Yes. For example, if an atheist brings a certain value to our encounter. Let's say if he is against abortion – I, too, am against abortion. So we can have a unity *in that value.*'

But in 1945 this question of different types or levels of unity did not arise. All the girls who followed Chiara and her 'way of Love' were Catholics, and so they shared a common credo. The numbers attracted to the Movement for Unity continued to grow. Between 1945 and 1947 two more residential communities were opened in Trent. As Chiara was the focus of unity in the 'little house', so she delegated others who lived with her there to go and be the focuses in the new focolares.

While they appreciated living close to Chiara and the graces that her presence seemed to bring, these others, like Graziella, who were sent out to animate the other focolares, didn't dwell on their loss of living in the same house as Chiara. Graziella remembers that being with Chiara was a real privilege because her charism was already evident. 'Every time Chiara spoke, what she said was so strong. It just turned you upside down, it transformed you. You felt that what she said could be lived, could become real. And we would just throw ourselves into it.'

Yet when Chiara sent her to animate a new focolare (first in Trent, then later elsewhere in Italy and then abroad), 'It was like a cut that you would feel. But it was always an opportunity to see the Ideal more clearly. Until then I had *received* it, and once she sent me out, I would have to *give* it myself. And in giving it, I would find that I received it again in a deeper way.'

Since those first two new 'foundations' in Trent after the first focolare around Chiara in the 'little house', the growth and spread of
the Focolare Movement and its Ideal has not stopped to this day.

During those first two years – 1945 to 1947 – Chiara and her
companions were already beginning to travel outside Trent to give
their witness to people who had invited them to speak of their experience. Graziella remembers their first big journeys. 'First of all we
used to go into all the villages around Trent – and then we got to the
point of travelling to Rovereto, which was *half an hour away* by train!
It seemed like the end of the world at the time! And then to
Bolzano…little places not really far from us, but which to us seemed
far away. Then one day I went with Chiara and we had to go to
Milan and Turin; I would go to Cuneo and Chiara was to go to
Genoa. These were our first external journeys.'

In 1948 Chiara made her first journey to Rome. She had discovered some writings by a priest about the Crusade of Charity and
found that some of the ideas in them were similar to her own. She
thought she should meet this priest. 'We were speaking about
unity,' she explains, 'unity with God and among the brethren; unity
which was found at the heart of Jesus' testament and which is an effect of reciprocal love. But nobody in the Church, as far as we were
aware, was speaking about unity at that time. The Communists
spoke about it, but in another sense. I had heard that there was a
certain Father Leon Veuthey in Rome who had written some tracts
on this subject.

'We wanted to get in touch with him. We had no fears or apprehensions, nor any particular hopes; we just followed the interior
voice.'

Chiara did find Fr Veuthey. She also got to know a Fr Tomasi
who had been Superior General of the Order of the Stigmata, and
she sought advice from him when there were important decisions to
be made. She had been put in touch with him by the Archbishop of
Trent, who was a member of the same Order.

Through Fr Veuthey, Chiara and then the others were introduced
to many people in the capital city of Catholicism. In particular they
made contacts with many priests and nuns in religious orders.

Chiara was pulled between Trent and Rome, spending an increasing amount of time in the latter. So many were the people who wanted to meet her, and who had already heard about the Movement, that she soon enlisted some of her first companions to respond to the requests.

Again, Graziella recalls that she often travelled down to Rome, sometimes with Chiara, sometimes separately. So much was happening so quickly that it is difficult to put precise dates on anything in those years. But the message of unity preached by Chiara and the Focolare Movement was being widely sown. Often it fell on fertile ground, particularly among the religious. (It was partly through these contacts that the Movement first spread beyond Europe, when religious missionaries invited Focolarini to come to their mission territories.)

One Luigi Alvino and his wife Elena put an apartment at Chiara's disposal in Rome. The couple were in contact with Archbishop De Ferarri through their friend the Bishop of Assisi. They introduced Chiara to various members of the Roman nobility in their enthusiasm for this new spirit, but not a great number of these understood the spirituality being proposed.

Elena Alvino continued to help and provide for Chiara and the Movement down the years, and Chiara nicknamed her 'Frate Jacopa' in reference to the lady who defended St Francis of Assisi and his first band of followers and provided so much for them.

Graziella remembers speaking to a packed salon in a palazzo belonging to some Roman nobility. When she had finished her presentation, one elderly Contessa remarked, 'But this is only the Gospel. This is nothing new. We've all come here to hear something new, and all you are telling us is already in the Gospel.'

Of course, the lady was right and it was all in the Gospel, but those who responded to this 'ever-new' way of living it found that it was indeed new, and that it caused what Chiara called the 'Christian Revolution' wherever it was lived.

The abiding memory of those times for Graziella is that of speaking to packed halls and finishing only just in time to dash to the next meeting. 'I remember that once I was invited to speak in a parish hall. It was the parish of Christ the King. And all I could see before me was a sea of religious: priests in clerical dress, friars in their habits, nuns looking at me through their wimples! There was I, a 23-year-old girl with two long blonde plaits, standing up to speak to all these priests and religious. It was a scandal at the time! And I spoke for three hours, without notes. Chiara wanted us to speak without notes, even though we should, of course, prepare ourselves with ideas and prayer. Well, after that the Vicar Apostolic of Rome [the bishop designated to run the diocese by the Pope, who is the Bishop of Rome] asked me to speak in other public places – and at that point we weren't even officially approved by the Church!'

For Chiara, it seems to have been a time of promoting unity among the Baptized, but guarding like a jewel the abandonment of the Forsaken Jesus for herself and her closest companions who were called to this particular vocation. Over the years this option has become the hallmark not only of the consecrated Focolarini, but of all the members of the Movement. This is confirmed and illustrated in a letter which Chiara wrote on 30 March 1948 to Brother Jerome, a young Franciscan student in Rome:

'My God, my God, why have you forsaken me?'

My dear Brother in Jesus,

As soon as I received your letter, I went straight into town. Jesus had to be the first and last witness to the joy that filled my soul. [She means she went straight to the Eucharistic presence of Jesus reserved in the tabernacle of the Catholic church.]

It could only be like that. I am convinced that unity in its most spiritual, most intimate, most profound aspect cannot be understood except by the souls who have chosen as their portion in life...Jesus Forsaken who cries out: 'My God, my God, why have you forsaken me?'

Brother, now that I have found in you an understanding of what the secret of unity is, I would like, and could, speak to you for days on end. I want you to know that Jesus Forsaken is everything. He is the guarantee of unity. All light on unity flows forth from that cry.

To choose him as the one aim, the one goal, the destination of your life is...to bring countless other people into unity. The book of light which the Lord is writing in my soul has two aspects: a page shining with mysterious love: Unity. A page glowing with mysterious suffering: Jesus Forsaken. They are two sides of the same coin. The page of Unity is for everyone. For me and for all those in the front line in Unity, Jesus Forsaken is our everything.

We have chosen to climb a summit towards total abandonment. For the others Unity, for us the abandonment. Which one? The one that Jesus (made man so as to deify us) endured; extreme suffering, the synthesis of all sufferings, sorrow as great as...God! 'My God, my God, why have you forsaken me?'

Look for Him as the bridegroom in the Canticle of Canticles did. This is the priority for those whom Infinite Love has thrust into the front line.

Seek Him out in our brothers, sinners who are without God. He is there crying out: 'My God, my God, why...?'

Seek Him in the abandonments around us, but most of all in those deep within us, those we find on life's journey.

Brother, there is no fuller nor harsher joy than when the soul is suspended between Heaven and Earth. Alone with him, abandoned even by the Father, even by God!

My brother, if you choose to follow this way of life, soon you will experience the stigmata of the abandonment! Then the Lord will dig out a space in your heart...which you will fill immediately with Jesus Forsaken.

Dear Brother, not everyone understands these words. We must treasure them so that Love, Forsaken Love, may be surrounded by hearts which understand Him because they have glimpsed Him in their lives and have seen in Him the answer to everything.

For the others Unity and for us the abandonment. Yes, because the bride cannot be different from the bridegroom.

Jesus is without God. To console Him, let us promise Him that He will always find Jesus amongst us. 'Where two or more...there am I.' Jesus will console Jesus who cries out. My Jesus! Our Jesus!

Chiara of Jesus Forsaken

NINE

WHAT ABOUT THE MEN?

1948 saw the creation of the first men's focolare. Marco Tecilla was in the air-raid shelter after the first siren sounded on the afternoon of 13 May 1944. It was the second great air-raid on Trent following the one on 2 September 1943. His family's house near the Capuchin church was destroyed. His father had died in January, and now with his mother and brother and sister he, like the Lubich parents, headed for the mountains. They found refuge in the small town of Centa.

Marco was 18 and had been working as a clerk since he was 14. While the family was living in Centa, he became interested in what his sister Maria and her friend Liliana Lubich were up to. They had been school-friends in Trent and they used to sneak away from the house and sit on the grass reading letters that came from the city. But the two girls never told anyone else what was in those letters.

Marco recalls, 'My younger sister Maria had been causing a bit of tension in the house. We had all noticed how she would often go out to meet a group of friends and how she wanted to give away clothes which, according to her, were superfluous. The rest of us were under the impression that we were already pretty poor ourselves. I agreed with our mother that Maria's behaviour was somewhat exaggerated. We were of the opinion that in order to be a good Christian you went to church on a Sunday and did no harm to anybody; that was enough.'

Marco started some enquiries about these friends of his young sister, because as far as he could see they were all a little strange. He was not pleased when Maria managed to get her mother's permission to go back to Trent to be with these friends. It was dangerous. Didn't she know there was a war on? Trent was occupied by the German army and besides, she had to walk all the way. Maria made the journey, and she got a job in the Capuchin school alongside

Lilliana's sister Chiara. This Chiara seemed to be at the root of all the trouble, filling all those young girls' heads with these extreme ideas!

A year later, on 25 April 1945, the War was over for Trent at least, and Marco moved back into town with his mother and brother. The two brothers had joined the Third Order Franciscans after their father had died the previous year. Now their friend the Capuchin friar invited them to attend a meeting he was holding one Saturday afternoon. It was held in the Cardinal Massaia Hall, the same place where the Third Order used to meet every month.

The two brothers went along. Marco remembers that they sat on one of the benches lining the walls in order to leave the seats for others. He says he wasn't quite sure why he was there, but as he was shy, he had decided not to open his mouth but just to listen and observe.

'We had been sitting there a few moments, when the door opened and a group of young women came in. They certainly appeared very joyful. One of them sat at the table in front. Everyone fell silent and she began to speak. That was a surprise for me – or perhaps I should say a bombshell! Those young women were none other than my little sister Maria's friends! And, in fact, the person who was speaking was the very ring-leader of the group, Chiara Lubich!

'My first impulse was to get up and walk out – but because of my shyness and a sense of good manners, I remained. I really had to fight against my own prejudice to listen to this young woman.

'Chiara was speaking about God who is Love, and she was doing so with extraordinary ardour and conviction. I found myself being captivated and attracted.'

His friends who were there at the meeting did not have the same reaction. At the end of Chiara's talk they began a debate about what she had said. Marco thought that her words had been very clear and logical. All he could say was that what he had heard was beautiful.

He left with his friend the Capuchin friar to walk home together. The friar was not in a talkative mood. In fact, he was deeply disappointed by the reaction of the other young men who had been at the meeting. They walked along in silence until they reached the Capuchin Friary. Then the friar pointed out a little house which had its entrance on the Piazza Cappuccini. 'There, on the second-floor apartment,' he said. 'Those young women live there. They really have nothing because they give everything to the poor. You're a good worker and a handyman – couldn't you give them a hand if they need things done in the house?'

A few days later he brought Marco to the house and introduced him to the young women. His first task was to fix a small electric stove. From then on, he was called on to mend things in the little house, which he did in the evening after his own day's work. He became fascinated by life in that little house. The conversation between Chiara and her companions seemed always to be of a spiritual nature. He never said anything – he just carried out the tasks he had been asked to do, and he listened to the conversation of these girls.

'One evening,' he remembers clearly, 'I was at the top of a ladder while Chiara was sewing at a table and another young woman was washing the dishes. When I finished my job, Chiara surprised me by inviting me to sit down and relax for a moment. I did so without saying a word.

'Chiara looked at me and began to speak about Jesus. I believed in Him, but I felt He was very far from me. She said to me: "Many Christians are like actors. They put on their make-up, they go to Mass, they come home, and then they take off their 'Christian make-up'. But, if Jesus came in this century, he would be Jesus 24 hours a day. He might even be an electrician like you." '

That evening, and that conversation, changed Marco's life. His whole outlook on life and religion was changed. He was called to be another Jesus, '24 hours a day'.

His way of approaching his work altered. His thoughts of other girls his own age, amongst whom he hoped to find someone to marry and start a family with, changed and began to fade. He became confused, and he didn't know what God wanted from him any more. One Sunday towards the end of 1947 he approached his friend the Capuchin friar and began, with great difficulty, to explain what was in his heart. He was somewhat deflated by the friar's reaction after he had listened to Marco for only a few minutes.

He says, 'The friar turned around, took a sheet of paper and began to write. I remained in silence, rather surprised, to say the least! He hadn't even given me enough time to describe fully the drama that was going on inside me, and now he had turned his back on me and seemed to be busy with his own affairs. When he had finished writing, he turned back to me and handed me an envelope.

"Take this to Chiara," he said.

'I ran down the stairs from the monastery and reached the Piazza Cappuccini. I rang the doorbell and found myself standing in front of Chiara, who opened the door. I gave her the letter and she told me to come back in an hour. I thought it a rather strange answer and didn't know what was happening to me any more.

'I began to pace up and down a nearby street. Every so often I would ask a passer-by what time it was. Those 60 minutes seemed an eternity! Finally, I was back at the door of number 2. Chiara opened the door again. She gave me a letter. "This is for you," she said.'

Marco ran home and went straight to his room to read the letter Chiara had given him. 'As I was reading it,' he says, 'I felt that a strong light was invading my soul; that every dark corner had vanished and a complete happiness had invaded me. Chiara had hit the nail on the head. She was repeating to me the words of Jesus to the rich young man: "If you seek perfection, go, sell your possessions... Then come follow me." '

In that moment, Marco says, he understood that he had to abandon his previous plans, even of marriage, in order to share the same experience that Chiara and the girls of the 'little house' were living.

There was no 'little house' for men, like the apartment where Chiara and her friends lived – the Movement had not yet even been approved by the Church. Nothing was formalized or regularized. Marco seemed on his own. He continued trying to 'live as Jesus 24 hours a day'. But it is not easy to remain enthusiastic without companions to share one's ideal. Worried about his failing zeal, he went to see Chiara.

She asked him, 'Are you upset by this?'

'Of course I am,' he answered.

'Well,' said Chiara, 'this suffering of yours is also contained in His suffering. Now is the moment to tell Him that you love Him. Love, in reality, is not a matter of sentiment, but of the will.'

Marco understood and told Chiara that what he really wanted was to follow the same way of life as she and her companions.

'So you want to follow this way?' asked Chiara – as if she didn't know! 'You know that we've not been approved yet? And then, you are alone. What are you going to do when you're old? Who will look after you?'

Marco burst out immediately, 'Chiara, I will do what you did! I'll choose God as the ideal of my life!'

Over the next months the desire remained strong in Marco to live the life of a Focolarino. It came to be shared by a friend of his, Livio. After a trip to Rome in September 1948, Chiara heard of a room to rent at 13 Via d'Antonio da Trento. It would be ideal for the first two male Focolarini, she decided.

And so, late on the night of Saturday 27 November 1948, Marco embraced his widowed mother and set off with Livio for their new home. Their worldly goods – two beds and a wardrobe that Chiara had given them – were loaded on to a little cart which the Capuchins had lent them.

By this time the companions of Chiara had learned to take all the different 'words' of Scripture at face value, so the two male Focolarini decided a week later that it was time to make an appointment with Archbishop De Ferrari. 'He who hears you, hears me...'

As soon as they entered his presence the prelate asked what they wanted. They told him that they had just opened a men's Focolare household and had come to ask for his blessing.

'How many are you?' His Lordship asked somewhat sternly.

'Just the two of us,' they replied.

'Well, according to the provisions of Holy Mother Church you need to be five people, or in exceptional cases just three, to form a community.' The two men were completely unaware that the Supreme Pontiff Pope Pius XII had made such a provision in his document on the religious life.

Marco immediately pictured himself having to borrow the Capuchins' cart again to remove their few possessions. 'If that's the case, Your Grace,' he volunteered, 'we are prepared to return to our homes at once.'

The Archbishop's tone of voice changed from one of authority to a quite paternal one. He asked them about their jobs and discussed life in general for a while. As the appointment drew to a close the Archbishop stood up to give them his blessing and said, 'Go ahead, my young friends. For the time being I'll be the third member of your community.'

So the first men's focolare was born. But just a few weeks later, on 10 January 1949, Chiara called Livio to come down to Rome.

Marco, who was now working on the railway, continued living in their one-room focolare, even if a hermitic Focolarino was a contradiction in terms.

Five months passed, and it seemed as if it was an experiment that had failed. A Focolarino was not meant to be alone. Moreover, the family who had rented out the room needed it back. Instead they offered him a wooden shed in the garden that had until then been used as a chicken coop. Just then, in June 1949, two young men from Rovereto, who had been similarly 'captivated' by the Ideal communicated to them there by Graziella and Valeria on one of their first 'speaking engagements', asked to move into a Focolare household.

The newly constituted men's focolare was a mixed bunch: Marco the electrician, handyman and railway worker; Aldo Stedile, an artist who was currently wielding another type of brush as he worked as a painter and decorator; and calm, sensible Carlo Cimadoma, a shopworker.

The trio scrubbed out and painted the erstwhile chicken shed which had become their home, their place to live with 'Jesus in the midst' of them. They managed to get it clean, but it always remained a damp dwelling-place.

In the immediate post-War period there were still many people suffering from poverty in Trent, as indeed throughout Italy. Every month the male Focolarini would divide their salaries, and the first portion would go to the 30 families whom they were helping. After this they paid their rent and electricity bills and had to make do with whatever was left.

From day to day they lived what Chiara calls 'the adventure of unity'. As she wrote in an early letter, 'unity has to be earned.' The three Focolarini, through clashes of personality and different outlooks on life, seemed to rub the rough edges off each other and learned to put unity and harmony – Jesus in the midst – at the centre of their common life.

All three passed a remarkable summer with Chiara and all the other Focolarine that year. Bonds had been strengthened and the 'flame within' them burned even stronger.

As Christmas approached, Chiara came back up north from Rome to spend the holiday with her first communities in Trent. As is still the case, wherever Chiara went, many others wanted to go too, just to be near her. And so she has had to get used to travelling with an entourage.

The women were put up in the various women's Focolare households which now existed in Trent and its environs. There were now several men involved in the Movement in Rome, and those who travelled up were lodged with families friendly to the Movement, and some even squeezed into the former chicken coop. Two other young men also arrived: one was from Florence and the other was a young man of a rather serious disposition from Pistoia. He was called Pasquale Forese.

Christmas Eve 1949 found 20 of them squeezed into a sitting-room in one of the women's focolares, all squashed round a couple of tables which had been put together and laid with all sorts of odd bits of crockery and cutlery – all that they could rustle up between them.

Pasquale was 20 years old. He had already spent two years study-ing philosophy in the seminary of his own diocese before being sent to Rome. He read everything he could, 'absorbing it all like a sponge', he says. But one book he read again and again. A priest friend had suggested he read the Gospel of Mark, which he did first in the original Greek. He was fascinated by the life and person of Jesus as portrayed by Mark.

It was the beginning of a period of crisis for Pasquale. The radical message of Jesus' life and person in Mark's Gospel was not what he saw being lived around him. The Church, it seemed to him, was in fact a structure that actually suffocated the authentic evangelical spirit. There no longer seemed any point to becoming a priest. He re-turned home to Pistoia, to the affluent home of his parents (his fa-ther was the local Member of Parliament).

He looked up the Catholic organizations there, but didn't find this radical Christian outlook that he had discovered. He felt com-pletely alone and dejected. Then one Monday morning a visitor ar-rived at his family home. Her name was Graziella De Luca, one of Chiara Lubich's first companions. She was expecting to meet his fa-ther, who had invited her to speak at a meeting. Graziella had missed her train and had arrived late, so Mr Forese had gone ahead to the meeting. Out of politeness, Pasquale accompanied her to the meet-ing in town, which his father and a local priest had organized.

As he chatted to her on the way to the local seminary where the meeting was to be held, her answers to his questions completely disarmed him. He remembers in particular that as they were walking through the market-place he asked Graziella, 'What exactly are you and your friends trying to achieve?'

Her reply, he says, was frank and crystal clear. She told him, 'We want to relive the Trinity on earth.'

Pasquale was astounded. Here was this young girl speaking of mysteries which he had spent so long studying in his theological classes; she and her friends were bringing the whole thing into the arena of everyday human life and experience. He soaked up everything that she said, there and at the meeting which followed.

Graziella stayed on another day and arranged to meet the rather serious young man who was searching for his 'way'. They talked together for seven hours! Pasquale recalls that among the myriad questions he put to her was, 'What do you think about the Eucharist?'

Graziella did not know the whole crisis the young man had been through with regard to the question of the priesthood. She answered, 'For us it is so important that we couldn't even imagine a day without receiving Holy Communion.' Unwittingly she had triggered off a reaction that would change Pasquale Foresi's life – and would have boundless ramifications for the life and development of the Focolare Movement.

'Her answer hit me like a ton of bricks,' says Pasquale, 'because in that instant I understood that in order to have the Eucharist you had to have the priesthood, the hierarchy. I understood then that you could not separate the Church from Christ. I realized also that we are all Church, each one with his or her own role and responsibilities in it. It was not the Church, or "the others" that had to change. I had to change. I had to start a new life.'

And so Pasquale found himself invited to that gathering in Trent where he would meet others who lived this Gospel lifestyle – and even Chiara Lubich herself.

As it happened, he found himself in even closer quarters to her than he had expected. In the crush around the table in the tiny little living-room, he was seated right next to Chiara, squashed up beside her at the head of the table.

Chiara began to share with the assembled company the very particular experience that she had lived with others of the Movement that summer at Tonadico in the Dolomites. Others who were present remember that a very special atmosphere seemed to surround them as Chiara shared her experiences. Pasquale says, 'There was such a warmth in what she was saying in that completely clear, transparent way of hers that my heart and mind felt completely full. I can't remember now what words she actually said, but it would be no exaggeration to say that I felt I was in Heaven.'

Then Chiara began to ask the others what they thought about what she had just shared. Pasquale was terrified that she would ask him. 'If I say the wrong thing,' he thought to himself, 'I'll ruin this beautiful atmosphere.'

He says that he was aware of the great chasm that separated what he was and the reality that was being lived by these people. But just then Chiara looked straight at him and said, 'And you, what do you think?'

Pasquale surprised even himself when he said, 'In this Ideal I see the reality of the Mystical Body of Christ being realized.'

A few days later, in early January 1950, he left for Rome on the same train as Chiara. In the Eternal City he lodged with a family, ate his lunch at the friary of a religious friend, and spent as much time as he could at the focolare where Chiara lived. At that time she was living in a small three-room apartment along with Graziella and two other early 'companions' in the Roman suburb of Garbatella. Pasquale remembers that he spent about five hours a day on the bus.

He realized that as he was not yet 21, he needed to go home and obtain permission from his parents to move permanently to Rome and live in a focolare. His plan was to live in the focolare and work in a factory.

Chiara and her household had in the meantime moved to the port town of Ostia, where a family had offered them the use of a house. Pasquale travelled down to visit them whenever he could. One day he was walking through the hallway of the house when Chiara, with a broom in her hands, suddenly stopped him and asked, 'What would you think about sharing with me the burden of responsibility for the Movement?'

Somewhat dumbstruck, he nodded his head in acceptance. His life was going to move at top speed from then on. Later that year, in September 1950, a whole group of those first Focolarini were on holiday at Tonadico. As some of them were walking along a country road one day, Chiara suddenly stopped and suggested that Pasquale should study theology. She couldn't have known that in recent weeks he had been feeling an urge to return to studying for the priesthood. Or could she?

A week later she approached Pasquale after Mass and said, 'I've got something to tell you, but first I want to know if you have already understood it yourself.'

Pasquale remembers, 'In fact what I really wanted to share with her was this desire I felt since meeting the Movement to go back to training for the priesthood.'

Up to then, of course, the Movement was entirely made up of lay people and was seen and understood by them all to be a specifically lay movement, after the fashion of Chiara's 'fourth way'.

'After a moment's hesitation,' says Pasquale, 'I told her exactly how I felt; of the certainty growing within me that I should be a priest.'

'That's exactly what I wanted to tell you,' Chiara replied.

So Pasquale continued his studies at Rome's Gregorian University. Archbishop De Ferrari ordained him to the priesthood four years later, on 3 April 1954 (the year designated by Pope Pius XII as a special 'Marian Year') in the Cathedral of Trent.

In the same week that Chiara had first asked Pasquale to share the responsibility of leadership with her, she had actually outlined what she thought his role would be. With his help, she told him, she believed it would be possible to 'incarnate into new structures all the light of our Ideal'. And that's how it has been. When official approval of the Movement came from the Holy See in 1962, Fr Pasquale helped Chiara to write the first set of statutes of the Movement which would be submitted to and accepted by the Universal Church. Already in 1951 Pasquale had been entrusted with responsibility for all the men's households in the Movement.

Today the partnership with Fr Pasquale remains as firm as ever. Although Chiara considers him as a co-founder, it is she who is the figurehead and point of reference for everyone. When she moves her base to a house donated to her in the Swiss Alps, Foresi and his

household move to a nearby men's house. When Chiara noticed that
he was slowing down a bit recently, she encouraged him to take
more physical exercise to offset all his desk-bound and academic
work. He dutifully paid heed and acquired an exercise bicycle which
he puts to good use every day in his home at the Rocca di Papa
complex. A case of 'on yer bike'!

When she speaks of him, Chiara's respect is evident. 'Father Foresi
is an important person in the history of the Movement. Since 1949
he has made an essential contribution, and continues to do so today.
He was the first Focolarino priest, and his ordination in 1954 paved
the way for a whole train of male Focolarini who would also want to
be priests. Thanks to his great theological expertise, he brought about
the creation of the Centre of Theological Studies for the cultural formation of members of the Movement and for the theological presentation of the Movement to the Church and the world.

'He was instrumental in the foundation of our New City publishing house as well as the numerous Mariapolis centres set up for the
on-going formation of members of the Movement. His role in the
establishment of the little town of Loppiano was crucial, and this in
turn led the way to numerous other little towns being founded in
different parts of the world.

'In fact he contributed immeasurably to the Movement's insertion
into the Church. He was the first Ecclesiastical Assistant and played a
key role in the elaboration of the different statutes which have had to
be developed. I would say that I cannot consider Fr Foresi as a col-
laborator but rather as a co-founder of the Movement during its different phases – a co-founder just like Giordani.'

TEN

A HEAVENLY SUMMER – AND
DOWN FROM THE MOUNTAIN

Igino Giordani, whom Chiara describes now as a co-founder, was a well-known Italian writer and journalist. Wounded in the First World War, he had gone on to become a linguist, writer and well-known librarian. He spent a year in Washington DC studying the system of classification used in the Library of Congress. On becoming the Director of the massive Vatican Library, he overhauled it with this new system, which became a model studied and adapted world-wide. He also founded the School of Librarianship in the Vatican. After the Second World War, he became a member of the first group of Christian Democrat MPs, along with Alcide De Gasperi and others.

In the immediate post-War period, he was in the Chamber of Deputies representing the constituency of Roma-Tivoli. In 1947–48 Chiara was constantly going back and forth between Rome and Trent, and it was in September 1948 that some of her collaborators in Rome invited her to come with them to meet this renowned parliamentarian.

In his memoirs published in 1981, Giordani wrote of that first encounter: 'Exercising the courtesy of an MP meeting possible electors, I met in Parliament one day a group of religious. They represented the different Franciscan families and with them was a layman and a young laywoman.'

The first thing which struck Giordani was the fact that these members of the various branches of Franciscans were all acting together and in harmony. That he considered a miracle, and he told them so!

Then, he says, the young woman began to speak: 'I was expecting to hear the sentimental propaganda of some utopian voluntary association. Quite the contrary. From her very first words, I could see that there was something new here. In her voice there was an un-usual timbre: the timbre of a deep and sure conviction which came from mystical experience.'

In his lifetime Giordani published some 94 books as well as trans-lating nine other major works into Italian. He wrote in 42 different newspapers and reviews. Much of his earlier works concerned the lives of the saints and the early Church Fathers. He had written two works on the Social Teaching of the Church, which still remain on the reading lists of many seminaries. As early as the 1920s he had written about ecumenism and the unity of the Church. This was someone who was no stranger to trends and movements in the Church throughout history – and to the work of the Holy Spirit in forming saints in different times.

His perception of Chiara at that first meeting was that she was someone 'who put holiness within reach of everyone. She tore down the grille which separated the world of the laity from the mys-tical life. She rendered God near, she caused people to discover Him as father, brother, friend, present to humanity.'

Giordani had already published books dealing with the gulf in the Church between clergy and laity. He once wrote that 'in the Church's calendar of feasts there is not even one married saint.' It was a gulf and an exclusion which he felt keenly. Something, he knew, had to change to encourage married people in the Church to be fully recognized as being called to the same heights of sanctity as popes and bishops, priests and religious.

Two of his major books had been on St Catherine of Siena. She and St Teresa of Avila would later be declared as the first women Doctors of the Church. Within a short time of making the ac-quaintance of Chiara Lubich, Giordani was not afraid to describe her to friends and parliamentary colleagues as 'a second St Cather-ine of Siena'.

For her part, Chiara was completely unaware of the gigantic im-pression which their first meeting had made on the respected MP. She says, 'It was just a simple meeting. I wasn't aware of the impact it had on Giordani. I only learned something of that afterwards when he sent a letter to me in Trent. In it he spoke of Jesus' last Testament in such a clear and profound way that I began to think that he was someone who had been put on our path by God.'

In fact, a major reason why Chiara had agreed to meet the MP in September 1948 was that she was looking for a house in Rome to use as a more solid base for the Movement. Giordani found her one. He also asked her to write down for him what she was working for – in fact, an outline of her ideal of unity. Using this as a basis, he published a long article about the Movement in *Fides*, a monthly review in which he wrote at the time.

It is clear from his later writings and testimonies that Igino Giordani really believed that he had met someone of the calibre of a St Catherine of Siena. This husband and father of four children somehow came to look on this young woman, who was then nearly half his age, as a sort of 'spiritual mother, as a guide and sister. Igino and Chiara henceforth kept in regular contact. However, while Giordani's wife, Mya, accepted her husband's involvement with Chiara and the Movement, she never really understood it or entered fully into it.

During the summer of 1949 Chiara and her first companions and early followers had a formative experience while on holiday together at Tonadico in the Dolomites. Giordani went up to Tonadico to pass a few days with these young people whose ideal he understood and shared, and whom he had come to admire. While there he found himself caught up in a period of extraordinary spiritual experiences in the lives of Chiara and her first companions.

During that period Chiara had a number of particular intuitions or insights. She is reluctant to speak about them. Perhaps she experienced them because she was to become the foundress of a vast movement. They were to do with the new spirituality of communion which was emerging among them, and she shared them regularly with her first companions, both the women and the men. They sprang from the mystical experience which both she and the first companions had had of what happens when Christians take seriously Jesus' New Commandment to 'Love one another as I have loved you', and when their nourishment is the Eucharist, the bond of unity.

In a sense it was about identifying oneself (while retaining the distinction) with Jesus himself, who is present in the heart of the Father. It is as St Augustine wrote in his *Confessions* about the words heard on high regarding the Eucharist: 'You shall not transform me into yourself, but you will be transformed into me' (*Confessions* VII.10.16).

The period in which all this happened came to be referred to in the Movement as 'Paradise '49'. It is difficult to get the full story of what happened over those weeks spent together, because so many things happened and they weren't writing them down. However, because what they experienced with Chiara was obviously something so sacred, there is still a hesitancy to speak about it too lightly. But they were all touched by it. And as was and is common within the Focolare Movement, whatever was happening to and around Chiara, was also shared with everybody else, even though they weren't there in person.

Thus Natalia, who had only had a week's holiday and then had to return to her work at the Chamber of Commerce in Trent, remembers the experience of 'Paradise '49' as if she were there herself. When I asked Chiara how Natalia seemed to know everything that was going on up at Tonadico while she was down in Trent, Chiara replied, 'Of course she knew and followed everything, because I communicated to her everything that was happening.'

This is something Chiara insists on now, and it was also something she felt strongly right from the start. Whatever was happening at the centre of the Movement, or whatever spiritual experiences or 'lights' she received on particular subjects or Gospel phrases, all of this had to be shared with all the others. Both the Bishop and her confessor had told her that she was the possessor of a charism, so she knew that these extraordinary insights and graces were meant not just for her but also for the up-building of the whole community. In embracing Jesus Forsaken and, later in a similar fashion, the Desolate One, His mother, Chiara learned more and more to 'let go' of everything that happened to her. It was not her 'property' but was for all the others. This explains why, after giving Marco and Livio two beds and a wardrobe when they went to set up the first men's focolare household in Trent a few months previously, her second gift was a telephone.

It continues to this day. She has an all-consuming desire to make sure that there is constant communication between the Centre of the Movement near Rome and all the houses of the Focolarini in 198 countries. This is not to impose anything on them, but rather continually to build up unity. Thus a little Focolare community in a shanty town in Brazil or in the African bush will join in regular telephone conferences in which the whole world-wide Movement is linked up with Chiara and the Central Council at the international headquarters.

'They have to feel involved,' she explains. 'Part of our vocation is to put all our goods in common, and that includes spiritual goods. So we all want to share in the progress, joys and sorrows of each other, wherever we are in the world.'

Of course, while Chiara wants to know and feel close to all that is happening to her 'friends' in their own disparate situations and locations, they treasure the opportunity of direct contact with her, the woman at the very origin of this 'Work' to which they have given their whole lives.

So all those closest to Chiara in the summer of 1949 became aware that something special was happening in the group up there in the mountains. As it is considered to be something sacred and delicate, all the first companions of Chiara will refer to it, but will say things like, 'I'm sure Chiara is the best one to explain it to you' or 'This is how we lived that time, but you should really ask Chiara about it.'

Chiara, as I pointed out at the beginning of this book, is very reluctant to talk about the very deepest spiritual experiences she has had. She always wants to shift the emphasis away from her to 'us', the collective, the community. While there are things about her private spiritual life which will always remain secret as long as she is alive, I persuaded her to talk about some of her other 'lights' or insights insofar as they were to do with the creation or development of the Movement.

She illustrated the idea to me by making a comparison with another celebrated foundress in the history of Catholicism: 'St Teresa of Avila says that there is a lot of suffering we cannot suffer ourselves, so we empathize with some of the suffering in others. And just as the children of St Teresa shared fully in her mystical experiences, I think the Focolarini do the same, to the point where they participate fully. They feel that this experience which was fundamental to the birth of the Movement is actually their own. It belongs also to them.'

So, just five and a half years after Chiara had made her own consecration to God and five years since Natalia was the first one to follow suit, already the future make-up of the Movement was being made clear. There would be communities of consecrated virgins, women and men, as well as married people who would also live in total consecration to God according to their state of life. In that same year, 1949, Chiara also confirmed Pasquale Foresi's desire for the priesthood, and in the future priests, monks, friars, religious sisters and even bishops would become members of this Movement.

'Paradise '49' was clearly a founding experience which set the path for the future of the Movement. Igino Giordani, the first married person in the group, was central to this. It was he who had to tell Chiara to 'come down off the mountain.' One day he told her, 'You have to come back down to the world. You have many children whom you must lead to God.'

In silence, Chiara acknowledged that what he said was true. She knew it in her heart, but the thought of voluntarily leaving this veritable foretaste of Heaven was heart-rending for her. She left Giordani, went to her room and through her tears poured out her heart in writing:

I have only one Spouse on earth: Jesus crucified and forsaken.
I have no other God but Him.
In Him there is the whole of paradise with the Trinity
and the whole of earth with Humanity.
Therefore what is His is mine, and nothing else.
And His is universal suffering, and therefore mine.
I will go through the world seeking it
in every instant of my life.
What hurts me is mine.
Mine the suffering that grazes me in the present.
Mine the suffering of the souls beside me.
Mine all that is not peace, not joy,
not beautiful, not lovable, not serene…
So it will be for the years I have left:
athirst for suffering, anguish, despair,
separation, exile, forsakenness, torment,
for…all that is Him
and He is Suffering.
In this way I will dry up the waters of tribulation in many hearts nearby,
and through communion with my almighty Spouse,

in many far away.
I shall pass as a fire
that consumes all that must fall
and leaves standing only the truth.

Many theologians have since wondered at and studied and analysed this poem written from the heart, whose mystical language betrays a searing intuition of sacred mysteries: suffering, the Mystical Body, the very Incarnation…

And it is part of the Christian paradox that although the writer decides to take on herself all that is 'not beautiful, not lovable, not serene', it is these very qualities that most people see in her. She is today the epitome of serenity, of harmony, of amiability. This whole question of being and non-being and even of 'being when not being' is explored today in the thought and writings of Chiara Lubich, and I will touch upon it in greater depth in Chapter 14.

During their summer vacation gathering of 1954, the specific role of each of those first companions in the future development of this Work became clear, and those individuals have found their vocation confirmed in this and still carry out their allotted tasks to this day.

'During our summer gathering of 1954,' Chiara explains, 'I understood clearly the different tasks of my companions. I understood, for example, that Giosi had the gifts to safeguard the interior life of our community, to keep alive our spirit of sharing everything, and this aspect would develop to include our economy and our daily work. Another, Graziella, would take up the more external aspect of our apostolate, our outreach. Natalia, for instance, emerged as someone who would keep the focus on our spiritual roots, our union with God, whilst another companion would be entrusted with the aspect of health, both spiritual and physical. Yet another would deal with study, with the wisdom to be drawn from the Scriptures and the early Fathers of the Church. Giulia would be entrusted with everything to do with communications, audio-visual media and all the means available to enable us to remain united.

'In this overall picture of the Movement I saw that another five of my companions had a different task. They would take on the world. Each one would follow up the development of the Movement in a different continent. This is how I saw it and how the foundations were laid for the building of the Work.'

As with the men's focolare in Trent, other communities of Foco-larini were formed during 1949 in other towns and cities outside Trent for the first time. After the summer vacation gathering in the Dolomites, Chiara understood that she had to move definitively to Rome, and did so in September of that year.

Like the founders of so many religious orders and congregations, she had understood that her place was in Rome, at the heart of the Church. Except hers was not a religious order for monks or nuns. In fact, it was completely new, defying classification, as it allowed for one organization for both male and female consecrated celibates. More than this, it had married consecrated people in the same orga-nization. And then, priests and members of religious orders, both male and female, would want to become part of this community. No, it did not fit into any category of society or community which the Catholic Church had ever had to deal with before! It still does-n't, and it has its own unique relationship with the Holy See which involves it being overseen by the Pontifical Council for the Laity.

But for Chiara Lubich in 1949 there would be many more nights of tears and years of suffering before that stage was reached.

ELEVEN

THROUGH THE CRUCIBLE –
YEARS OF ENQUIRY

In accordance with tradition, Pope Pius XII declared 1950 a Holy Year. The 1,950th anniversary of the Incarnation would be for the Church a 'jubilee year' similar to that called for in the Covenant of the Book of Deuteronomy. Catholics were encouraged to 'return to the sources' and to make pilgrimage to the sites of the Apostles Peter and Paul and the catacombs of the Early Church.

Many religious orders had come to know of Chiara and her Movement through the article published by Giordani in *Fides*, a re-view read by many religious, and through the talks which Graziella and others had been giving in Rome in the late 1940s. But word among the religious orders would spread much wider as many of them came on pilgrimage to Rome and lodged in their 'mother houses' during the Holy Year.

The renown of Chiara Lubich and the Focolare Movement was growing steadily. For their part, they were increasing in numbers and influence and were organizing as best they could to cope with it. They were no longer just a little group of young idealistic girls. They were being taken seriously by people, from MPs to heads of religious orders. The official Church had to take an interest and investigate. In 1950 Chiara had her first meeting with officials from various congre-gations of the Vatican. The Vatican Curia is the 'executive' of the Holy See, the 'civil service' of the Pope and the Magisterium (the teaching body of the Roman Catholic Church). Chief responsibility for safeguarding the deposit of the Faith fell on what was then called the Holy Office but is now called the Congregation for the Doctrine of the Faith (and was once known as the Inquisition).

They were to keep a close eye on Chiara and her 'disciples' throughout the 1950s. What is interesting is that in all their inter-views of Chiara Lubich she was never 'called in' to see them. They always went to her. In fact, she remembers that on more than one occasion, while the Movement and her Ideal were under question, the investigators who came to interview her left in tears! They were so moved by the simplicity and beauty of her message that they actually wept.

The Curia may have been forced to instigate investigations into Chiara and her Movement by the allegations which were made against them. Once, when pushing Chiara to find out if in fact everything had progressed easily, if all was 'sweetness and light' and only joyful and beautiful things happened to her and the Movement – as one would think by her recollections – I did get her to admit that 'We did have our little persecutions, you know.' That is the strongest language she has ever used to describe what happened to her and the Movement at the hands of their detractors.

Even in the first few years of their activities in Trent, there had been some who had denounced them as Communists – or, even worse, as Protestants! 'But,' says Chiara, 'they were always people who didn't know us.'

This is a striking characteristic of Chiara. She will never accuse or condemn anyone. This also makes it somewhat difficult to find out exactly what happened during those years of enquiry by the Church authorities. Although we learn from others that it was an extremely painful time for her, being under suspicion from the very Church she loved and sought to serve, she genuinely finds it difficult to remember, or rather to recount, the details. Her opinion is, and always has been, that the Church, as the guardian of the deposit of the Faith, is Mother. You don't criticize your own mother, for goodness' sake! And a mother wants what is best for her child and for the whole family, even though the child may not understand the reasons for such a course of action, or such a refusal of permission, or such an exercise of prudence.

Some who were living with Chiara in Rome at this time refer to her 'years of silence' and to the atmosphere of suspicion that reigned in certain quarters. They report that there were even some wild rumours that Chiara was forbidden to speak publicly, under pain of excommunication! She herself categorically dismisses this idea, saying that no such threat was ever made. Whatever the case, obviously there was a certain climate of fear among the Focolarine, and Chiara herself seems to have kept a low profile during these years of investigation. She did not cease or slow down her activities, but certainly avoided putting herself in the forefront, even to the extent that at the large summer gathering held in the Dolomites in 1959 she wrote the talks and teachings, but they were delivered by her first companions.

But this is not how she would see those years. Rather, as with all that has happened in her life, she seeks only to know the will of God for her. She understood during those years that to some extent she was meant to 'let go' of the rapidly expanding and developing work which had grown up around her – just as in the 1940s, when in Trent she had insisted that her companions should destroy her letters and written meditations after they had absorbed the content, because she did not want them to rely on her or to cling to any earthly writings. The Gospel was to be their book and rule of life, and each one was to develop his or her own prayer life and relationship with the Lord, not some vicarious relationship through the experiences of Chiara Lubich. In the intervening years Chiara's understanding and that of her Movement has further developed and matured so that the idea of a 'collective spirituality' has arisen. This, it would seem, needs still further refinement in order to avoid problems in the future. At the moment, everyone, from the rank-and-file Focolare members to the Church hierarchy, seem to accept that while the foundress and holder of the charism is still living, they are all living in a constantly developing situation. That is one reason why the Vatican is so insistent on formulating official statutes to embody each state of development.

Some of those who were young followers at the time no doubt found it all very exciting to be under investigation by the stuffy old Holy Office. Understandably, they could have fallen into a belligerent attitude of 'them and us'. But they remember that Chiara would not countenance any sort of derogatory remarks, even in jest, about the Holy Office or individual investigators. They took the point. In fact, at one summer gathering or Mariapolis held in the Dolomites, during a musical presentation of the history of the Movement so far, some of them adapted a local mountain song, substituting the original words with: 'In the Holy Office we've found a mother. / Whoever sees the Church as Mother will never go wrong.'

In 1951 another key figure entered Chiara's life. Today, wherever Chiara is, you will also find Giulia Folonari, her 'right-hand woman'. Officially she is Chiara's secretary. She is also her driver. And that is how she came to live with Chiara!

Giulia is the eldest of eight siblings. Her family are the producers of the famous Folonari wine. She had graduated in Economics and Business Studies from the Catholic University of Milan. In 1951, at the age of 25, she was living at home with her parents and younger brothers and sisters in Brescia. The family was well off and she certainly did not need to work.

Despite graduating in commerce, her main interest throughout school and university had been philosophy and religion. This caused a little tension at home sometimes when Giulia tried to live the Gospel. For example, as a youngster she would be told off when she played with the poorer children in the street, or when she wanted to give away surplus clothes. Eventually she came to the conclusion that the Gospel was for 2,000 years ago; it couldn't be lived today, even by Christians.

A Franciscan priest who moved to Brescia had met one of Chiara's first companions, Valeria Ronchetti, when he was stationed in Padua. She had spoken in many monasteries and convents in that area, just as Graziella was doing in Rome. In the spring of 1951 he asked Valeria to come and speak to a meeting in Brescia, and he invited Giulia Folonari to attend. She remembers that Valeria spoke for an hour. She talked about not a movement or organization but about how she and her friends in Trent had discovered and tried to live the Gospel, one phrase at a time. Giulia remained quiet and sat at the back of the room, as the rest of the audience were priests and religious brothers. At the end she spoke to Valeria and discovered that she was staying with the family of a local MP. They agreed to meet the next day.

Then Valeria told her the whole story – about Chiara Lubich and this radical choosing of God above all else. Giulia remembers that as she listened to this she thought to herself, 'This is it!' It was just what she had been looking for. If she didn't say 'Yes' to God immediately, 'it might be the last time the good Lord would give me such an opportunity. So, in my heart I said "Yes." It was really like that. I made the decision, without telling anyone else.'

A few days later her father sent her to a holiday town in the Dolomites called San Martino de Castrozza to find a house to rent for the summer holidays that year. Valeria had given her the address of the Focolare community in Trent in case she ever found herself there. Giulia seized the occasion and made her journey to San Martino de Castrozza via Trent. She turned up, unannounced, at 2 Piazza Cappucini. There was no one there!

It just happened to be the very day that the members of that first Focolare household were moving from that apartment to another in Via Bellenzani. Giulia learned this from the neighbours and made her way to the new address. She met two of Chiara's first companions.

Later in the year, during the summer holidays, it also just happened that the first Focolarine were holidaying only a few miles from where Giulia and her family were staying. The Folonaris were in San Martino de Castrozza and the Focolarine were in Tonadico. Giulia twice travelled over to Tonadico to visit. She remembers her first meeting with Chiara. It was in the street. Another Focolarina introduced her and Chiara simply greeted Giulia before continuing on her way. But the 'look' of Chiara struck Giulia. She says that there and then she was reminded of the Gospel phrase which says of the rich young man that 'Jesus looked on him and loved him' (Mark 10:21). 'I didn't say a word,' she remembers. 'I was just struck to the core by this look of love which came from her.'

By this time, of course, Chiara and some of her companions were living in Rome. In September Giulia told her mother that she had met some girls who lived the Gospel and that she wanted to go to Rome. 'Of course, dear,' replied her mother. 'We're all trying to live the Gospel. But does one really have to go to Rome to do it?' Mummy's opinion was 'No.'

The next day, though, Signor Folonari called his eldest daughter into his study and asked her to go to Rome to sort out a business matter for him there. It was an excuse. He knew next to nothing about the Focolare Movement but he knew his daughter had had some sort of experience which had changed her life. The following morning Giulia boarded the seven o'clock train carrying only a small suitcase with a few clothes. She was going to join the Focolare. En route she realized that she had told no one in Rome that she was coming. While changing trains at Verona she sent a telegram to the Focolare household: 'I'm coming. Stop. Giulia. Stop.'

She laughs as she recalls that perhaps someone in Rome knew her from Tonadico, or even from Brescia. 'But this "Giulia from Verona" – nobody knew who she was! So when I arrived at Rome there was no one to meet me. Undeterred, I had the address and found my way to the Focolare house. And I stayed. I had told my Mum that I was going for a day or two, but once I was there I just knew that this was my life.'

Two of Giulia's sisters and one brother, Vincenzo, eventually also joined the Focolare, and while at first Giulia's 'elopement' caused a rift with her parents, this was later healed.

As all the Focolarini have to support themselves, Giulia quickly found her first job, teaching in a commercial college. While she was living in a household with other Focolarine, she remained fascinated by the person of Chiara, but she did not fawn over her or keep seeking her attention. She respected her privacy. Perhaps because of this, and because Giulia could drive and had secretarial skills, she was eventually called on more and more by Chiara in this capacity. Eventually it was more practical that she should live in the same house as Chiara. Apart from a couple of interruptions, she has done so up to this day.

In March 1956, during a trip to Jerusalem, there were several people interested in the Ideal, so Chiara left Giulia there to live with them. She remained in Israel for about six months. (By 1995 the Focolare households in Israel were just part of the 'Middle-East zone' of the Movement, which has thousands of members – Catholic, Orthodox, Coptic, Jewish and Muslim.) Then in 1961, as the Movement was expanding, Chiara sent Giulia to Belgium to look after things there, just as she sent out all her first companions and closest friends to respond to the needs wherever the Movement was taking root. From Brussels Giulia also visited England, where there were already some people interested in the Ideal.

After Giulia had left her home and family to move to Rome, Chiara had one day told all her friends there that they should not let a day pass without sharing the Ideal with someone new. Giulia, who was herself new to Rome, racked her brain to think of someone whom she could tell about the Ideal. 'Among others, I thought of

Monsignor Montini,' she says now. 'His brother was married to my father's sister. So, although we weren't directly related, his brother was directly my uncle, so we knew each other.

'He didn't know the Movement at that time, but he would surely have heard on the family grapevine that I had left home and had come to Rome somewhat abruptly. So I phoned him at his office in the Vatican and said, "I'm in Rome now; perhaps we could see each other some time?" He said, "Yes, of course. Come round." Just like that. And when we met I told him about the Focolare and the Ideal. He was the chief Assistant for the whole Catholic student population of Italy, and he came from a Catholic family which had been very actively anti-Fascist, so he was delighted to hear about the Movement and my response to this evangelical call I had felt. Later he also got to know Palmira and Valeria, two of Chiara's first companions, and then Chiara herself.'

Monsignor Montini assured Chiara that the investigation by the Holy Office was a necessary protection for the Movement. He told her: 'For you this study is protection and guarantee. Protected because you're in the heart of the Church and guaranteed because you are sure that what you do is Christian, you're studied by the Church.'

Montini's brother Ludivico was one of a group of MPs who had come into contact with the Movement through Igino Giordani. Another was the Prime Minister, Alcide De Gasperi. Chiara had met him in 1950 when Giordani brought him along to a gathering of young people associated with the Movement held at Fregene. She saw him again privately some time after that, and a letter written by him to Chiara on 21 April 1951 has survived. In it De Gasperi (whom Chiara says was one of those people who associate with the Movement, and whom she called 'adherents') reveals something of his own state of soul. It reflects a man of spirituality who, like his French politician friend Robert Schuman, saw politics as a Christian service. In the turbulent post-War years De Gasperi's task was not an easy one. He wrote to Chiara:

> To feel united under the wings of the divine paternity gives a feeling of serenity and confidence even in time of tribulation.
>
> And the hour of tribulation is upon us, when the one responsible for governing is assailed by the fear that our country faces bitter days

and that we shall not be equipped with the necessary cohesion and solidarity to face the trials ahead. If I were not obliged to share the responsibility for this part of history which Providence accords to the freewill of man, I would retire and resign myself to the will of God.

But for the Christian who sees politics as an expression of his faith and above all as a service and therefore as his highest obligation towards his brethren and our common Father, this anguish and upheaval become an inescapable duty.

In a letter to Chiara dated 28 December 1953 he expressed regret that he did not have the time he would like to dedicate to 'heartfelt friendships' because of his ever-pressing duties and the many difficulties he had to overcome. He asked her to pray to the Lord, 'not for me but for our troubled country...'

De Gasperi and Giordani had been friends for many years. In 1925 Giordani was already being persecuted for his strong denunciation of the assassination of Matteoti and Father Minzoni by the Fascists. The newspaper which he ran for the Italian Popular Party was closed down, so he promptly set up the *Official Bulletin of the Press Office of the IPP* instead. He was tried in court but was then given an amnesty because he had been a hero in the First World War. He defended De Gasperi when he was attacked by the Fascists. When De Gasperi was released from prison in 1928, Giordani, who had by then set up the Vatican School of Librarianship, obtained a post there for De Gasperi from Pope Pius XI.

De Gasperi and his friend Giordani seem to prove that unity was not only the preserve of the Communists. Chiara's brother Gino, who by 1950 was working on the Communist newspaper *Unita*, wrote to Giordani following his speech in Parliament on 21 December in which he called on Italy to be a mediator to bring an end to the Korean War. Giordani was at the time also a director of the review *La Via*, in which he published Gino Lubich's letter on 30 December. It sheds light also on the spirit in which Gino Lubich, still a committed Communist, looked on politics:

Dear Giordani...

Forgive me for using this plain paper – it was the nearest to hand – to write and tell you of my joy, how I was moved, my gratitude – yes, truly, my gratitude as a man, as an Italian, as a friend – although we are not on the same side – that you took the floor of that Chamber, which for so many years now has been shadowed by hatred, to speak words of wisdom, of understanding, of brotherhood...

For so long we have been responding to one another with insults and jeers that it was hard to get used to the idea again that an exchange of ideas might be possible, although I knew it was absolutely necessary...

So today you spoke to the House. And I admit this to you (but don't tell anyone) – I saw, with tears in my eyes and a lump in my throat, that for the first time the whole House applauded. They were applauding you, dear Giordani, because you had spoken good, just and holy words; words which demolished the atmosphere of hatred, of preconceived and absurd suspicions, of rivalry. Words? They are not just words. With your courageous gesture you swept away the Babel of language from the tower...Dialogue has been taken up again among us...Italy is taking up the noble role of being a mediator of peace.

Thank you, Giordani. Thank you in the name of the millions of ordinary people such as the one writing to you now – all prepared to struggle with all their strength so that a further catastrophe might not descend on our people, on our homes, on our families. May Italy's history mark this date as one of the most decisive post-War moments.

Monsignor Montini was a confidant of Pope Pius XII, having been appointed by him to head up a section of the Secretariat of State before the Pope made him Archbishop of Milan. Through him a private audience with the Pope was arranged for Chiara and some of her closest collaborators.

She remembers that when they were presented to the Pope, he immediately showed that he knew of them. 'Ah, the Focolarini! Good! Good! Where's the leader?'

Chiara says, 'He turned towards me with a really genuine and paternal friendliness. He wanted to know about each one of us, what we did and where we came from. I explained to him that we represented different regions of Italy where the Movement was present. He was particularly interested in Tuscany and Emilia, explaining that in those regions, where Communism dominated, you could sense more strongly the influence of materialism.

'One of us replied, "We want to bring Jesus to the world. Each one of us has hundreds of souls behind her, and we follow each one of them personally...We want to be the joy of the Church."

' "And the Church needs it so much," replied the Pope. "Continue your work. Go forward!" At the end he gave us a solemn blessing, and as he was being led away to his next appointment, he kept looking back and waving to us.'

Despite this private meeting with the Pope, the investigation into Chiara Lubich and her ideas continued, as did the denunciations coming from various quarters. Chiara was said to be leading young people astray. They were breaking off marriage engagements to follow her! She was promoting Communism within the Church. She was encouraging people to read Scripture without the guidance of the Church to interpret it. In fact, it was only in 1943 that Pope Pius XII had opened up the whole area of Scripture study to Catholic laity with his encyclical letter *In Divine Afflante Spiritu*. In any case, Chiara submitted all her commentaries on Scripture, right from the very first one, and even short passages such as the *Word of Life* commentaries, to the Archbishop of Trent for his imprimatur.

It was he who received the bulk of the accusations against Chiara and the Focolare. To make his position on the Movement clear once and for all, he published the following statement in 1956:

To whom it may concern.

What I think about Focolare can be summed up in a few words. I witnessed its birth in my diocese and I have always regarded it as an exceptional company of very fine souls whose lives were edifying in every respect. Their genuine spirit of charity and zealous sense of apostolate are sure proof that in this poor world, 'set as it is on a course to ruin', there are still Christians who are able to scale the most demanding heights of virtue and mine the deepest recesses of goodness.

For 12 years now, I have been vigilant and attentive in my observation of them, and during that time, I have never had cause to reprove them. On the contrary, they have always been a joy, a rare experience for me in more than 50 years of pastoral ministry. I have already said this in the past, I have put it in writing on other occasions, and now I repeat it: Would that there were legions of Focolarini!

Signed: Carlo De Ferrari, Archbishop.

One day Chiara and her companions learned that as the Bishops had received a number of letters of complaint about this new Movement, the subject of the Focolare was put on the agenda for a Bishops' conference. Graziella De Lucca, in her airy and breathless manner, recounts what happened:

'I don't know if you know about this. It's quite funny really. There was one cardinal who wasn't favourable towards us – the Cardinal of Palermo – but then, he didn't know us. So, by chance, we heard that we were to be discussed at this conference of the Italian Bishops. So Chiara sent us out to all the bishops that we knew in Italy to tell them how things were progressing with the Movement – so that they could decide for themselves whether or not we were sound.

'And we prayed and prayed to the Eternal Father in the name of Jesus that this Bishops' conference would go well. The Cardinal broke his leg and was replaced by the Bishop of Trapani, who was a great, great friend of ours. Everything went well for us at that conference.'

The German Bishops' Conference had already approved the Movement a couple of years previously. The Cardinals Döepfner of Munich and Frings of Köln were very encouraging towards the Movement, as was Bishop Stimpfle of Augsburg, whose episcopal ordination Chiara attended.

Chiara says: 'It was a time of suffering for us. Until we received the official approval of the Pope, we passed through a period of suspense, uncertainty and forsakenness.

'Several factors came to the fore for us during those years. First of all, a deep love for Jesus crucified and forsaken, which always sustained us. We had chosen him and now he was making himself known to us in grand style. It was an opportunity to prove our genuine love for him. And then there was our strong belief in the Church's maternity, which must have come to us directly from Heaven. Finally, it was a period of extraordinary fruits. The Movement, which had already spread to different parts of Europe, now began to reach other continents. We saw the beginning of its ecumenical work and its initial penetration of countries behind the Iron Curtain so as to help the Church in Eastern Europe. It was a time of blessings, immense blessings. "Unless the grain of wheat falls into the earth and dies, it remains alone; but if it dies, it bears much fruit" (John 12:24).'

Pope Pius XII died in 1958. The Focolarini learned, again 'by chance', that the old Pope had left a note regarding the Focolare Movement and his wish that it should be officially approved. After discussion at the Italian Bishops' Conference in 1960, Pope John XXIII appointed a papal commission to oversee the process of fully integrating the Movement into the structures of the Church. Once the commission had completed its task, Pope John officially and publicly approved the Focolare Movement on 23 March 1962. There would be no more restrictions on its public activities.

TWELVE

SUMMER HOLIDAYS – WHOSE CITY IS IT ANYWAY?

As Chiara and Graziella have testified, during the years of investigation and suspicion throughout the 1950s, 'the Movement carried on.' From that first holiday together in the Dolomites in 1949, every summer saw a Focolare gathering somewhere in that region. It was a time when Chiara wanted to get away from the city and, with her companions, enjoy the mountain air and take some rest. It never worked out that way.

Graziella and other 'first companions' state that wherever Chiara was, they wanted to be too. After the extraordinary experiences shared by Chiara and the early companions during 'Paradise '49', the next year hundreds arrived up in the mountains. Everything was done on the hoof. The first companions had to cope with the crowds. They slept in little towns and villages all around the area. Where there were beds, someone slept on the base and someone else on the mattress on the floor. Some people slept in barns, while others came with tents and camped out.

In 1957, following the previous year's public statement by the Archbishop of Trent and the Italian Bishops' decision not to censure the Focolare, some bishops also attended the summer gathering. At the summer gathering those who were associated with the Movement but were not consecrated members experienced the lifestyle of the Focolare. Chiara described it as 'building the City of Mary', as Mary brings Jesus to the world. The participants would then take this experience back to their own towns, villages, parishes, families and places of work. The summer gathering thus became known as the Mariapolis.

Every year a new aspect of the spirituality and the Ideal of the Focolare would be developed. Chiara would prepare the talks and others would deliver them. They all realized that they could not just welcome all these people during the summer and then abandon them during the rest of the year. In 1956 Fr Foresi collected the names and addresses of some 3,000 people who were in contact with the Movement and, back in Rome after the Mariapolis, he ran off a first newsletter. That stencilled circular later became a magazine called *New City*. As with nearly all of the branches and activities of the Focolare, it bears the prefix 'New'. Chiara doesn't like sameness or staleness: 'Behold, I come to make all things new!' (Revelation 21:5). Christians are born to new life in Baptism. Even as adults making a new commitment to God as their Ideal, they are putting off the 'old man' and putting on the 'new' (Ephesians 4:22–24). They are children of the New Covenant between God and Man. 'Behold, I make all things new!'

New City is now a full-colour magazine published twice monthly in Italy, monthly in many other countries and bi-monthly in some others. Altogether it is now published in 39 different national editions and 24 languages, totalling over a quarter of a million copies. (The American edition is called *Living City*, as there was already another American magazine called *New City*.)

The Movement now has 27 *New City* publishing houses in 26 countries. They publish some 300 new books each year. Among the regular magazines and reviews which they produce are *New Youth News*, *Youth for Unity News*, *Gen's* (for ministers and seminarians), *Unity and Charisms* (for those in religious orders), *New Humanity* (a referenced academic cultural review), and the monthly tract entitled *Word of Life*, which contains a spiritual-theological commentary by Chiara Lubich on a text of Scripture. It is published in 90 languages and has a print-run of some 4 million copies.

An audit carried out in October 1995 revealed that 185 radio and television stations around the world carried information about the Focolare on a regular basis (daily or weekly or monthly). Many of these would be monthly readings of Chiara's *Word of Life* meditations. The combined audience of these programmes was put at over 100 million. This figure did not include the countries of Eastern Europe, where gathering audience statistics was more difficult. Neither did it include occasional radio or television broadcasts covering particular events. For example, in 1995 Genfest, the Movement's international youth gathering, was transmitted in whole or in part by 54 national television stations and by 288 regional stations.

In 1959, the numbers arriving at the summer Mariapolis in the Dolomites exceeded 12,000 people. They could no longer invade those small mountain villages for their summer gatherings!

In the 1950s the Movement had also taken root in other countries of Europe, and focolares were opened in Belgium, France, Switzerland and Germany. In 1960 the first Mariapolis outside Italy was held in Fribourg in Switzerland. By the following year, summer Mariapoli were being held in all the countries in Europe where the Movement was present, as well as in Argentina and Brazil. Today a Mariapolis is held in almost every country where the Movement has been implanted, so that in 1995 there were 178 such gatherings.

At the 1954 summer gathering, held in the Dolomites, a priest from Eastern Europe was present. He had been persecuted by the authorities in his own country and had been imprisoned in a forced labour camp. He eventually escaped and made his way to Rome. He was horrified to find that the Church in the West seemed to be almost completely unaware of the suffering of the Church in the East, which at that time was experiencing some of its darkest hours.

The number of people attending that summer gathering of 1954 had already reached several hundred, but the priest insisted on seeing Chiara. She agreed to hear him out, and was astounded by his account of the suffering of the forsaken Church in Eastern Europe – 'the Church of Silence'.

The priest, for his part, recognized the extraordinary nature of Chiara's charism and the revolutionary quality of the spirituality which she proposed. He quickly grasped her Ideal. He quite clearly saw it as the answer to the problem of Communism, and went on to write a private document (which remains in the Vatican archives) for Pope Pius XII. In it he made a total comparison between Communism and the Ideal of the Focolare. It was like a comparison of a negative and a positive. The Focolare Ideal was definitely *the* answer to Marxist theory (the worst heresy of the century), he concluded.

This meeting with the priest from Eastern Europe awakened a strong desire among the Focolarini to do something for those people who were without God. Anna Fratta, an Italian who later spent 30 years of her life in countries of the Communist bloc in order to implant the Movement secretly, says that although that desire to reach those who were far from God had been present from the beginning of the Movement, this meeting with an escaped priest from a country under Communist oppression 'fired it up' in them again. 'That meeting with him at Mariapolis '55 put into our hearts this particular love for Jesus Forsaken, who cries out in that portion of the Church. In fact, the Bishop of Erfurt in East Germany said, "The Church of Silence is a great Jesus Forsaken which cries out, 'My God, my God, why have You forsaken me?'" '

In September 1955, the three 'co-founders' of the Focolare Movement made a pilgrimage to the Marian shrine of Fatima in Portugal. They were accompanied by a niece of Pope Pius XII (her mother, the Pope's sister, had attended the 1954 summer gathering) who had arranged with her uncle that Chiara might meet Sister Lucia, the sole surviving seer of Fatima, at her Carmelite convent in Coimbra. Giordani wrote in his private, unpublished papers that they had in mind Russia and the consecration to the Immaculate Heart of Mary recently made by the Pope. What was said in that meeting between Chiara and Sister Lucia has remained secret.

That year Giordani had the idea to call the summer gathering of the following year a 'Mariapolis'. Until then, each year the gathering had been given a different name. In 1954, for example, it had been 'Giapolis', in honour of Jesus Forsaken (*Gesu Abandonato* in Italian). Ever since then the name 'Mariapolis' ('City of Mary') has stuck.

In Soviet-occupied and forsaken Eastern Europe, an attempt at revolution was made in Hungary in 1956. The Soviet tanks rolled in and put a bloody end to all that. Many erstwhile supporters of the 'Socialist empire' in the West were shocked and horrified. Liberal commentators and journalists who had been taken in by the apparent benevolence of the Soviet regime faced a crisis of conscience.

One journalist, who was a committed Communist and a chief reporter and leader writer on the Italian Communist newspaper, found his illusions about Communism shattered. He was Gino Lubich, the brother of Chiara. His faith in that system had already been shaken somewhat on the death of Stalin in 1953. Chiara wrote him a letter at that time, urging him to seek an Ideal that would go on for ever. 'Look,' she said, 'don't you see that even Stalin comes to an end?' From then on, he began to have more contacts with the Focolare. He became friends with several journalists who were involved with his sister's Movement. The crushing of the Hungarian rebellion was another blow to his faith in Communism. In 1959 he even attended the great summer Mariapolis in the Dolomites. He was impressed by the talks which were given by the companions of Chiara (but which had been written by her). Chiara says, 'It was not so much our idea, or ideas, that impressed him, but the Word – our ideology, if I can use that word – and it replaced his ideology.' Gino gave up his membership of the Communist Party and returned to the Catholic Faith. He wrote lives of several saints and also a popular and much-appreciated biography of Pope John XXIII. His work for unity had not stopped – it had merely taken a completely different direction. He became a journalist on the Focolare's Italian magazine, *Citta Nuova*.

On that morning in December 1943 when she had consecrated herself to God, Chiara had written a note which the priest had placed under the chalice. It had simply said, 'For the conversion of my brother Gino.'

With the bloody repression of the Hungarian Revolution and the Suez Crisis in 1956, Pope Pius XII lamented that everyone was speaking of crises, but where were the people who would bring the solution? The solution was, 'God…God…God', to fill the void of atheism, he said. Chiara determined that she and her Movement would take the Pope's cry seriously.

In October of that year, 1956, the first 'branch' of the Focolare Movement was formed. Until then there had been the female and male Focolarini, consecrated to God with promises of poverty, chastity and obedience and living in community. Then, with the arrival of Igino Giordani had come the section of married Focolarini who lived the same promises according to their state of life and lived in their own families – what Vatican II would call 'the domestic Church'.

Thus, Chiara sees 1956 as the year in which the Focolare was reinforced in its nature as a lay movement, with those first volunteers who, she says, 'wanted to share in the spirituality of the Focolare and take God as their Ideal…as a reply to Communism.' Today there are 16 different branches, and while there are nuns, priests and bishops involved, the vast majority of members are lay people.

Shortly before the summer Mariapolis of 1957, Chiara and one of her first companions were driving from Rome to Grottaferrata when their car skidded, sending them right off the road and into a ditch. Chiara suffered a broken collar-bone but still insisted on going north a few days later to take part in the Mariapolis. There she had to take to bed for a few days and had her shoulder in plaster. One of the people who came to see her during that summer gathering was a Jesuit priest, Fr Lombardi, who had founded the Movement for a Better World. He was a well-known preacher in Italy who drew massive crowds and was nicknamed 'God's Microphone'. He was held in high esteem by Pope Pius XII.

Chiara and he had known of each other and their respective movements for some time. Now Lombardi came with a proposal that, in view of the many similarities and goals of the two groups, they should merge into one.

While the Focolare often co-operates with other movements in the Church for a common service, Chiara says that 'Despite their similarities, charisms are far more different from one another than you might imagine. Working together at the request of ecclesiastical authorities, for specific purposes and practical activities within set periods of time, such as our joint work at the World Youth Days, or events for things like The Year of the Family, are not only useful but of great value.'

But that, she implies, certainly does not mean amalgamation. When she and Fr Lombardi sought advice from their respective superiors – for him, the Superior General of the Jesuits, and for her at that time, the Archbishop of Trent – they were advised not to fuse the two movements. The two had specific contributions to make, and these could be confused if both groups lost their specific identity. Chiara quotes this as another instance when seeking advice from and obeying the due authorities in the Church safeguarded the specific charism proper to a particular founder/foundress and the Movement.

The following year another well-known charismatic preacher and priest, Fr Werenfried van Straaten, met Chiara. She recognized that in his work of collecting aid for persecuted Christians and refugees from oppression, he too was reaching out, in his own way, to console Jesus Forsaken.

Two young women Focolarine went to work at Fr Werenfried's depot based at his monastery in Tongerlo in Belgium. A male Focolarino, Aldo Stedile, became Werenfried's secretary and driver for some months.

In the December of the previous year, 1957, Aldo had accompanied Chiara to Munster in Germany. While Aldo addressed a group of seminary teachers and students on the Ideal, Chiara remained at her hotel in town and had a meeting with the exiled priest from Eastern Europe who had spoken to her about the Church of Silence at the 1954 Mariapolis.

In Aldo's audience at the seminary was a Fr Lubsczyk, an Oratorian priest from Leipzig in East Germany. At the end of the talk he confided to Aldo: 'This is the spirit we need behind the Iron Curtain. The Focolare must come to East Germany.'

Aldo told this to Chiara the next morning, and she wondered aloud if this Oratorian priest might not be the instrument for the Focolare to enter the Communist countries.

In May 1958 Chiara visited the small Focolare community which had moved to Belgium to work with Fr Werenfried. She also visited the World Fair, Expo '58, which the Belgian capital was hosting and whose symbol, the Atomium, still stands as a lasting reminder. The Focolarini were particularly interested in the stands of the USSR and Czechoslovakia. Chiara was impressed by this giant world-wide 'expo', which she described as reaching 'a summit of style, beauty, technology'. She couldn't help but notice that 'Christ crying out to the world, "Who is like God?" was not exhibited.' She felt she would have wanted to make room at that giant exhibition 'for God present among people through a display of fraternal charity, where one is at the service of the other, where titles are given little relevance and the beatitudes are proclaimed.'

Very well, she decided: her summer gathering of the Focolare would be 'God's Expo'. When a group of Focolarini, Aldo among them, travelled back to the seminary in Munster to hold a day seminar there on the Movement and its Ideal on 29 June, they shared this idea with their audience. A similar group did the same at a meeting which they organized for those interested in the Movement in Grenoble, France.

That summer Mariapolis was held in Fiera di Primiero. Thousands flocked there from Italy, Germany, Belgium and France. The Mariapolis had become international.

Chiara made another visit to Brussels in September 1958, and from there she and some companions travelled by car to the

French Marian shrine of Lourdes. Events were moving so quickly that she needed to get away with only a few close companions for a few days of prayer and quiet. Above all she wanted to entrust this sudden expansion of the Movement to the Blessed Virgin who had appeared at Lourdes a hundred years before. While there she understood and accepted that the Movement in the rest of Europe outside Italy should become its own 'zone' (the 'zone' was to become the geographical administrative unit of the organization).

At the Mariapolis the idea had emerged of laying the groundwork for an eventual expansion into North and South America by sending several Focolarini there. A group of men and women left for Argentina and Brazil later the same year.

The years of 'learning to let go' as the Church carried out its investigations seemed to be producing fruits far beyond the work of any one woman – well, any ordinary woman! Chiara had entrusted the whole Movement into the hands of an extraordinary woman: Mary the mother of Jesus. The official title of the Movement in the Church documents which Chiara and Fr Foresi had to draw up was 'the Work of Mary'.

In 1959 colleagues persuaded Chiara to allow them to publish a first book of some of her collected writings. It was called simply *Meditations* – a compilation of some of her thoughts written down over the previous 15 years. As of February 1995 it had gone through 100 editions and almost half a million copies.

A meditation in that collection shows something of the fire burning within her after she had seen Expo '58 and desired to put the mighty love of God on display. One can see how at the Marian shrine of Lourdes she should succumb to an ambition that this Ideal which she and her companions followed should be brought even beyond the oceans to the other side of the world. She wrote:

> If a city were set on fire at different points, even by a small fire, but one that resisted extinction, in a short while the whole city would be aflame. If a city, in the most diverse points, were set alight by the fire that Jesus brought to earth and, through the goodwill of the inhabitants, that fire resisted the ice of the world, we would soon have the city aflame with the love of God.

The fire that Jesus brought to earth is himself. It is charity: that love which not only binds the soul to God, but souls to one another.

In fact, a lighted supernatural fire means the continual triumph of God in souls who have given themselves to him and, because they are united to him, are united among themselves.

Two or more people united in the name of Christ, who are not afraid or ashamed to declare explicitly to one another their desire to love God, but who actually make of this unity in Christ their Ideal, are a divine power in the world.

And in every city these souls can come to exist in families; father and mother, son and father, mother and mother-in-law...It is not necessary for them to be saints already, or Jesus would have said so. It is enough for them to be united in the name of Christ and that they never go back on this unity.

Naturally, they will not remain two or three for very long, for charity spreads of itself and grows by enormous proportions.

Every small cell, set alight by God in any point of the earth, will necessarily spread, and Providence will distribute these flames, these souls on fire, wherever it thinks fit, so that the world in many places may be restored to the warmth of the love of God, and hope again.

But there is a secret by which this lighted cell may grow and become tissue and give life to the parts of the Mystical Body. It is that those who make up the Body should throw themselves into the Christian adventure, which means *making a spring-board of every obstacle*. They should not just 'put up' with the cross in whatever guise it presents itself, but should wait for it and embrace it, minute by minute as the saints do.

On reading this extract from her meditations, it is not difficult to understand why Igino Giordani described Chiara as 'a second St Catherine of Siena'. Catherine's spirituality is described as 'fire and blood'. Chiara obviously understands and shares that same fire. The blood she leaves to another type of spirituality, as she understood from her prayer vigil the night before her total consecration to God back in 1943. 'I understood,' she says, 'that my suffering would be spiritual suffering.' And when the priest told her that morning that she was now a 'bride of blood', she replied in her heart, 'No. I am a bride of God.'

In the same book published in 1959 there appeared another of Chiara's meditations – 'On the lives of the Saints'. Forty years after it was written, one cannot help but marvel at its insight and depth, and ask if the one who wrote it has not shared in the same experiences which she seems to discern and understand so well in the lives of the saints. In the 1950s Chiara often referred to a period of 'tears and light' through which she seemed to be living. Among her thoughts on the saints one finds written:

The saint's life is made up of abysses and peaks: bottomless abysses, nights as black as hell, dark tunnels where the soul, invaded by an absolutely superior light, is dazzled in a dark contemplation and submerged in a sea of anguish or near desperation due to its clear awareness of its own nothingness and wretchedness. The saint lives through months, years, during which his only yearning is to die into the bosom of God, from whom at times he feels hopelessly separated. Life is an atrocious death and sleep a relief, a respite, almost a caress for the wounded soul. A long time passes in which the saint cries out, calling for pardon, for salvation, with no longer anything in his heart but God, his God.

Then, after a long time of being worked upon in a crucible comparable to purgatory, the soul of the saint is slowly drawn by its divine Craftsman into a life that is serene, full, radiant, active and immune to any blow. But *now* in the soul it is no longer itself that lives. In it, glorious and strong, honoured and heeded, there lives the Creator and Lord of every human heart.

This is the hour when an unknown, unique, divine strength flourishes in the saint which fuses together the most contrasting virtues in his soul: meekness and strength, mercy and justice, simplicity and prudence. He rejoices in his life in God and offers to his Lord 'sacrifices of joy' (Psalm 27:6) with a joy that this world does not know. He is forced to admit that no dream is comparable to the Life he possesses, a Life which is divine and extraordinary (because it is a life of love), full of harmony and fruits.

Then God uses him for his great works that make up and adorn the heavenly city, the Church, which is destined to ascend to God as the spotless and worthy *Bride of Christ* who founded it.

Human beings are only given one life. It would be in the interest of each one to place his life in the hands of God who gave it. This, in a rational and free person, would be the highest possible act of intelligence, the most effective way of maintaining and extending his own freedom to a divine level. It would mean the deification of his own poor self in the name of the One who said: 'You are gods, sons of the Most High, all of you' (Psalm 82:6).

I believe it would be difficult to find anything more like the writings of St Teresa of Avila. Giordani compares Chiara Lubich to St Catherine of Siena, but I think it would also be fitting to describe her as a modern-day Teresa of Avila. And while Chiara may have been writing about saints in general, and particularly canonized saints, such insight, one feels, has to be linked to personal understanding through experience. The late Jesuit retreat-master Anthony de Mello wrote in his book *Awareness*:

> St Teresa of Avila said God gave her the grace of disidentifying herself with herself. You hear children talk that way. A two-year-old says 'Tommy had his breakfast this morning.' He doesn't say 'I', although he is Tommy. He says 'Tommy' – in the third person. Mystics feel that way. They have disidentified from themselves and they are at peace.

In the 20 years between the publication of her first book and that experience of finding her 'fourth way' in the little house of Loreto and the intuition that a whole host of other people would follow her in it, Chiara had surely understood that she had been, and was being, used as a 'foundress' herself.

In any case, when I remarked to her in 1996 that the progress during the 'birth period' of an order or community often seemed linked to the level of sufferings of the founder, she replied quite definitely: 'That's true.'

Up to what point can this be true? How far can a founder or foundress take this? To what extent of suffering? In a rare moment of self-revelation, she told me: 'The life of a person who has been given a charism has two names: abysses and heights. And it's the heights – the mountain-tops, the union with God, the intuition of what God is, of what God does – that's what fills the abyss. There *is* suffering but there are *these great heights* which you reach with God.'

THIRTEEN

CHURCH SOUL – A KINDRED SPIRIT

In one of her books (her ninth) published in 1973, Chiara includes a chapter on St Catherine of Siena who, along with St Teresa of Avila, had been declared the first woman Doctor of the Church by Pope Paul VI.

As a picture of the life of Chiara Lubich builds up, it is not difficult to see comparisons with the great Catherine of Siena, even though six centuries separate the two women. Chiara's obvious empathy with the saint is evident in her written appreciation of her:

CATHERINE OF SIENA, CHURCH-SOUL

The calendar for April presents again to all Christians the great figure of the saint who was proclaimed a Doctor of the Church by Pope Paul VI a few years ago: Catherine of Siena.

But what is so special about this woman who, despite the passing of the centuries, lives more than ever in the Christian consciousness and is rediscovered by each period as she who always has a word to say, a fascination that attracts, a supernatural beauty that charms and especially such a relevant and modern spirit?

How is it that so very many Christians live or eke out their Christianity leaving little or no trace behind them, while in the case of *this* Christian, the more time goes by, the more the Church honours her and the Church's children are delighted by this?

It would take volumes to answer this adequately, to cite the countless wonderful graces, miracles and wisdom that fill up her extraordinary life.

Yet I believe one single word can answer this: the fact is that Catherine is a *Church-soul*.

Now just as the Church will never pass away and, notwithstanding that the unavoidable struggle which must characterize it will never see the sun set, so Catherine, having become one with the Church, has, one may say, a like destiny.

It is through this, her being 'Church', that Catherine still has something to say to all of us Christians today, intent in thousands of ways and as much as we can, on understanding, on loving, on bringing a lacerated Christianity together again into the one and only Church which is *her very own word*.

Catherine is a creature in whose heart charity burns so strongly, that it is like Christ's, with a love that becomes true, holy passion for the Church.

Let's look at her in action.

Although she inspired a religious current, the 'Catherinites', who followed her spirituality which is summed up in the two words, 'fire' and 'blood', this is not her chief work, but rather her chief work is her untiring effort to bring the Pope back to Rome. Quite clearly here she is facing the problems of the Church with complete openness.

If her apostolate is analysed, we are struck by the same impression. At a certain moment, Catherine passes from a private to a public level. The immediate reason for this was the fact that among her followers there were also noted personalities from the political as well as from the religious field. And she saw them all not through the distorting lens of restricting interests, even though religious ones, but in terms of their complete personality.

If Catherine has something to do with a Cardinal, for example, she considers him in the context of the influence he has in the Church. If she has dealings with a prince, she also follows him in his political action. He is a follower of hers, but Catherine loves him for the Church, for mankind.

She shares with all her children their struggles, their anxieties, everything they are living through.

And if she maintains a prolific correspondence, not only with men and women in the humblest of circumstances, but also with the Church and State authorities, if she interests herself in news of current affairs, this is because her openness has the measure of the Church and mankind.

Then if we hear her pray, we have not the slightest doubt that she has only one great love. Her desires and requests to God are for the Church: 'Oh eternal God, receive the sacrifice of my life in this mystical body of the holy Church. I have nothing to give other than what you have given me. Take my heart and spend it for the sake of this Beloved Spouse.'

Catherine has no peace until the Church finds unity again around the Pope. She lives and loves the Church so passionately that her every move is inspired by this flame.

Nor is the doctrinal side secondary in the virgin of Siena if she has been declared a Doctor on account of her wisdom.

Catherine writes books that Jesus himself dictates. And yet she is grateful to Brother Raymond for what he does for her with his doctrine. He guarantees that she remains faithful to the teaching of the Church.

Catherine acts like the true reformers. They submit their illuminations or revelations to those who can tell them the thought of the Church, and let themselves be guided by those for whom they themselves are at times, in another way, the guide.

The false reformers, on the contrary, stigmatize error with cold judgement and separate themselves.

Catherine is not scandalized and does not withdraw in the face of the disconcerting deviations of the Church at that time, and she always finds a way of living her 'being Church'.

When, for example, she herself seems to be an object of discontent to the Pope at that time, she exploits the very situation to lodge herself even further within the heart of the mystical body, and writes to the Pontiff like this: 'Most Holy Father…if you are displeased and are indignant towards me, if you abandon me, I shall hide myself in the wounds of the crucified Christ, whose vicar you are; and I know that he will receive me since he does not will the death of a sinner. And since I am received by him, you will not chase me away.' So Catherine concludes that, still together, 'we will stand in the front line to fight dauntlessly for the sweet Spouse of Christ.'

Catherine, just when she feels weakest, considers herself most Church and makes her weakness its glory, and completely forgetting herself, she sees nothing else and loves nothing but the interests of the Spouse of Christ.

Because the fire of Christ is burning in her heart, she experiences strongly the sense of the Church as a family.

She has a spiritual family herself and, of course, lives for them. She goes out of her way so much for them that Brother Raymond can confess: 'All of us because of this, call the virgin "mamma", giving birth to us day by day from the womb of her mind, until we become copies of Christ.'

But at the same time, Catherine's family is the entire Church. She is so taken up with love for it that she can with amazing directness assume the authority of a mother, often cutting short the intricate controversies of the Church by stating her determination with a peremptory formula: 'It is God's will and mine.'

Somebody might ascribe her behaviour to the following reason: Catherine speaks like this because her will coincides by now with God's will.

Yes, her will coincides with that of God, but it is also her own because she is Church and shares in some measure in the motherhood of the Church for all.

In the forcefulness with which she affirms her own will, we do not feel a juridical authority, which Catherine does not have, but that maternal authority which has given everything to keep God's family united together: an authority similar to Mary's.

Not only is the Church her family, it is her home, her city.

Without doubt, everything that tears apart the net of relationships of peace which should make the Church the city of light for the world, tears apart her own inner being.

It is enough to think of certain painful moments in the last years of her life.

The Pope had returned to Rome at last, but in the meantime an anti-pope had been elected who had his see at Avignon, and many cardinals had sided with him.

Catherine then went through the darkest night of her whole existence: perhaps she felt herself responsible for that schism, through having persuaded the legitimate Pope to leave Avignon for Rome?

But look at her, as though desiring to concentrate in herself that entire trauma of the mystical body, as though desiring to suffer at the centre of this pain, making her way to St Peter's, where she feels nearer the Pope, to pray there the whole day for unity and peace to return. And this is what she writes to Brother Raymond: 'When it is still dawn you may see a shadow of a woman going to St Peter's...There I stay like that almost until the hour of Vespers: and I would not wish to leave that place day or night until I see this people quietened a little and settled down with their father.'

This is significant: Catherine feels the need to make her way even physically to the centre of Christianity, making St Peter's her parish church.

Church-soul, Catherine teaches us that the Church is itself if it is *one* in faith and in love.

For lots of well-known reasons, today too, we need to learn from such a great teacher, and our hearts will be enflamed by her ardent passion and we can all effectively serve our Mother Church wherever we are on earth, whether the position of responsibility we hold is big or small.

FOURTEEN

CHIARA'S 'BROTHER RAYMOND'
– THE ABBA SCHOOL

Comparisons with Chiara's own life are not difficult to find in what she writes about Catherine of Siena. Whereas Father Raymond drew out the doctrine from Catherine's spiritual teaching, with Chiara there is a whole study group. Known as the Abba School, they meet twice a week with Chiara at the Movement's administrative centre in Rocca di Papa outside Rome. The group consists of 14 academics including a philosopher, a theologian, a historian, a psychologist and medical doctor, an expert in exegesis, a sociologist and a professor of spiritual theology.

The group was founded in 1990–91 and used to meet every day, with Chiara attending once a week. Since 1995 it has met twice a week, both times with Chiara. In a sense, though, the idea of formulating 'doctrine' or 'theology' from the charism and spiritual insights of Chiara had been there from the earliest days of the Movement. Chiara herself had seen one of Fr Foresi's tasks as being to elaborate a theology resulting from the charism. Up until his death in 1993, the late Bishop Klaus Hemmerle had greatly contributed to this process. He was a respected theologian, a Focolarino and the Bishop of Aachen in Germany.

Since the group has started meeting twice weekly with Chiara, she herself presides. They accomplish so much work in each two-hour session that sometimes they think afterwards that it must have been at least a whole-day meeting. They appreciate Chiara as someone who asks the deepest, most practical questions.

Giuseppe Zanghi, a philosopher who sits on the group and who also edits the Movement's academic review, *Nuova Umanita*, says he feels as if he is 'bathing in light' when he sits in those meetings exploring ideas with Chiara Lubich. He is responsible for co-ordinating the on-going study programme which is compulsory for all consecrated Focolarini and is also open to other members of the Movement. (Von Balthasar had said that, 'The true tragedy in the Christian world are not the confused Christians but the absence of lay theologians.') Zanghi appreciates the fact that although Chiara's university studies in philosophy were interrupted, she has, in fact, never stopped studying. He describes her as being 'very intelligent' and as having 'a very strong speculative intelligence'.

Zanghi's own particular interest is in rediscovering a deep dialogue between philosophy and theology. If the basis of Western philosophy has been the notion of being – *essere* – and then non-*essere* and so on right up to nihilism, then he feels the need to overcome these two apparent irreconcilables of being and non-being. 'I believe we have this solution in love and *agape*. Chiara says, "Love is when it is not." That is, when it is given. If the subject of the gift is being, isn't it therefore non-*essere*, non-being?'

This new line of thought is generating considerable interest. So far, over 30 doctoral theses have been written, and some published, on various aspects of the thought of Chiara Lubich.

The philosophy which is emerging from her thought and spirituality, suggests Zanghi, is Jesus Abandoned: the being who is not. 'When He felt abandoned even by His Father, apparently no longer even the Son of God, that is when He was most precisely Himself. That is when He was accomplishing His task, that is when He was precisely the Redeemer and Son of God, Jesus Abandoned.'

Chiara says: 'Jesus Abandoned, the being who is not.' Zanghi adds: 'We, if we are, we are not; and if we are not, we are.' It is a theology-philosophy of total donation – the practical application of Jesus Forsaken.

Several books have already been published on these aspects of Chiara's thought. Bishop Hemmerle wrote *The Ontology of Non-Essere* and also *For an Ontology of the Trinity*; Anna Pelli wrote *The thought of Chiara on Abandonment*; Piero Coda compared the form of Hegel's thought with that of Chiara in his book about negation in the philosophy of Hegel.

If Catherine of Siena 'founded a spirituality', so too has Chiara Lubich. It is Jesus Forsaken, the spirituality of unity, the discovery of 'the Desolate One'. Chiara's understanding of the Desolate Mother who lost her only Son – and worse still, was then given another in replacement – is one that has deeply touched many Buddhists and Muslims.

When I was once waiting to meet Chiara, I witnessed the arrival of a Japanese Buddhist family who had come to meet Natalia and Enzo, Chiara's companions who were charged with the work of inter-religious dialogue. On a previous trip to Rome the husband had been presented to the Pope. When he and his family visited St Peter's Basilica, what struck them was not the architecture of Bernini or the tomb of St Peter, but Michaelangelo's portrayal of the Desolate One in his famous statue of the Pieta.

When Natalia later visited the family in Japan she saw that they had set up a shrine in their home to the Desolate One, with a large photograph of Michaelangelo's Pieta.

While the husband and wife talked with Natalia and Enzo that day in March 1995, their two young daughters sat drawing. Before they left, they presented Natalia with their day's handiwork. One was a drawing in the style of the Pieta; the other was Jesus on the Cross. As the group paused for a souvenir photograph in the foyer of the Focolare Centre before leaving, the two little Buddhist girls instinctively slid their hands into the outstretched hands on the sculpture of the Virgin Mary which decorates the entrance.

Chiara Lubich has founded a spirituality and has inspired a following as Catherine did, but Chiara's spirituality finds resonance not only with Catholics and Christians of all denominations but also with Jews, Muslims, Buddhists and many others.

If Catherine passed at a certain moment from a private existence to a public one because among her followers were politicians and prelates, so too did Chiara. Her meeting with Igino Giordani and other MPs, including De Gasperi, and the admiration of first the Bishop of Trent and then Monsignor Montini (later Pope Paul VI) and Pope Pius XII propelled her from being a provincial girl from Trent to being a public figure both in society and the Church, first in Italy and then world-wide.

It is said of St Thomas Aquinas that he dictated to two secretaries simultaneously. It is not uncommon to find in historic figures in the Church this unbounded energy and intellectual vigour. When St Catherine was returning from Avignon after persuading the Pope to regain Rome, she encountered the Papal fleet at Genoa. The reason

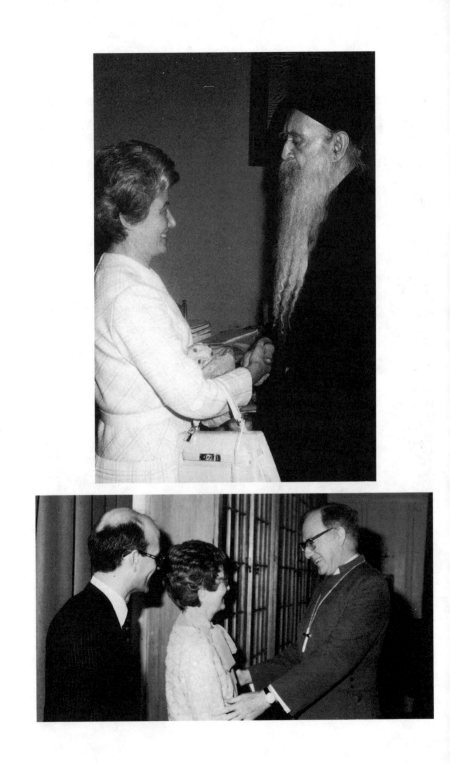

why she had stopped there? Two of her secretaries had fallen ill, and she was detained there a month. Chiara has a whole building full of staff at the Centre of the Movement. They sometimes struggle to keep up with her and her prolific output of work and ideas – yet she herself insists that she leads 'a very serene life; serene and very ordered'.

As Catherine was willing to leave Siena whenever the good of the Church and the people required her presence elsewhere, so with Chiara. If she believes it is the Will of God for her, she will travel to the ends of the earth to meet with her Focolarini working in a shanty town in South America or the remotest village in Africa – or if the unity of the Church may in any way be nurtured.

Enough! As with so many aspects of Chiara Lubich, there is scope for a book just about a comparison between her and Catherine of Siena! Catherine of Siena is now a Doctor of the Church.

FIFTEEN

'MOTHERS OF HUMANITY'
– OUR BROTHERS THE COMMUNISTS

While Chiara may have passed through a 'dark night' and learned to 'let go' of the Movement during the years of the 1950s, the late 1950s and early 1960s saw an enormous expansion. In hindsight its pace is dizzying and yet, seeing how Chiara lives today – her 'serene and ordered life' – it is not difficult to imagine that the same serenity reigned in and around her then, even when she was living an interior torment.

Chiara almost never speaks about these phases of her life but, somewhat reluctantly, she did admit to having more than a theoretical knowledge of those nights of the senses and of the spirit which the Carmelite mystic St John of the Cross wrote about. She told me, 'Whilst in 1949 it seemed to me that I saw God beneath everything – all Creation, as a light which illuminated everything – now this light went out, so that what I saw seemed to me to be made of paper, no longer sustained by God. So faith was less to me, hope was less. The greatest blow to me was in regard to charity, because this is my very ideal.

'There was a moment once when I had a strong temptation to stop loving one of my companions. Once Natalia was near to me and it seemed as if I heard something saying, "Don't love her, don't love her, don't love her." I said to myself, "But Natalia is such a good person that I'll continue to love her anyway." That's how I got out of that temptation, because it was a temptation against charity, which is against the Gospel.

'The night of the senses comes through illnesses and other things. But the night of the spirit is different. And of course there are many other complications: there are sicknesses, temptations, doubts and more doubts, scruples. Everything serves to make your soul suffer to the maximum – so that the soul feels it is almost abandoned by

God. But then it re-abandons itself to God, over years, and what re-
sults, over years, is that the soul emerges completely different from
this experience.

'Because the night of the spirit has as its task to uproot the vices.
First in the night of the senses and the purification which we prac-
tise ourselves with penance, we *cut* the vices, but the *roots* stay within us. With the night of the spirit, the roots are taken out.'

When someone is living through this experience, I wondered, is
she aware that it is going to end, that it is for a limited time? Or is it
an experience of living abandonment which she thinks is never
going to end?

'The confessor continues to say that it will pass, that the dark night
will pass. But even the words of the confessor don't console, they
don't give any tranquillity. No...because it's terrible. It's like Hell.'

Hell is often defined as the complete absence of God. Is this
what Chiara Lubich experienced? Has she identified so totally with
Jesus Forsaken that it is that which gives her the compassion and
commitment to console Him in His brothers and sisters to the ends
of the earth?

She has often referred to Jesus in the Eucharist as the 'Great Con-
soler', but she admits that in this period of the 'dark night', the time
of total dryness and feeling abandoned, she couldn't find God anywhere at all.

In 1956 Chiara, Giulia, Don Foresi and some others travelled to
the Holy Land to visit some friends. She was totally captivated by
walking in the places where Jesus had once walked, by being in the
land in which the Son of God had lived as a man. But the division
was just as strong an impression. Even Jesus' tomb was divided.
Christians fought over the custody of the holy places.

Above all, though, she was able to relax a little. She entered into the
spirit of pilgrimage and forgot all about the Movement and organization and responsibility. When the time was coming to return home,
she says she was encouraged because 'I thought in Rome there is
something more than the holy places of the Holy Land, which is the
Eucharist – it's Jesus Himself. This gave me the courage to go back.'
(For as well as going back to the warmth and family atmosphere of the
Movement, she was going back to an atmosphere of suspicion in certain quarters and on-going investigation by the Holy Office.)

There were already some people there who had expressed an interest in the Movement, and Chiara left her faithful secretary-driver Giulia there with them to lay the foundations for the Focolare in that country. Today there are Focolare communities of Jews and Muslims in the Holy Land. They meet together regularly. Giulia, after some months, returned to Rome. Her mission was to help Chiara.

One day Chiara felt herself impelled to go before Jesus Eucharist in the tabernacle and ask the question: 'Why have you wanted to stay on this earth at every point in the Eucharist, yet you haven't found a way to make your mother be present?'

The thought that came into her mind was: 'I have not left her because I want to see her again in you. Even if you are not immaculate, my love will virginize you, and you – all of you – will open your arms and hearts as mothers of humanity, which, as in times past, thirsts for God and for His mother. It is you who now must soothe pains, heal wounds, dry tears. Sing her litanies and strive to mirror them in yourself.'

In 1958 the Soviet leader, Khrushchev, declared that he wanted either to annex Berlin to East Germany or else see an 'internationalization' of the former Reich capital. The Berlin Wall would be erected in 1961.

With the contacts they had had with priests from Eastern Europe, the Focolarini knew that they had to 'open their hearts as mothers of humanity' to this portion of Europe, which was cut off from the outside world and, apparently, cut off from God.

At the time there was one relatively easy way to visit East Germany. It was the twice-yearly Leipzig Fair. In the Spring of 1958 Chiara sent Valeria and Aldo to attend as tourists. Valeria recalls that they arrived on the very day when Khrushchev was coming to open the Fair, 'So the police were far too busy to be concerned about us.' She and Aldo clandestinely met with friends of the Movement there, who were connected with Fr Hans Lubsczyk, the Oratorian priest who had met Aldo at Munster in December 1957.

Chiara visited West Berlin several times over the next couple of years. She decided that there should be a community of Focolarini there which would serve as a point of reference for the Movement in East Germany – which she later described as sharing the vocation of the Desolate One (Mary Desolata). As the Foundress and President of the Movement which was spreading world-wide, she had to stay at the physical centre of the Work – even though her heart would have had her go to those people suffering under the yoke of atheistic Communism.

She did the next best thing. She sent Natalia, her first companion, the first who had followed her in consecrating her life to God in this 'fourth way'. With the consent of the local Bishop, Cardinal Döepfner, a focolare would be opened in West Berlin which would be specifically for the needs of the people in East Germany. It was still possible at that point to pass back and forward fairly easily, using the Berlin underground system, although they had to make themselves inconspicuous and not go around in groups or draw attention to themselves in any way.

On Chiara's visits, hundreds would pass over from East to West; from Erfurt, Leipzig, Dresden and Halle. In July 1960 the Bishop of Leipzig, the only German diocese which was in fact totally contained in East Germany, met Chiara. Although only 10% of the population in his diocese were Catholic, the Church was particularly active in social and charitable works, being aided by Catholic charities from the West. The Bishop surprised Chiara by asking if she could open a focolare in Leipzig. She needed no second invitation!

Ten months later, on 13 May 1961, two men Focolarini took up posts at the Catholic St Elisabeth's Hospital in Leipzig. Enzo Fondi was a surgeon, and Giuseppe Santanche was an anaesthetist. They were housed in two miniscule rooms in the hospital and had to lie low for the first six months, unable to contact any of the many friends of the Movement in the city. They were being closely monitored and could not take the risk of endangering everyone else and the whole of the Movement's future work behind the Iron Curtain.

That summer the political situation deteriorated rapidly. Fifteen thousand people had fled to the West in just one month. The Communists would no longer accept this human haemorrhage. On 13 August the hitherto invisible wall between the two Berlins became one of stone, concrete and barbed wire. The Berlin Wall had arrived. People from the Warsaw Pact countries would no longer be permitted to leave the East. Thousands of families were caught up in the trauma, many even being able to see the apartments of their loved ones on the other side of the Wall, but not able to meet.

Natalia Dallapiccola, responsible for the Focolare household in West Berlin and in constant telephone contact with Chiara, planned her move. Two German women in the Movement – a doctor and a nurse – applied with Natalia to emigrate to East Germany to work in Leipzig. At the time, when everyone wanted to leave the country, here were three who wanted to go in! However, the country needed qualified medical personnel. In January 1962 the three women crossed over. For the two Germans the procedure was slightly easier. For the Italian among them, it was a different matter. Natalia, who was going as a maid to the other two, was held in a detention centre for two weeks.

The guards in the camp were used to dealing with a certain category of people and suspected that many of those coming into the country were either spies or criminals, and their initial behaviour towards the inmates reflected that attitude.

The camp detainees underwent daily interrogation. Why were they coming to East Germany? Did they know anyone else here? Every detail of their past lives was scrutinized. Natalia had chosen as her guiding motto, 'Prudence must be the expression of my love towards all.' The inmates slept in dormitories dominated by huge portraits of Ulbricht, the then President of the Republic, and their lockers and personal possessions had to be open and available for unannounced inspection at any time of the day or night.

During her time of incarceration, Natalia befriended a young woman who was pregnant and quite ill. Her Spanish husband was being held in the men's section. Natalia nursed the young woman and took on her share of work in the camp. It is a typical reaction of Natalia and the Focolarini: 'How can I love Jesus Forsaken in this person?'

When her time came for release, the two German Focolarine were waiting in a street near the camp (not right outside, so as not to be seen) to meet Natalia. They had found a house in Leipzig where they set up a medical practice.

Some months later, one of the local Catholic priests asked Natalia if she knew a Spaniard with a young German wife. The young woman had approached the priest, asking him if he knew an Italian lady called Natalia, for by now the couple's baby had been born – a little girl named Mercedes – and they wanted Natalia to be at the Baptism.

When the baby was only six months old, the mother died. The mother was an Evangelical Christian. Through the friendship of the Focolarine she had become Catholic. She died asking to see a Catholic priest. The three women now felt responsible for looking after the young father and his baby. He entrusted little Mercedes to them, and she was unofficially 'adopted' by the Focolare household with whom she went to live. Her father, Gonzalez, was a regular visitor to the Focolarine's house on Machinastrasse. When Mercedes was two years old, Gonzalez married again – to a friend of his first wife who already had a child by an Arab who had now left the country. They took Mercedes back to live with them.

The Focolarine were happy that Mercedes was back in a family, and the parents and children continued to visit regularly. Then one day they heard that the two little children were on their own. The parents had been arrested. The women went to the police. It turned out that Gonzalez had been a secret police agent, but had become disillusioned and had gone over to the CIA. He was discovered and arrested. The women asked if they could take the children, rather than see them put into an orphanage. An official application was made, and they were reminded in court that they would have to bring up the children as Socialists. They told the judge quite clearly that they were Catholics and would bring up the two children as Christians. 'If only all Catholics were like you!' said the judge, and granted custody to the doctor, the nurse and their domestic.

Some time later there was an exchange of prisoners. Gonzalez and his wife were handed over to West Berlin, but the authorities did not want to release the children. The Focolarine went through all sorts of procedures, contacting the Red Cross and various other organizations to have the children returned to their parents. It took another two years before the family could be reunited.

Margarethe, the doctor of the trio, took the children to West Berlin to hand them over to the parents. It was then that she learned Gonzalez's remarkable story. He told her that he had been an agent of the secret police even while in the detention camp, and he had been given the job of keeping Natalia under observation. In Leipzig she had been put under his control again. The women remembered how he used to say sometimes, 'Natalia, don't come home too late at night' or 'Natalia, don't let yourself be seen talking with the priest.' But Natalia had shown such kindness to his wife and had made her so happy in her final months. Natalia had then become a surrogate mother to his little daughter. So he didn't betray her to the secret police. Her exercise of charity, her loving Jesus Forsaken in the other, had been the protection for that first women's focolare in East Germany.

While Natalia and her two companions started preparing as soon as the Berlin Wall went up, and had then moved to East Germany in January 1962, Chiara knew this was only a beginning. (She herself had also visited Hungary along with Aldo Stedile in 1961 and so knew at first hand what life was like for those living under atheistic Communism.)

She sought others who could follow. In October 1962, she met with one of the hundreds of bishops who were arriving in Rome for the opening of the Second Vatican Council on 11 October. He was Cardinal Bengsch of Berlin. They had previously met in Berlin, and he knew that some doctors belonging to the Movement were working in Leipzig. Could Chiara provide some doctors for his hospital in Berlin?

Chiara shared the result of this meeting with her colleagues later the same day. By that evening three young doctors – two women and a man – had volunteered. Within a week they were in West Berlin to learn German. They applied to enter East Germany and received their permits in August 1963, when they officially entered that country.

One of them was Anna Fratta, a 24-year-old newly qualified general practitioner. She and the other two began to work in the Catholic hospital in East Berlin. She describes it as being 'like the time of the first Christians. We had to be very prudent. We were undoubtedly being watched and observed all the time. The community began to grow. We would meet one person here, a family there, a priest in a parish…That's how things developed.' Later Anna transferred to Leipzig and lived there in the same focolare as Natalia.

While Natalia, Anna and the others were quietly working away in East Germany, others in the Movement were penetrating Yugoslavia from Trieste in the north of Italy and from Austria. But in East Germany things were much more strict. The country was really under Soviet control and was meant to be the model Socialist state. It was very difficult, if not impossible, to have contact with people in the other Communist countries, and the Focolarini determined to work as best they could – and to love Jesus Forsaken in all things and in everyone they met. He would do the rest.

In 1969 the frontier was open for visitors, and Chiara crossed into East Berlin as a guest of Cardinal Bengsch. East Germany – which had been part of the Nazi Third Reich and which was now being held up as the ideal Socialist state while suppressing even its own people – now had another vocation, Chiara told her companions and the followers of the Movement there:

'God wants to make East Germany a place from which he will radiate this charism, this spirituality, to the whole of the Church in the Communist bloc. East Germany, divided and isolated, where families are split from their relatives in the West, will share the role of the Desolate One, of Mary Desolate.

'Here, where there is such suffering, pandemonium, chaos and aggressive atheism...this place will be the mother to pass on the charism and spirituality of unity to all the other suffering countries of the Communist bloc.'

Anna Fratta, like the others, had no idea how this might be fulfilled or what they could do to bring it about, but she remembers, 'From that time, it was as if the Ideal just began to seep like an oil-spill into the other countries, and we were making more and more contacts in those places.'

Already in 1967 a young newly ordained priest in Czechoslovakia had organized a 'touring club' whereby he and other priests and religious who had been touched by the Ideal could travel into the Tatra mountains. Under this pretext they could conduct a retreat there. He had also been given the task of keeping in contact with figures in the Church in East Germany, as that country had more contact with Rome than any other.

He made a trip to East Germany and gave Anna a list of contacts in Czechoslovakia. The Focolarini were planning to hold some sort of meeting – a 'mini-Mariapolis' – in the Tatra mountains of Czecho-slovakia during the following summer.

The young priest left Berlin to go and lead a group of priests on one of his 'hiking tours'. On that trip he fell and died. He had given all his contacts to the Focolarini.

The mini-Mariapolis went ahead the next summer with about 50 people. Many of the contacts of the young priest came, along with some others from East Germany who were able to travel under the guise of 'tourism' in the slightly relaxed atmosphere of the Prague Spring. (But that summer ended with the crushing of the Prague Spring by Soviet tanks on 21 August 1968.) Two Italian Focolarine obtained visas later that same year to study Slovak in Bratislava. So the Movement took off in Czechoslovakia.

Encouraged by Chiara's visit to East Berlin, Anna Fratta organized a gathering in the Tatra mountains of Poland in the summer of 1969. The 50 or so people who came all slept in a tiny house in the mountains. Anna says, 'Every day we had to have a trip somewhere so as to make out that we really were tourists. We would walk for hours and hours until we found an isolated place. There we would stop and talk about the Ideal, and then we would walk back again for hours.

'We would have Mass in a little mountain chapel, always a different one; to do it twice in the same place would have been risky. I remember that one day when we had found a spot and stopped to talk, some other tourists arrived. Immediately we all jumped up and started singing and dancing as if we were having a party! But it was wonderful, because as soon as the strangers had left, we immediately picked up where we had left off, and the spiritual atmosphere wasn't in the least disturbed.'

Little by little, individuals in other Communist countries came to know the Focolare: for example, a family of doctors in Lithuania, and a couple of scientists in Russia through an exchange visit of Polish scientists who already knew the Movement. In each case, the Ideal spread from those first native contacts.

Anna Fratta says that they lived just like the first Christians. The local people and the State knew they were there, but they didn't know who they were. 'We had to live quietly, almost underground,' she says, 'and just love every person we met.'

The young Dr Fratta integrated so well that she was awarded three different medals by the Communist authorities! She believes that in the Communist bloc there was a great thirst for ideals. 'Marxism,' she says, 'had many good ideas. But it was like a negative reflection of Christianity. They even felt the need for some sort of quasi-sacraments – look at their "naming ceremony" and their *Jugendweihe* [youth rite] for example.'

She believes that so many people readily accepted the Focolare Ideal because they were constantly living in a climate of mutual suspicion which wore people down in the end. Through the Focolare they discovered confidence in the other person, and solidarity and mutual love.

Anna laughs as she remembers the elaborate ceremonies that would take place on various Socialist 'holy days' and anniversaries. One of her medals presented on such an occasion was for 'exceptionally good work'. Another was for having formed a 'Socialist Brigade work cell' whose aim was to create harmony and unity in the workplace. Anna had merely tried to create a family atmosphere. The third medal she was awarded on some anniversary of Socialism was for being one of the best Socialists in the area! Her medal was engraved, 'We work, we live, we think in a Socialist way.'

She likens the spread of the Ideal to the flow of an underground river. It is there, constantly flowing, undermining foundations, and people aren't even aware of its existence.

Because of this discretion, prudence and complete integration into the environment in which they lived, the Focolare Movement grew steadily and without persecution. On the whole.

One Focolarino who used to travel on business regularly from Italy to Prague ended up in jail. Guido Mirti set up an 'import-export' business in 1955. He would import wine into Czechoslovakia and bring out typical Czech toys.

On 19 January 1963 Guido left his hotel to meet a regular contact. As he waited near the famous fifteenth-century astronomical clock in the city centre, Guido recognized the usual signal. But it wasn't Jan. He was supposed to meet Jan, a priest who had already been secretly ordained a bishop. Instead, his housekeeper had come. Ashenfaced, she told him that Jan had been arrested.

Guido recognized the danger of the situation and didn't hang around. He thought it best to return to his hotel, meet the other contact he was due to see that evening – a Jesuit – and return to Italy as soon as possible.

But he never made it back to the hotel. On the way a Skoda pulled up beside him. Three secret policemen jumped out and arrested him. He was taken to Ruzyne, a prison for political prisoners. He was questioned until midnight, woken at 5.30 a.m. and questioned again until mid-day. The afternoon interrogation lasted again until midnight.

This was the pattern for the next three months until he finally faced trial on 3 April, Easter Saturday. He was brought back to court the following day for sentencing. He had been found guilty of plotting to overthrow the government of the country according to Paragraph 10 of the Penal Code.

It was true that once, when being questioned in the prison, he had told his interrogators that this world would pass away. Both communism and capitalism were destined to collapse, he told them, and a new order of civilization and love would come one day.

He was sentenced to four years' imprisonment. Then came a surprise. The judge told him that his sentence would be transmuted to immediate repatriation. What Guido did not then know was that an Italian MP who was also a Focolarino, Enrico Roselli, had taken up his case with the authorities. To head off an international incident, they decided to deport Guido.

As he was taken to the airport the following Thursday, he gave whatever he had to his captors. To one, his cigarette lighter, to another his cigarettes. To the commandant who had led the interrogations, Guido said, 'Look, when you speak and especially when you are angry, you use the term "Jesus and Mary". I want you to promise me that when your hour of death arrives, you will do the same thing. For my part, I promise to pray for you always.'

After meeting some Polish people at the summer gathering of 1969 in the Tatras, Anna Fratta visited Poland again at Christmas that year. Thereafter contacts grew between the increasing numbers of people following the Movement in Poland and the focolares in East Berlin and Leipzig.

The Movement continued to grow in Poland, and some of the people were being called to live as consecrated Focolarini. In 1972 Anna asked Chiara if she should apply to go and live there. At the time there was a surplus of doctors in Poland – and most of them would have left if they had the chance. Here was an Italian doctor applying to come in! Finally, all the formalities were completed in 1974. Anna obtained a visa to work in Poland. A few months later an

Italian Focolarino doctor, Roberto Saltini, transferred from Leipzig, where he had already been working for nine years, and opened a men's focolare in Breslau. Doctor Fratta was posted to a 'new town', an industrial complex which the Communist authorities had built right outside the ancient city of Cracow. That city has long been the cultural centre of Poland, and even during the Second World War a top SS official who was an art lover had ensured that the city would not be destroyed.

With one of the oldest universities in Europe and a concentration of the intelligentsia, it was a hot-bed of resistance to Communism. The authorities built this giant steel-works on its doorstep. Cracow lies in a valley, and so the polluting smog would hang over the ancient city. The Communists shipped in convicts and criminals from all over Poland to work in this new steel plant. They paid them to relocate and gave them apartments to live in. The Communists called the place Nowa Huta, and that is where the Archbishop of Cracow, with material aid from Fr Werenfried's Aid to the Church in Need, built a church in defiance of the Communists.

Anna Fratta was assigned to work in the occupational health clinic of one of these giant factories. As is typical with the Focolare, she went immediately after her arrival to meet the local bishop. Monsignor Wojtyla already knew of the Movement by then, as two lay-people from his diocese had already visited Anna and Natalia in Leipzig in 1966 and told their archbishop all about the Focolare on their return. He had studied charisms and admired the charism of Chiara and the Focolare. He told Anna, 'You are the ones with the graces of this charism. If I interfered, I would only spoil it. Go ahead with your work. Do whatever you have to do, and then tell me.'

He and his private secretary, Fr Stanislas Dziwisz, were always completely supportive of Anna and the Focolare. In May of 1978 the Archbishop visited a large Focolare gathering that Anna had organized in Cracow. He told them their Movement represented a 'sign of the times'. 'This spirituality is a return to the Gospel roots,' he said. He had brought the rector of his diocesan seminary along with him. Fr Makarski told Anna, 'This is a difficult spirituality. It's like a climb which goes immediately upwards, but it takes you directly to God.'

Father Makarski was soon to replace Wojtyla as Archbishop. In the second conclave that would take place that year, in October 1978, Archbishop Wojtyla of Cracow accepted election as Supreme Pontiff of the Universal Church. He would be known as Pope John Paul II.

SIXTEEN

'THAT THEY MAY BE ONE, FATHER'

If the 1960s saw a spreading of the Focolare Movement throughout Eastern Europe, it was also the decade which saw the expansion to other continents. One of the most striking aspects of the Movement would also begin – the contacts with other Christian churches.

In 1961 Chiara, who had visited West Germany several times, was invited to address a community of Lutheran women religious, 'Marienschwestern', at Darmstadt. Some of them had previously attended a summer Mariapolis in 1958. Chiara remembers: 'At the request of these women I had been speaking about our spirituality, and in the audience there were also three quite well-known Lutheran pastors. At the end, their comments surprised me. They said, "What? Are Catholics living the Gospel?" From that moment on the bond between us became stronger. They asked us to bring this spirit into their community and into the Lutheran Church generally. And now, wherever the Focolare Movement exists in Germany, it is to be found also among the Lutherans.'

Indeed, in 1968 Chiara inaugurated a Centre for Ecumenical Life at Ottmaring, near Augsburg in Germany. Now it is a permanent centre of the Movement, a 'little town' inhabited by Catholics and Lutherans. For this and all her ecumenical work, she was awarded the Peace of Augsburg Prize in 1988.

In 1961 Chiara also met the Anglican Archdeacon Bernard Pawley for the first time in Rome. Canon Pawley had been sent to Rome to be the Anglican Observer at the Second Vatican Council, which was already in preparation, since Pope John XXIII had so unexpectedly announced its convocation on 25 January 1959. The Canon later said, 'The first people I came across, or rather, the ones towards whom God led me, were Chiara Lubich and the Focolarini.' Their first meeting took place on 19 May 1961.

When he later tried to explain to friends back in England who and what exactly he had encountered there in Rome, he said, 'It is extremely difficult to sum it up or to say exactly who they are, but I would describe them in these words: They are an evangelical phenomenon.'

Canon Pawley and his wife Margaret were so taken by this phenomenon they had encountered that during the second session of the Vatican Council, which was held in 1963, he organized a meeting for other Anglican clergymen to meet Chiara. Also present were Dr Lukas Vischer, the first Observer to the Council from the World Council of Churches, and Professor Albert Outler of the Methodist World Council. The meeting lasted four hours, and at the end the participants asked that there should be other such encounters.

In 1961, after her first meeting with Lutherans and then with Canon Pawley, Chiara established a Secretariat for Christian Unity within the Movement. It was based in Rome and was known as 'Centro Uno'.

At Pentecost 1965 that centre organized a meeting in Rome with representatives of other churches who were interested in the spirituality of Chiara and the Focolare Movement. As part of the programme, Chiara and some of her companions accompanied them in pilgrimage to some of the treasured sites of the Early Church in Rome. Thus together they visited the tomb of St Peter, the site of St Paul's martyrdom and the catacombs. At the end of the week, Chiara, quite unplanned, said:

'For centuries we have been separated; cathedrals and religious monuments belong to one church or another. But here, right now, we give all that we have to you. Not only does the heritage of the Early Church belong to you, but all that we as a Movement possess is yours also. As in the Movement we pool all our resources, temporal and spiritual, so from today all that we have is yours.'

To say that the week-long encounter finished on a 'high' would be an understatement. The representatives of other churches went home determined to spread the good news about this wonderful discovery they had made. Many were astonished to find that there should be such an evangelical grass-roots movement in the Catholic Church, and one that had been fully tested and approved by the Church authorities.

In 1962, following a two-year-long study by a commission appointed by him, Pope John XXIII granted approval for the official statutes of the Work of Mary.

After Pope John's death on 3 June 1963, the Conclave produced Pope Paul VI. His would be the task of bringing to completion the Council convened by his predecessor. The new Pope was no stranger to the Focolare. He was the very same Monsignor Montini, the relative of Giulia Folonari, who as an official at the Vatican Secretariat of State had encouraged Chiara and her companions when the Movement had been under investigation in the 1950s.

On the Eve of All Saints, 31 October 1964, His Holiness received Chiara in a private audience. She brought him up to date with all that had been happening in the Movement and outlined to him the developing structures which had been put in place to cope with the expansion of the Ideal in so many different areas, including the ecumenical work of Centro Uno. The Pope approved everything.

The private meeting with the Pope made a profound impression on Chiara, and ten days after the event she was still writing in her diary: 'After the meeting with the Holy Father something new is being released in my soul: the capability, such as I never had before, to live the Ideal under every aspect.'

Those around her have witnessed ever since that whenever she has direct contact with the Pope, whether Paul VI or, in more recent years, John Paul II, Chiara seems to find a new energy. And they certainly know when she has been to see the Pope or even spoken to him on the telephone. For weeks afterwards, they have to struggle to keep up with her.

While she had been received with a group of her companions by Pope Pius XII, that audience of Paul VI on 31 October 1964 was the first truly 'private audience' that she had experienced. There were only her and Giulia Folonari present with the Pope in his study. In her diary the next day Chiara wrote:

> We walked through room after room, passing by pontifical guards dressed in a variety of uniforms. Then we were offered a seat in one of the parlours. At 11.30 we were led into another room, the one immediately next to the Holy Father's study. The Holy Father asked me how the Focolare was doing...

While I spoke, the Holy Father listened to me with a silence of soul that I have never found in others. It seemed to me that this last subject [the ecumenical aspect of the Movement's work] interested him very much; so much so that he then said to me that 'this dialogue' is something we should learn to carry out better and better, making ourselves specialists, and that we would do well to open it up also with non-believers, as far as possible.

I don't know at what point in our conversation the Pope said that ours is a 'Work of God', but he said it in such an emphatic and convincing way that we were amazed.

Toward the end, the Holy Father asked if we had something to ask of him, to which I responded, 'Your Holiness, are you pleased with our work?' 'Yes, my daughter, with all my heart. If there is something that you should know, I will tell you. If all goes well, you will have my encouragement and satisfaction...' He added other beautiful words.

When he got up he presented Giulia and me with a rosary, asking us to say a few Hail Marys for him too.

Then, as he accompanied us to the door and as if to complete what he had wanted to give us, he told me that later on he would also receive my collaborators and all the others too. Before we took leave, he gave us his blessing. I left there with a lump in my throat...

The relationship between Paul VI and Chiara grew ever closer over the years, and their mutual esteem was evident to everyone who saw them together. After Pope Paul's death in 1978 on the Feast of the Transfiguration (6 August), the Movement published in book form a collection of all the addresses that Paul VI had given to the Focolare Movement in his 15 years as Pope. During his pontificate he had met each branch of the Movement several times. The last time he addressed a special word to them was just two weeks before his death, when at a general audience at Castelgandolfo he singled out the 400 priests and 350 volunteers of the Focolare Movement who were present.

After that first 'ecumenical week' organized by Centro Uno at Pentecost 1965, the Anglicans present wasted no time in spreading the news about this 'evangelical phenomenon'. Back home in England they invited members of the Movement (a women's focolare had been opened in Liverpool in 1963) to address a meeting in

Liverpool's Anglican cathedral. In the same spirit of urgency, Chiara herself was brought over to England to address a further meeting in Liverpool Cathedral and several others throughout England in November 1965.

The following summer saw her back on English soil, and on 1 July she was received by the Archbishop of Canterbury, Dr Michael Ramsey, at Lambeth Palace. After he had heard her outline the Focolare spirituality, Archbishop Ramsey told her: 'I am very grateful for the hand of God in this work. I hope that you will be able to visit us for longer next time. You have much to offer the Church of England...I give you my blessing.'

Within six months Chiara was back in England again. This time, with the approval of the Archbishop of Canterbury, she was invited to address a gathering of Anglicans and Christians of other denominations at Canterbury during the Week of Prayer for Christian Unity. That event was a springboard for ecumenical activity by the Movement throughout Britain. Invitations poured in for Focolarini to address gatherings of Christians all over the country. Weekend gatherings of 200 to 300 people were held in different regions for those interested in learning more about the Movement.

Today about a third of the Movement's membership in England is Anglican, and they have an Anglican Bishop Guardian, currently Bishop Robin Smith of Hertford, who replaced Bishop John Dennis of St Edmundsbury and Ipswich in 1995.

In May 1971 Chiara returned once more to England to meet in London with Anglicans who were part of the Movement and to discuss their way forward. Over the years Chiara and her companions who have been charged with the interdenominational aspect of the Work have had to seek a 'legal' framework within their statutes in Catholic Canon Law for the non-Catholic members.

A solution was finally reached which allowed members of other churches to be fully integrated into the life of the Movement. They would be described in official Church documents as 'associate members'.

Chiara next visited England in 1977 (see Chapter 19) and was on that occasion received by the Archbishop of Canterbury, Dr Coggan. In 1981 she was back in London again, and after a visit on 10 June to the Catholic Archbishop of Westminster, Cardinal Basil

Hume, she crossed the River Thames to Lambeth Palace to be received by the new Archbishop of Canterbury, Dr Robert Runcie. The previous year, just after his appointment, he had sent greetings to an ecumenical Anglican-Catholic gathering held in Rome under the auspices of Centro Uno.

Chiara was received extremely warmly by Dr Runcie, who told her it was a great privilege for him to welcome her to Lambeth Palace. He told her that he had met many members of the Movement on his travels as a Primate of the Church of England and as the honorary head of the world-wide Anglican Communion. He said: 'Whenever I travel I meet people who greet me. They have a special look of joy on their faces and they say, "We're from the Focolare." Now I'm getting to recognize them as soon as I see them and can say, "You're from the Focolare!" even before they have introduced themselves. They bring a real family atmosphere with them.'

After a chat about the Movement during which the Archbishop posed many questions about the organizational side of the Work and about the different vocations represented inside the one Movement, they were joined by several other, mostly Anglican, members of the Movement, as well as Chiara's secretary Giulia Folonari. Mrs Margaret Pawley, widow of Canon Pawley, the first Anglican Chiara had ever met, was also there. Before proceeding to lunch, the Archbishop presented Chiara with the Cross of the Order of St Augustine of Canterbury, in appreciation of her work done both within and for the Anglican Communion.

On her return to Rome, Chiara was interviewed on Vatican Radio about her meeting with Dr Runcie, and she said: 'What impressed me more than the words that we spoke was the welcome I received and the person of the Archbishop himself...'

In 1986, the Focolare Movement in Britain inaugurated an ecumenical centre in a former school in Welwyn Garden City. Cardinal Hume of Westminster, the Papal Nuncio Archbishop Barbarito and Anglican Bishop John Dennis, the then Guardian of the Focolare Movement in the Church of England, were joined by representative leaders of all the other main Christian denominations. The centre was put into immediate use as a week-long gathering of bishops of different Christian denominations who were 'friends of Focolare' held their meeting for the first time in England.

Before returning to their respective countries, those bishops, along with one or two of Chiara's 'first companions' whom she sent in her place, were received in audience by Archbishop Runcie at Lambeth Palace. He gave a warm speech of welcome and appreciation of Chiara and the Movement. He said: 'Many good things come out of the ruins of war, by the grace of God, and among them is this great Movement, through the inspiration of Chiara Lubich. I give thanks for her, and I am grateful for her message. I remember the day when she stood here.' Referring to her charism, the Archbishop said, 'Chiara Lubich has a special authority by the grace of God. And we remember her in our prayers here at this time.' The next day, 20 November 1986, Dr Runcie wrote a personal letter:

Dearest Chiara,

I am writing to thank you not only for the beautiful gift presented to me by the bishops of the Focolare Movement during their visit to Lambeth yesterday, but more meaningfully for the opportunity you gave me to meet a small group of bishops linked to the Focolare Movement. I was able to spend a little time with them in conversation and in prayer, and it was a moving experience for me. You know my warm support for the Focolare Movement. I also humbly acknowledge the help of prayer and love the Movement gives me...

I am sorry you were not able to get to Lambeth. I am sure, however, that it was right for you to rest a little. Even though you were absent physically, your spirit was there in the presence of those who follow you. You are always present in my prayers.

Yours sincerely in Christ,

Robert Cantaur
Archbishop of Canterbury.

Chiara's aim from her first 'call' by God is to love each individual as if he or she were the only one on earth. Her contacts with bishops, whether Catholic or of other churches, are first of all that: a chance to love them as individuals, and to love Jesus in them.

With her Ideal of Unity, inspired by the last testament of Jesus, she would be willing to do anything, go anywhere, if her presence might build or reinforce that unity; or repair it where it is ruptured. This is because, for her, in division there is Jesus Forsaken; suffering, abandoned in some measure, 'not being' what He is. For He is One and indivisible, and His Body is, or should be, one in faith.

One of the longest-running wounds of division in the Christian Church has been the split between East and West. Several schisms between the Orthodox churches – those Eastern-rite churches which do not recognize the Primacy of Rome – had led to a final break between the Orthodox and Catholic churches in 1054. The Patriarch of Constantinople and his adherents were excommunicated in that year by a visiting legation of the Pope led by a Cardinal Humbertus. The Patriarch and Synod of Constantinople in turn pronounced excommunication of the Papal legates, and the Patriarchs of Antioch, Alexandria and Jerusalem followed Constantinople into schism. Temporary reunions were effected by the Council of Lyons in 1274 and the Council of Florence in 1439, but in 1472 all such reunion was repudiated by a synod led by Patriarch Dionysius I of Constantinople.

The greatest breach in Christendom has remained implacably throughout the centuries. Since the beginning of his Pontificate, John Paul II has stated on many occasions that it is one of his prime concerns. Ambitiously, and perhaps in great faith, he even said that he wanted to see full reunion of the two churches by the end of the twentieth century.

In 1964 Pope Paul VI made an effort to overcome some of the obstacles to unity. At the beginning of that year, in between the second and third sessions of the Vatican Council, he had a personal meeting with Patriarch Athenagoras I of Constantinople during his pilgrimage to Jerusalem. Already at the Council the Pope had given official recognition to the rank of patriarchs in the Eastern-rite churches. As one of them had pointed out in a debate on the Decree on Eastern Catholic churches, the Pope himself is described in the Vatican Yearbook as 'Patriarch of the West'. The Orthodox Patriarch of Constantinople and Paul, Patriarch of the West and successor to Peter, publicly exchanged a fraternal embrace and privately discussed inter-church relations.

The resulting improvement in relations was so great that the following year, on 7 December 1965, the day before the closing of

Vatican II, Pope Paul and Patriarch Athenagoras simultaneously lifted the anathemas dating back to 1054.

Chiara was invited to visit Patriarch Athenagoras, and first met him at his Phanar in Istanbul in June 1967. They hit it off immediately and Chiara visited several times in quick succession over the following few months. In all, during the coming years, she would visit him eight times.

'At that first meeting,' says Chiara, 'when I told him something of my aspirations, of our work for Christian unity, he found a striking similarity between what I was telling him and what he himself felt about these things, and he said to me: "You are my daughter! You have two fathers: a great one in Rome, Paul VI [whom he regarded as a second St Paul], and another, an old one, in me, here."'

Chiara says that both at that first meeting and subsequently, the Patriarch spoke of the Pope in a way that she had never heard from anyone else. 'His personal love for the Pope was evident in his solicitude for the smallest details concerning him. For example, he would say to me, "Tell him to eat more, to go for walks sometimes and to get some fresh air." '

On learning of the Patriarch's death on 7 July 1972, Paul VI said, 'A saint has died.' In an interview soon afterwards, Chiara recalled her final meeting with him just a few months before he died:

In my last meeting with him, the first thing that he asked me was, 'How is His Holiness, the great and glorious Pope of Rome?' Such language did not sound rhetorical at all coming from him. On the contrary, beneath it there was a warmth and deep affection, which was typically oriental.

He also told me during our conversation where he drew his consolation from during the difficulties of his ecumenical activity. He said, 'I console myself by thinking that I spiritually live in a very, very tiny room in the Vatican. I don't need a big room; a little one is enough for me…'

I dare to say that this love for the Pope represented a special unity, almost of a mystical nature. This is so true that it is given voice in expressions such as this: 'I was with the Pope in Bogota. I was with the Pope in Bombay. I was with the Pope in Sydney.' Because wherever the Pope was, he was there too. It was as if he had a physical life located

in space, but also a spiritual life outside of space and always at the side
of the Pope…

Nearly 30 years after her first meeting with Athenagoras I Chiara recalls:

> I went eight times to Istanbul, called by the Patriarch. He shared
> much of the ideas of the Movement, above all the ideal of love, of rec-
> iprocal love, of unity. And he saw in me a possible private link with
> the Holy Father, and so he told me many of his thoughts – on the
> Church, on unity of the Church, on the possible reunification of the
> churches. When I came back, I used to write everything down and
> send it to the Pope. The Pope would then tell me what I had to say
> next in reply. This relationship was never published anywhere because
> it was something very private.
>
> Athenagoras really wanted to have a personal relationship with Paul
> VI, not just an official relationship. The Patriarch showed himself to
> be completely open to doing whatever could be done to arrive one
> day at complete reunion.

Pope Paul VI always wrote to Chiara in his own hand, and she has
kept those letters as a treasure of the Movement. They always began,
'To our dearly beloved daughter Chiara Lubich' and ended with him
expressing his 'profound thanks' and 'I bless you with all my heart.'
While she had a warm and close relationship with Pope Paul VI
and even more so with Pope John Paul II, the person of Patriarch
Athenagoras certainly had a profound impact on Chiara. In fact, she
found in him someone who had the same love and veneration for
the successors of Peter that she had and someone who had a similar
capacity to love others as she did. Of course, with typical humility,
she would never put herself on the same plane as the one to whom
Paul VI referred as 'venerable'. She says, 'What I learned from
Athenagoras was not only his extremely sensitive love for the Pope; I
also learned about the quality of charity that must always take priority over any conversation we might be planning…In addition, I saw
the great love he had for all peoples. During his long life he had got
to know many, and knew how to see goodness everywhere. I don't
know how he did it, but I am sure he had a very special gift in this

sense. From him I learned to love all nations, to find the good in them all…Athenagoras was truly great; it would be impossible to forget him.'

Chiara sums up her contact with Athenagoras by saying, 'My relationship with the Patriarch was a deep one, due partly to the fact that he knew Paul VI so well. Since I had personal contact with the Holy Father, I found myself acting as a means through which the Patriarch could communicate informally with the Pope.' In a handwritten letter of 3 March 1968, the Pope wrote:

> What comfort, what edification, what hope was produced in our heart by your letter following your conversations with the Venerable Patriarch Athenagoras, for whom we have such admiration and love in the charity of Christ. May the Lord help us with his light and with his grace in these shared steps that we are making towards perfect communion of faith and of love in the Church of Christ. Asking for, and assuring you of, prayers for this sublime task, we bless you with all our heart.

And from a letter of 5 April 1971, it is clear how Chiara's contact with both the Patriach and the Pope was enabling bridges to be built between the two spiritual leaders. At that time Paul was seen as a remote figure in the Vatican. Bound by protocol, it was not easy for him to have informal contact with the leader of another Church. Perhaps Chiara's greatest contribution was in being able to inform the Supreme Pontiff of the genuine love and esteem felt towards him by the Patriarch, who seemed to live an almost mystical union with the successor of St Peter in Rome. The Pope wrote:

> I'm pleased to tell you that I've read your letter of 2 April, in which I was so happy to learn the interesting and consoling news of your conversations with the revered Patriarch Athenagoras. And also what you told me about the sentiments he expressed towards my humble person and of the hope that he is cultivating in his venerable and august Church towards perfect unity in the one chalice.
>
> God wants a happy fulfilment to such a desire so much in conformity with that supreme wish of Christ 'that they may be one', that we might have this by virtue of the Holy Spirit and through the humble and loving disposition of our hearts.

With sincere thanks and wishes for a particularly happy Easter, we send you our apostolic blessing.

In honest simplicity Chiara judges: 'I believe this role of mine was important in helping to consolidate the unity between these two Church leaders.' Consolidating unity – nothing could have made her happier.

Chiara kept in contact with Athenagoras' successor, Dimitrios I, and with the present Patriarch Bartholomew I, who takes a keen interest in the progress of the Movement. The ecumenical group of bishop 'friends of the Focolare' held their annual gathering in Istanbul in 1984.

On the ecumenical front, Chiara also got to know another tireless worker for unity, Brother Roger, the founder and Prior of the ecumenical community of Taizé in France. He consulted her on various occasions on the way forward for the thousands of young people who were flocking to Taizé. He was concerned about how they would find the support to remain faithful to their personal commitments to God after their deep experience at Taizé.

Whenever she mentions him, a warm smile of recognition becomes apparent in her eyes. She says of him: 'I have always been struck by the way his face glows with light. It's a light unlike any other; it's the light of God.'

For his part, Brother Roger, now no longer young but still sharp of mind, told me from his community in Burgundy: 'Ah Chiara! Whenever I am in Rome with some of my brothers, we invite Chiara Lubich to our apartment, and it is always a joy. We put a white cloth on the table for tea and, whatever the season of the year, we insist on finding white flowers too.

'When Chiara arrives, we talk together, sharing what fills our hearts. Often the question arises: How can we communicate Christ today, by the lives we live? And together we ask God to fill us with the humble trust of faith, to such an extent that the well-springs of a peace of heart and a joy as light as air will never run dry.'

He had once said of her: 'The transparentness of this woman is like an open page of the Gospel. I do not forget that Chiara was chosen from the humble, the workers, in order to confound the strong, the powerful of this world. And I praise Christ our Lord for this...'

I think it is fair to say that Chiara greatly appreciates the childlike simplicity and serenity of Brother Roger, as well as the desire of his heart to see all things united in Christ.

This ecumenical activity may be all very well on the level of fraternal life and contacts. But what about the thorny questions of doctrine – of Rome's claim to primacy, of the question of intercommunion? Moreover, after the Anglican Church's radical decision to confer ordination on women, isn't the ecumenical movement now dead?

On the contrary, counters Chiara. 'Before, looking from the outside, I might have said the same thing, but since we have been involved in this whole ecumenical field, our outlook has changed. It's rather like the two views of water in a glass: some will see the glass as half empty, others as half full. I'm definitely of the latter camp!

'When you have the experience which we share on a daily basis with brothers and sisters in different denominations, you can only marvel at how much, in fact, actually unites us. It's like Pope John used to say: "Concentrate on what unites us rather than what divides us." '

But surely what divides are also key elements of the Focolare spirituality – obedience to the Pope and bishops, for example. From the earliest days Chiara and her companions had taken at face value the words of Christ, 'He who hears you, hears me', as applying to the bishops as successors of the Apostles. Surely, this is not a very fashionable position to adopt.

'No,' she acknowledges, 'it is not fashionable. But it is the truth. It wasn't fashionable when we started, and it's not fashionable now. The fact is that some people try to separate Christ from the Church, and you can't do that.'

Jesus said many beautiful things, she explains, like 'Love one another', and 'Look at the lilies of the fields.' The very same Jesus said, 'You are Peter and on this Rock I will build my Church.' He said, 'I will give the keys to you.' He said, 'As the Father sent me, so am I sending you.' So you cannot separate Christ from the Church, Chiara insists. It is all one and the same.

'They try to make this separation, but they are also throwing Christ out with this. It is also destroying Christ. Ours is a Movement born independently from ecclesial authority, because it was born within me. But always in unity with, and in obedience to, the ecclesial authorities. That is why it has so been so blessed.'

But with these differences of belief or even interpretations of certain parts of Scripture, how is it possible to live this 'unity' which Chiara and her Movement always aspire to?

She told me about the most recent meeting of ecumenical bishop friends of the Movement which she had attended and addressed. She used a term to describe the experience which she often uses for such gatherings: 'We created unity,' she said.

So what is this 'unity' which they created, when they even had to split up at the end of the day to go to different rooms to celebrate different Eucharists?

'Unity,' explains Chiara, 'is to live out what Jesus says in his testament. As Jesus is one with the Father, so we must be one among ourselves and also one with Jesus in the Father. And this is possible. Because what links Jesus to the Father is the Holy Spirit. And the Holy Spirit was brought on earth by Jesus through His Passion. And it is poured out in our hearts. That is, what He has put into our hearts is charity – Catholics' hearts and of course, through Baptism, into the hearts of all Christians – the same charity as there is in the Trinity. We can be united in some way like the three Persons of the Blessed Trinity.

'When we live like this, with mutual love, complete to the letter, as Jesus has loved us, so we create unity – which is not a personal effort: it is a grace which descends wherever we live perfectly the New Commandment of Jesus.'

Because Jesus has brought us the same Spirit who unites Him and the Father, we can live the life of the Trinity, says Chiara. That is 'creating unity'.

SEVENTEEN

FROM AFRICA TO THE AMERICAS
– AND 'INCULTURATION'

While the 1960s saw the beginnings of all this ecumenical work, it was far from being the only development which was taking place in the Focolare Movement. In 1960, Chiara and Fr Foresi realized that they needed to have a centre where the increasingly numerous young adults who wanted to follow in their footsteps and commit themselves to God as Focolarini could receive at least a basic formation and initiation into community life.

Work began that year on building a permanent centre for the formation of members of the Movement on a site that had been given to the Focolare at Rocca di Papa. It would not be finished and inaugurated until 1964, and rather than as a school only for Focolarini it would be a formation centre for all the branches of the Movement until becoming an administrative centre in 1986.

In the meantime, the first 'school' or year of formation for those wishing to become consecrated Focolarini continued, with the aspirants living in household communities, in houses rented or lent to the Movement in and around Grottaferata, Rocca di Papa and other villages in the area.

Doctor Dimitri Bregant, from an exiled Slovenian family, was one of that first year-group to do the 'school' in 1961–62. He had graduated in medicine at Turin in 1960. His first contact with the Focolare was in the operating theatre in 1959. He was struck by the atmosphere of harmony and unity around two visiting surgeons who were performing a particularly complicated operation on a patient who was himself a doctor (and also a Focolarino, as it turned out).

The atmosphere in the operating theatre had been remarked on even by the theatre nurses, one of whom asked Dr Bregant who these visiting surgeons were. One of them invited Dimitri to accompany him on a trip he had to make to Trent later the same day.

The visiting Focolarino surgeon was going to see the Archbishop of Trent, Monsignor De Ferrari. Dimitri was impressed by the surgeon's outlook on life and his peaceful manner. A few weeks later he again accompanied him, this time to a Focolare meeting being held in Trent. There were over 1,000 people present, among them a group who had come over from Brazil because they wanted to become Focolarini too.

In 1961 the young Dr Bregant joined others from all over Italy, from the rest of Europe and from South America who would together live a year of formation at Grottaferatta. At the end of the year's formation, after the summer Mariapolis in 1962, he moved to Rome.

Chiara and her focolare were living in an upper-floor flat in Via Palombara Sabina in Rome. Her parents lived in the flat directly underneath. Dimitri assisted in caring for Chiara's father, Luigi Lubich, in the last months of his life. He was present for Luigi's final hours and eventual death on 24 February 1963. Luigi had had an irregular heartbeat and eventually died of heart failure (as his son Gino would 30 years later). Dimitri remembers that Chiara, Gino and their two sisters were all there. While the younger sisters were very emotional, Chiara, he says, was outwardly perfectly calm. Everyone looked to her to lead the prayers for the dying. While she may have conquered her emotions to sustain the others, her own companions in her focolare household witnessed later how much she had suffered at her father's death.

The Second Session of the Second Vatican Council was held from 29 September to 4 December 1963. Many were the bishops who visited Chiara during their stay in Rome. One of them was Bishop Peeters of the Diocese of Buea in Cameroon. He was a Dutch member of the missionary Mill Hill Fathers.

Like many bishops in Africa, he had heard of Chiara and the Focolare from European missionaries working in his territory. He made it his business to ask Chiara to send him some medical Focolarini to work in his diocese. Within a few months, Chiara sent three doctors and three nurses. They were posted to a small hospital at Shisong and another at Nginikou.

When he returned from Rome to his diocese, Bishop Peeters received a visit from a delegation of the Bangwa Tribe. While Buea is about 3,000 feet above sea level, the Bangwa lived in the forested valley of Fontem, 280 miles further up in the hills. The tribe were at the end of their tether. A drastically high infant mortality rate of 85% meant that they were facing extinction. The elders of the tribe approached the Fon, the King, and said that the situation was now so bad that they had to seek any possible solution. None of their witch-doctors' spells or rituals had worked. Animists all, they decided to make a collection and send a delegation with this money to the Christian leader. They would offer him their gift and ask him to pray to his God for a solution to their problem.

When Chiara made a visit to Douala in Cameroon in 1965, Bishop Peeters spoke to her of the plight of the Bangwa Tribe and asked if some of the Focolarini doctors and nurses could be transferred to work there. In June 1966 Chiara visited Fontem for the first time. During the days she spent there she got to know many of the people and attended a gathering of several hundred members of the Bangwa, including the Fon and some chiefs from the different clans.

During the course of the conversation, which was simultaneously translated into both Pidgin English and the Bangwa dialect, she voiced her first impressions: 'Because of the Movement, I have trav-elled all around the world, but I can honestly say that nowhere – neither in America, nor in Europe or Asia – have I met such a wel-come and such an understanding of our Movement and our work as I have found here among you.'

The Fon outlined to her the most acute needs of his people, and in response Chiara made a commitment to the Bangwa Tribe: 'I un-derstand your great need of doctors, of hospitals, of schools. Today I want to assure you, both in my own name and in that of the whole Movement, that Fontem will have first place in our hearts. It will be the place where we will dedicate ourselves with the most love.'

That first trip to Fontem is one which Chiara has never forgot-ten. She delights in recounting how the Fon expressed his astonish-ment when he learned of the Movement: 'You are a woman, and therefore nothing, and yet you have accomplished this great work. Tell me, how did you do all this?' She says today, 'I remember that this remark didn't offend me in the least, since I knew only too well that what I had described to that African chief wasn't the work of a woman but the work of God. Now, many years later, I am even more convinced of that.'

Although she uses all her femininity in the accomplishment of her work, in her dealings with bishops and popes, Chiara says today that as the 'head' of an international Movement, she does not think of herself so much as being a woman in this extraordinary position. She quotes St Paul: 'In Christ, there is neither Jew nor Greek, male nor female.' What is important is that she is a child of the Father, sharing the life of the Trinity by the gift of the Holy Spirit.

During this exchange with the Fon, the Bangwa people from the village and the surrounding area gathered in a huge circle. The moment had come to celebrate their distinguished guest. With infectious enthusiasm they put on a colourful display of dances and songs – songs which told of their greatest pride and hope for the future, the children who had survived. The many wives of the Fon also danced gracefully in their brightly coloured gowns.

During a pause, one of the elders expressed to Chiara the tribe's anguish at the tragedy they were unable to resolve. He said, 'Why are our children dying? In a short time in this village, 400 of our children have died.'

Chiara replied, 'I think it is because in the world we do not yet live as brothers and sisters. It is because we do not help one another enough. But with the proper doctors here for the children, they will live.'

The elder then said, 'You, Chiara, and our Fon, and all of us present here must pray together for God's help so that your promise to us will be fulfilled soon.'

The three Focolarini doctors who had transferred from Shisong and Nginikou set up their rudimentary first-aid post in the mud hut where they would live like their neighbours, as Chiara herself had lived when she was there. They began to treat the infections, the scourge of the Bangwa people, against which they had no protection.

Chiara returned to Rome and sent out an urgent appeal to all the young people of the Movement in particular to raise funds for equipment and medical supplies. In the coming months and years, a hospital was built, then a secondary school – which, according to Piero Passolini, had been 'a cherished dream of the Bangwa people'.

Piero was a physicist and engineer who had first met Chiara at Tonadico in the Dolomites in 1950 and became one of her closest colleagues. While he was a brilliant physicist who had written books on the universe, the cosmos and evolution, he was also eminently practical. He was known to his Focolarini colleagues for his battered old motorbike, which he was forever repairing and which seemed to be held together with bits of wire. From the time of Chiara's first visit to Cameroon in 1965, he travelled constantly to Africa. He was responsible for many of the developments at Fontem, including the hydro-electric plant. In his diary on one of his working visits to Fontem, Piero recorded:

Fontem now includes quite a few villages and it is the capital of the district. It started when, in the middle of a plain and surrounded by a pleasant row of hills, the Bangwa people decided to build the permanent 'Mariapolis'... a town founded on the law of mutual love, open to anybody, and trying to spread its atmosphere to nearby communities and also to distant ones.

He describes how that point was reached: first the rudimentary first-aid post, then a hospital, then a secondary school. After this the school was expanded; dormitories and refectories, along with teachers' accommodation was added. Then some houses were built for young people 'who wanted to live together in order to deepen their understanding of the spirituality of the Focolare Movement which they had come to know.' The next project was a workshop built to train the young people in various crafts. A hydro-electric station was built to provide electricity. A factory was developed for the production of coconut oil. And the Church came too. Bishop Peeters himself visited to lay the foundation stone for a parish church. Just before it was time for him to return to Italy, Piero recorded:

The time to leave has nearly come. In these last few days I have dealt with the problem of the water...for the two new villages which make up the town of Fontem. We need a spring source high enough to provide water through gravitation for the whole village, without the complication of pumps and filter plants. I remembered a small waterfall I had seen during a walk in the dry season. It was not very far from the hospital. I decided to go and find its source. In the company of a chief, we went into the forest and, further up, noticed a very good well among the rocks, with plenty of water. After measuring the level, we discovered that its location was much higher than any other point of the Mariapolis, so we decided to use the spring. With the help of some men, I measured the distance to be covered by the pipes: about three miles. We had already received over a mile of piping from the workers of a factory in Genoa as a present. The remaining piping will come from somewhere. Everybody is very happy at the thought that perhaps, in a few months, they will have plenty of drinkable water.

Piero Passolini died suddenly of a heart attack during a visit to Nairobi in 1981. In his memory the Focolare 'little town' at Fontem became known as 'Mariapolis Piero'.

In 1969, three years after her first visit, Chiara returned to Fontem to inaugurate the new hospital. As the Landrover turned the hill and she caught sight of Fontem, her first words were, 'It's a miracle!' In her diary she wrote:

> I am amazed by everything I see. New roads, a spacious and beauti-
> ful hospital, a wonderful school, new houses – lots of them! And how
> has this come about? How has a forest lost in the heart of Cameroon
> become a centre of life, a magnet of generosity and love? It's because
> we have tried to live together the Lord's words, 'Love one another as I
> have loved you.'

To a gathering of her Bangwa friends before she left, she said, 'Do you remember that day three years ago when we came together? Then there was nothing here, none of the things that we can see here today. But what was most important was already here. You, my dear-est brothers and sisters, were here, and most of all, God was here with you, that God to whom you had prayed so earnestly for His help for your greatest needs, for your children and your beloved families.

'That day we all felt His presence with us, like a great sun which embraced us all. Whilst He gave you the certainty that He would provide for all your needs, He gave me and my colleagues the strength and the means to begin to do something. Now, don't let's stop here.

'God is all-powerful and if we obey Him, He will bless us. He is great and I can tell you that He will do great things. How I would like to stay here with you. I am at home here, among my people. But as you know, I have to go and wherever I go, I will tell everyone of Fontem, of what prayer can obtain and of what love can build. Let's promise one another always to love each other and to help one another to make a better world.'

A young student at the newly established Fontem secondary school, 17-year-old Charles Taku, wrote a poem which he gave to Chiara before she returned to Italy. It read:

The land is bright
The lamp is lit
The paths are straight
The gaps are mended.
Madame Chiara, Madame Chiara!
May the Lord be with you.
You who comfort the poor.
You who gave me the word of Life.
You who show the light to those in darkness.
The world needs your ideas to be saved.
How can we show gratitude
To our God-fearing helper?
To God, shall we pray, to give you long life
To help the world.

In 1963 Dr Dimitri Bregant, who had tended Chiara's father in his final illness, was posted to the United States, where he worked as a hospital doctor, first in New York and then in Chicago. In that vast country there were only three men and five women Focolarini. Chiara crossed the Atlantic in 1964 on her first journey to America to encourage them, and to go on from there to visit the flourishing Focolare Movement in Argentina and Brazil.

So few in such a vast country! It is true that they did sometimes feel a bit isolated. There were no telephone or video link-ups in those days. Indeed, there was no 'Centre of the Work' at that time and no Co-ordinating Council – that came about later as a result of Chiara's audience with Pope Paul VI in November 1964. All that there was by way of regular contact with what was happening 'back home' was the Italian magazine of the Movement, *Città Nuova*. Dimitri remembers that he used to read it avidly.

One day he answered the telephone in the New York apartment. It was Chiara herself! She had phoned to say she was coming over to visit them – and arrived on Holy Saturday, 28 March 1964.

She was immediately struck, of course, by the immensity of the place, describing New York City as 'endless'. When she arrived at the Church of St Ignatius for Easter Sunday Mass, Chiara spotted the women Focolarine immediately. That night she noted in her diary:

> They stand out because of the mantillas they are wearing. Today almost every woman and girl is wearing an Easter bonnet, generally covered with white, blue or yellow flowers – unusual perhaps, but dainty and delicate.
>
> For the Focolarine girls to look different is not in keeping with our spirit, which teaches us to be like others in all respects, provided we don't exaggerate. At this rate we'll develop a uniform!
>
> Adapting ourselves is a cross (although this is a special day, when even little girls are wearing that sort of hat, innocent enough in itself, and at mid-day we will see a whole parade of them), but it has to be done, to be like the rest. Perhaps then the Americans will feel more comfortable with us, and we will find the way to bring our Ideal to America.

From the beginning, Chiara had understood her 'fourth way' as being a life of total consecration to God as radical as that of any monk or nun, but being lived out totally in the world of today, in a family environment like that of the House of Nazareth. The members of the Movement were not to appear different or to stand out in any way, externally, from the population among which they lived. And certainly there were not to be any religious-style habits or uniforms. That was not the way of the Focolare.

In the General Statutes of the Work of Mary, which are constantly being modified and developed, and submitted to the Holy See for ratification during the life of the foundress, there is a chapter on 'Dress and Residence'. Article 54 states: 'In order to give witness to God who, being goodness and truth, is also beauty, persons who are part of the Work of Mary will seek to create harmony in their dress and in the environments in which they live.' Article 55 continues: 'Whilst dress should reflect the personality, the vocation and the environment in which one is living, it should also, by its simplicity and decorum, express our ideal of unity. It should bring to mind the words of Jesus: "Look at the lilies of the fields. They neither work nor weave. Yet, I tell you, not even Solomon in all his wealth had garments as beautiful as these" (Matthew 6:28–29).'

So, while travelling to bring comfort and joy to her Focolarini children on her different journeys, Chiara, as a 'mother' and as President of the Work, will also pick up on any little lack or default in their life and witness, and their observation of the Rule. For the Statutes also cater for matters of health and periods of rest and recreation. If on her travels or on their visits to the Centre of the Work outside Rome, she observes that any of the Focolarini appears overtired, she will gently question them to see if they have been having adequate sleep, rest and so on, and, if necessary, she will suggest that they should take some time off for a rest or a sabbatical.

But the question of dress and adaptation to local custom is not merely pedantry. She really is concerned that the Focolarini throughout the world should not seek to be different from their peers, except in the exercise of mutual love and charity. Mary is her model and the model for all the members of Focolare. Chiara would argue that just as Jesus, Mary and Joseph, in that first 'holy house' in Nazareth, lived completely as people of their time and region, so should her Focolarini today. That is precisely this 'fourth way'.

As with her experience at Fontem, she is also concerned that whenever Focolarini move from their own country to another, the Ideal should be completely inculturated. That is, everything that is good in the local culture must be respected. Chiara's Ideal, the Gospel itself, is for everyone and for every nation, language and culture. So the message is clear to her followers: in this respect, don't be different from those among whom you live.

But it does appear that this is an on-going task. While in Fontem and other parts of Africa, and also in Asia and Latin America, there appears to be no trace of any 'foreignness' associated with Focolare and the Ideal, in other places that barrier does not seem to have been overcome.

One area is simply a question of language. As the Focolare began in Italy through an Italian foundress and has its international centre in Italy, it is perfectly normal and understandable that the *lingua franca*, the everyday working language of and within the Movement should be Italian. The problem comes with translating that. No language can be translated quite literally into another. There are always expressions, turns of phrase and sentence structures that just do not translate and must be adapted and reworded and 'inculturated' into the local language and mentality.

While some religious orders exported from Italy used to keep the habit of closing down church and convent for siesta, this was always bound to mark them out as 'outsiders', foreign in a place such as Scotland or Scandinavia where such was not the local norm. That is precisely the kind of thing Chiara would not want the Focolarini to do. If they are moved to another country, they must love that country and its culture and traditions as their own.

While the Focolare Movement has spread like wildfire in its country of origin and in other Latin countries, how can one explain its phenomenal growth in, for example, Germany, a country in which the national temperament differs markedly from that in Italy or Brazil?

If the Movement can be adapted and embraced so widely in Germany, then why not in the Anglo-Saxon countries of Britain and the USA? Chiara says it may be that the early Focolarini sent there from Italy and elsewhere did not 'inculturate' themselves and the Movement enough and that the Italian way of expression and of doing things may have been somewhat perpetuated with successive generations.

But the 'head' of the Movement's British zone believes the explanation lies elsewhere: 'You have to look at the history and experience of each individual country,' he says. 'Germany and Italy suffered similar experiences of defeat in the Second World War. While the Movement was native to Italy, perhaps the Germans, in the aftermath of all that they had experienced, were ready to embrace Jesus Forsaken: they found an answer in Him and in the figure of the Desolate One.'

It is true that in Western Europe, Britain stands out from most of the other countries in that she has not experienced being invaded and occupied by a foreign power. Likewise with the United States. Is that the only answer, or simply a partial one? Chiara is anxious to explore the whole area further. As her representative in Britain points out, Britain is also an island with an imperial past and a strong sense of identity which has never lightly taken on board foreign ideas or movements.

In fact, other movements in the Church have a similar experience. Movements which thrive and spread easily in Italy and Spain, Latin America and even in Germany, never find the same response in Britain or the United States.

In recent years, the whole question of 'inculturation' has been a much talked-about question in the Movement, as it has been in the Church. When she went to lay the foundation stone of a new permanent Mariapolis near Nairobi in Kenya, Chiara also founded a 'School of Inculturation' along the lines of the Movement's school for ecumenical dialogue in Germany and its school for inter-faith dialogue in the Philippines.

On that occasion she said: 'Inculturation requires that we "make ourselves one" by entering into the soul, into the culture, into the mentality, into the tradition, into the customs of the others so as to understand them and to bring out the seeds of the Word already present there.' She then went on to delight her audience of some 1,000 representatives of the Movement from all over Africa by illustrating how she saw 'seeds of the Word' already present in some aspects of African culture and folklore. She said:

> I brought a few proverbs with me to give you an idea. In Kenya there is a proverb which says, 'One head alone does not contain wisdom.' This is the Ideal. I always say, 'Do you want to spread the Ideal? Do you want to advance the Movement? You need wisdom. Keep Jesus in the midst'...
>
> Another one comes from Madagascar: 'It is better to lose a considerable amount of money and wealth than to lose unity.' This one is easy to understand.
>
> In the Focolare, we must always place unity above everything else. In the life of the Ideal we must always place unity above everything.
>
> Then, this is truly remarkable, because it is a phrase from the Gospel and it's a motto from Zaire which says, 'A tree is known by its

fruit.'...We say, 'You will be able to tell the tree by its fruit.' It's the same thing. It's incredible. They are seeds of the Word.

Then there are also many names that remind you of the Ideal. For example, there is a surname which means 'People are not God'. This reminds you to put God first always, because people are not God.

Another is this: 'Nothing is greater than God'. Truly this phrase would be enough to help us become saints...

On Chiara's first trip to New York, as she had arrived during Easter weekend, the Monday was a public holiday. She spent it with the three men Focolarini. They took her to see the sights, and Dr Dimitri Bregant, who was part of that first men's household there, remembers that the time travelling from place to place in the car was a great opportunity for Chiara to speak to each one of them. As was the time spent in the queue to visit the top of the Empire State Building, then the tallest skyscraper in the world.

Dimitri is visibly moved as he remembers that day. As Chiara had spent time with them both individually and altogether, they came to understand that Jesus present in the community reinforced the presence of Jesus in the individual, or rather rendered the individual more sensitive to the voice of Jesus within him.

It was an important realization for Chiara, and one which she has often used since in her teaching. In her diary for Easter Tuesday, 31 March 1964, she wrote:

> Yesterday I spent the day with the men Focolarini. Today they are at work. They were so desirous of God and were so attentive that they seemed to have rendered 'tangible' the action of the supernatural. At one point Jesus seemed so present in our midst that we were moved...
>
> With them I understood that Jesus in our midst is like the loud-speaker of Jesus in each soul. His presence among us makes His voice inside each of us grow and makes us better able to receive it: to receive and consequently to live the *new man* in us.

On 2 April Chiara and Giulia flew from New York to Buenos Aires in Argentina, where they stayed for two weeks. Chiara's health took a turn for the worse, and her planned activities were scaled down. She attended the ordination of a Focolarino as a priest. The next stop on her journey was Brazil, where she saw the ordination of another Focolarino. She also visited the newly completed permanent centre for the Movement in that country, noting:

> I have been at Loreto House. I had never seen it before. It is the first house in the whole world that has belonged to the Work of Mary for its own use. At Rocca di Papa we are now putting the finishing touches on the Mariapolis Centre, and that will be the second.
>
> I liked Loreto House. It has the minimal necessities for whoever lives there, poor but with its inexpensive furniture arranged in good taste. The walls are brightly coloured. Inside, the rich won't be ashamed and the poor will not feel out of place. As a centre, everything is just right.

She admits in her diary just before leaving Brazil that 'A physical illness has accompanied me during the course of this whole trip. At times I had to make a constant and continuous offering to God. He knows all things.'

Before leaving to return to Rome and because her activities had been slightly curtailed through poor health, Chiara read the many letters from members of the Movement who, because they were so numerous, could not spend time with her individually. She wrote in her diary:

> I read some letters that the Focolarini wrote to me. What true children of yours they are, Mary our Mother! How you work on them and how very different each one of them is from the other! I'm happy I said my 'Yes', because you, Mary, and the Church have a new family with new spiritual blood, which will be able to produce saints.
>
> If I don't manage to become a saint, there will certainly be others, and this consoles me and gives me peace...

In 1996 the Focolare counted almost 700,000 members and 'adherents' in North and South America, being present in Canada and the United States, Argentina and Brazil, as well as Bolivia, Chile, Colombia, Ecuador, Mexico, Paraguay, Peru, Uruguay and Venezuela. In Africa, the Movement is present in 50 countries and counts some 130,000 members and adherents. Chiara visited the communities in the USA, Argentina, Brazil and Cameroon three more times during the 1960s and founded Mariapolis centres in each of them.

Following Chiara's private audience with Pope Paul VI in 1964 and their discussion on the structure of the Movement, that structure was implemented. There was to be a Co-ordinating Council, on which every 'branch' and 'zone' of the Movement and every 'aspect' of the Movement's work would be represented. A President was elected. In her lifetime, it is unlikely to be anyone other than the foundress, Chiara Lubich herself.

The Mariapolis Centre (now known as the Centre of the Work) was completed on the land given to Focolare at Rocca di Papa. On 13 May 1965, Chiara left her apartment in Rome to take up residence at the Centre of the Work, where she has lived ever since. In her diary entry of 7 November 1965, she noted:

> Yesterday, I sent the first letter since the will of God gave me this responsibility as President (let us hope above all in charity) over the Centre of the Work of Mary.
>
> Last night it seemed to me (when I looked at them again) that our Rules of Life are very profound…I will use them for meditation because they contain the ideals which I have to be worthy of 'sowing, promoting and representing'. In them it is written that their general purpose is the 'perfection of charity'.

In those first approved Statutes and in their every mutation over the years, the Preface has remained the same. The first page of the Rule reads as follows:

> *General Statutes of the Work of Mary*
>
> The Preface to Every Other Rule:
>
> Mutual and continual charity,
> which renders unity possible
> and brings the presence
> of Jesus into the community,
> is for the person who is part

of the Work of Mary
the basis of their life
in all its aspects:
and the norm of norms,
the preface to every other rule.

EIGHTEEN

AM I MY BROTHER'S KEEPER? – TOWARDS AN ECONOMY OF COMMUNION

While the Centre of the Work was being built on the land inherited by Enzo Fondi at Rocca di Papa, Chiara had often remarked, half in jest, 'If we have to have a headquarters, what we should really have is a city headquarters. If religious orders or other groups have a mother house, we should really have a "mother town" because our spirituality is a collective one and our Work is a lay movement, and so we would need all the normal activities: a bank, shops, factories and so on.'

In the summer of 1961 Chiara, Giulia and some others were on holiday in Switzerland. Out on a drive one day, they stopped the car and got out for a walk. As they came to the crest of a hill, they paused to look down. There, spread out below them was the little Swiss town of Einsiedeln. The town grew up around a very famous Benedictine Abbey, and many visit the Marian shrine which it houses.

Chiara says, 'We looked down on the imposing structure of the abbey, with the beautiful church at its centre where the monks prayed, with the two wings where they lived and studied, with the school building and the surrounding fields where they worked and raised livestock. It seemed to us that we were looking at the fulfilment of St Benedict's ideal: "pray and work". We felt great admiration for holy founders like him who after many centuries still live on in the works they gave life to.

'With that splendid sight before us, another vision took shape in our hearts. It was the dream of a modern "little city" with houses, workshops, craft centres and industries where we could bear witness to our ideal of unity. It was a powerful intuition.'

The idea just would not go away. Even back in Rome, Chiara and Giulia spoke of that intuition. After Giulia had arrived so unexpectedly at the door of the Focolare in Rome on 12 September 1951, her brother had come to pursue his studies, with the permission of his mother, since his eldest sister was there. He became a Focolarini two years later, and two of his sisters were later to follow suit.

After their father's death in 1952, in agreement with their mother, the children decided that the family wine business should go to the other brothers and that those who were in the Focolare would receive another patrimony. Vincenzo inherited a farm and estate near Florence, at a place called Loppiano. As the Focolarini put everything into common ownership, this now belonged to the Work of Mary. Chiara and some Focolarini visited it one day in early 1964, and it became clear that this was the place for Chiara's 'dream of a modern little city'. A few young men Focolarini moved there immediately. They renovated some barns and sheds to provide accommodation. Soon, some others joined them and laid roads. Next, an old farmhouse was renovated to accommodate some girl Focolarine, and then some families arrived. Chiara spent a lot of time there helping with the work and supervising plans and designs for the future college.

On 12 July 1964, after Mass and a community meeting, Vincenzo Folonari was asked to take a visitor, a young man called Gabriel, for a run in the car. They drove to Lake Bracciano, where Vincenzo hired a boat. Vincenzo dived in to take a swim, but hardly had time to shout 'It's freezing!' and to tell Gabriel, 'Go for help!' before he went under. He drowned at the age of 33.

That same night Igino Giordani recorded in his diary that Vincenzo's tragic death was 'the picking of a magnificent flower by God, who was in love with it.' Alluding to the earlier death of the Folonaris' father, he wrote: 'He will be welcomed into Paradise by all the saints and angels, gathered around Mary who will have been holding the hand of his father, now his brother for all eternity.'

Chiara's diary reveals a sudden interruption after 11 July. It was over a week later before she could take it up again, having been caught up in the shock of Vincenzo's sudden death and the practical arrangements of the funeral. On 19 July she wrote:

> we can still hardly believe what's happened. Every work established within the Focolare needs a cornerstone, and Vincenzo was the first stone of Loppiano. I am saying this to state what many others have

been saying…Now he is with Jesus, whom he loved, and with Mary, and with our people, who – we hope – are in Heaven.

By the end of the summer, there were enough buildings either restored or built to welcome the international group of young people who had come to do the 'school' – their preparation to make their consecration as Focolarini. The school which had been running for three years at Grottaferrata in one-year cycles transferred to Loppiano and later became a two-year programme. Today young people wishing to become Focolarini can do the first year of their formation at Loppiano and the second in one of the other Focolare 'schools' around the world, usually at Montet in Switzerland.

Loppiano is the first and the most developed of the 'little towns'. It has its own town hall, church, school, factories and farms, its own wine industry and even its own radio station. At weekends it is flooded with thousands of visitors from far and near who come to see a 'new society' in action. In an article in *New City* magazine in November 1975, Gordon Urquhart wrote that while there were just over 400 people living in Loppiano at that time, 'all the components of a complete society are present. With the difference that every structure is a consequence of the Gospel lived out by individuals and at a group level.'

Franco Zeffirelli, the renowned Italian film director, said during a visit to Loppiano in 1987, 'I am amazed and humbled, because I feel that I have not seen what really counts. I have raced through the world, I've chased shadows, illusions, hopes; then I see something like this which breaks my heart with joy. You are immersed in a dialogue with the most essential values, true values which redeem us. In this glorious celebration of nature, everything is beautiful, resplendent, even the smallest things speak of God.'

In its scenic setting in the Tuscan hills, Loppiano recalls the first Mariapolis in the Dolomites. It has truly become what Chiara called the Movement's 'mother town' and is the base for all the Movement's schools of formation: priests, religious, volunteers, families, young people – they all spend time on courses there, as well as the Focolarini. Today almost 1,000 people live there and hundreds of others work there but live in the surrounding area. The little city might have developed further up to this point except that, until recently, the local regional council consistently denied planning permission for expansion on the 600-acre site. Communist opposition on the council has now eased and new buildings have been approved.

Since the 1956 summer gathering had been called a Mariapolis or 'City of Mary', every summer gathering of the Movement has come to be known by this name. The 'little town' of Loppiano, like others which would follow, is known in the Movement as a 'permanent Mariapolis'. For, according to Chiara, their purpose is the same: to live Jesus in the midst and to give him, like Mary, to the world.

During one of her regular visits to Loppiano, in March 1972, Chiara made a speech to the assembled permanent residents of the town and especially to the 'new arrivals', the young adults who had come to live their year of formation. She addressed them as 'Dear Citizens of Loppiano' and went on to outline the purpose of such a 'little town':

> The Mariapolis...teaches you the way to make Christ continually rise among all of you, Christ alive in your midst.
>
> This, I would say, is the specific vocation of the Mariapolis, the reason for which God brought this citadel to life, a foretaste of the heavenly Jerusalem of which it is written, 'And I saw the holy city, the new Jerusalem, coming down out of Heaven from God, prepared as a bride adorned for her husband; and I heard a loud voice from the throne saying, "Behold, the dwelling of God is with men. He will dwell with them, and they shall be His people, and God Himself will be with them"' [Revelation 21:2–3].
>
> God, Jesus, spiritually alive in your midst here must never fail to exist.
>
> If he isn't here, if his presence grows dim, the vocation of the Mariapolis is compromised...
>
> There are many Christian citadels in the world. To have a citadel, to build a citadel which reflects and incarnates one's ideas, has often been the dream of those who had a strong philosophy or an ideology or a spiritual line of thought in the Church. And every citadel which was built has, or has had, its idea to say to the world. For example, the City of Mary Immaculate of Maximilian Kolbe keeps alive the devotion to Our Lady through its intense publishing activity.
>
> The characteristic of our cities is life. And not, of course, a life that is normal or only Christian in one way or another. The Mariapolis

lives because in it shines forth He who said of Himself, 'I am the Life'...

But then, if it is life, we know that life cannot exist without a Mother...And here I could go on speaking for ever...Our work is not a work of ours; it is Mary's...Don't forget the invisible but real and constant presence of Mary, who watches Christ in you and among you develop, as once, in Nazareth, she watched Jesus grow in age, wisdom and grace.

If you do this, the vocation of the Mariapolis as the city of life will never grow dim. Where there is a mother, where the mother is recognized, there cannot be anything but life.

As related in Chapter 19, 1966 saw Chiara open a permanent Mariapolis at Fontem in Cameroon. The following year work began on permanent Mariapoli at Tagaytay in the Philippines and at Sao Paolo in Brazil.

By 1996 there were 19 permanent Mariapoli throughout the world, counting thousands of inhabitants between them and several more thousands who live around them and are associated with them through work or community projects. The most recent to be founded was in Poland, near Warsaw. (See Appendix 1 for a full list of permanent Mariapoli.)

From the beginning, the Focolarine had put their goods in common. As one of them remarked, there was never any rule which made people do this. It just came naturally, and if anyone didn't do this, it merely showed that he or she had not grasped the Focolare family spirit. The economist Alberto Ferrucci wrote in the *Living City* of June 1994:

> In a family the members do not constantly monitor who earns and who spends. In fact, the decisions that often receive the greatest considerations are those involving the care of the elderly family members and the education of the children, those very members who contribute little or nothing to the family's income. All of us have experienced the joy of taking care of the needs of others in the family, not only when we give gifts, but also when we provide for the future.
>
> Why is it, I wondered, that the human person lives one way at home and assumes another posture when outside of it? Why, when they leave their homes, do people become takers, competitors rather than givers?

Chiara Lubich had also pondered this question and, on her journeys to Africa and Latin America, had been all too aware of its fruits. In 1991 she and Fr Foresi spent several weeks living at the Movement's little town of Aracoeli, near Sao Paolo in Brazil. While all the little towns share a common way of life, they also all have unique characteristics according to the society in which they are situated. The citadel of Ottmaring near Augsburg in Germany, for example, is clearly an ecumenical town, with its population made up of Catholics and Lutherans. The citadel in the Philippines gives special place to dialogue between Christianity and the major Asian religions.

In Sao Paolo, Chiara could not fail to notice the expanse of skyscrapers, the dominant minority rich class, the growing but struggling middle class, and the vast spread of wretched *favelas* (slums) where the poor lived. The very same year Pope John Paul II had issued an encyclical letter on social concerns. Called *Centesimus Annus*, it marked the centenary of the famous letter, *Rerum Novarum* of Pope Leo XIII, which is considered as the founding document of the modern development of the Church's social teaching. From her earliest embracing of Jesus Forsaken as her model and guide, Chiara had understood not only how to embrace the Cross – be it pain, misunderstanding or the sorrow of division – but also how to go beyond it, to seek a solution. She had written in that heart-rending meditation when she had to come down off her 'Mount Tabor' in 1949:

> I have only one Spouse on earth: Jesus crucified and forsaken …And *His* is universal suffering, and therefore mine. I will go through the world seeking it…In this way I will dry up the waters of tribulation in many hearts nearby, and through communion with my almighty Spouse, in many far away. I shall pass as a fire that consumes all that must fall and leaves standing only the truth.

The injustice and the indignity of masses of the population living as outcasts in *favelas* and on rubbish dumps was clearly something that must one day fall. But Chiara's contribution would not be 'liberation theology' or the Marxist promotion of the class struggle. No, she is far too practical for that.

Christian solutions had to be like the action of God, who respects completely the free will given to man. Class struggle and hatred were a road to nowhere. Much better to seek the good in people and their free and willing co-operation in promoting justice. Justice without mercy is also a dead end.

For Chiara, Mary's Magnificat represented a social charter, where 'the poor shall be filled with good things and the rich sent away empty-handed' – not because the rich had their goods wrenched from them but because they gave freely when their hearts were filled with spiritual treasures.

The Church has always recognized and promoted the right to private property, perhaps more so in the last hundred years to counter Marxist philosophy. Today, with John Paul II's centenary encyclical, the emphasis has also widened somewhat to remind society of the 'universal destination' of goods. So, there is a fundamental right to property and heritage, but we must be aware that this is in the light of the universal destination of goods; that God gave us mastery of the earth, and the fruits are for everyone.

Towards the end of May 1991, Chiara announced a new scheme, a new activity of the Movement that should begin first there at Mariapolis Araceli in Brazil and then spread throughout the world-wide Movement. It was to be known as the 'Economy of Communion'. Each little town of the Movement had its own little businesses by which the inhabitants earned their keep. Why could not this be extended to reach out to those in the surrounding areas, especially those in places like the Brazilian *favelas*?

The plan was to set up businesses, including those co-operatives which were already running at Loppiano and elsewhere, and invite other businessmen and women to collaborate. Yes – here is what was new – as a Movement they would own and share capital, but the profits would be put in common. And the profits would be used for good works. Precisely one third of the profits would go to helping those in need so that, like the early Christians, there should be no one in need among them. So the profit would be put in common to fulfil the universal destination of goods. Another third of the profits would be reinvested in the business itself – but so that it would grow and develop, not as a means of accumulating wealth. The final third would be used to build, develop and support the little cities of the Movement, because their purpose was to form 'new' people who would be 'pillars' of a new society where there would be a communion of goods.

The news spread through the Movement like wildfire. It had struck a chord, and just one day after its announcement, news was coming in that businesses in Italy, Germany, the Philippines and the United States wanted to participate in this new economy.

A few days later, on 29 May 1991, Chiara addressed a gathering of inhabitants at Araceli. She placed the inspiration for what one resident of the little town had described as this 'bombshell', the announcement of the new Economy of Communion, precisely at that first sight of the Abbey of Einsiedeln in Switzerland 30 years previously. After recalling the scene, she said:

> At one point, it was as if that very beautiful sight of the church and fields in the dazzling sun dissolved, and I felt that I understood that God wanted something similar from us. Einsiedeln appeared almost like a little city, because of its vastness, and it seemed that God also wanted a little city from us, but not like that one. He wanted a real and true little city, with houses, especially little houses, but also larger ones, with pavilions, with factories, with businesses and industries. This image has remained so deeply impressed that it is as if I can still see it, even now.

That was the original inspiration, but she went on to explain how it had recently been revived in her:

> Recently a book was published in Italy by a priest who is also a sociologist and a scholar. It is entitled *Protagonists Today* and in it he considers the movements to be the protagonists, the champions of change today. And since he speaks of the movements, he also speaks of the Focolare.
>
> I was struck by a point he made. He is an expert on the social and religious situation of our times. He says: 'Certain achievements of these movements point to the possibility of a third way between communism and capitalism.'
>
> Those words made an impression on me because I remembered when I spoke of this many years ago, at the launching of our youth movement. At that time I said to the young people: 'no to capitalism, no to communism. What we need is something animated by Christianity in the social field.' And this 'third way' reminded me of what I had said then.

Chiara regularly reads all the Church's social teaching and any major document issued by John Paul II. She went on to explain to her Brazilian audience how she had been reading the Pope's recent encyclical on social issues, *Centesimus Annus*:

> It's a wonderful encyclical because it gives a perfect picture of the economic, social and political situation of the world today. It's a *dramatic* situation, as you know, in many parts of the world, not least here in South America.
>
> In this encyclical the Pope dedicates a lengthy chapter to Communism, and rightly so. Because in our day an ideology which had invaded a third of the world has crumbled. The Pope, who lived under a Communist regime when he was in Poland, speaks about this, coming out again against Communism and reaffirming Christian social doctrine, which holds that private property is a right. He says that free enterprise is a right, that freedom to form associations [i.e. co-operatives, unions, etc.] is a right. He says that we must safeguard human rights under all aspects. However, he also speaks very much about solidarity, about the need to consider not only ourselves but others.
>
> So now you know how we've been thinking in recent days: Einsiedeln; this book *Protagonists Today*; the encyclical *Centesimus Annus*. And at this point we began to consider our Ideal. We understood that our Ideal is a charism, but in our charism there is also a social aspect; it's a charism with a social background too. It's a charism which leads to sanctity; it's a charism which leads to ecumenical activities; it's a charism which leads to evangelization; it's a charism which can help to resolve social problems.

The atmosphere grew more and more enthusiastic, and Chiara was repeatedly interrupted by applause as, in her animated manner, she went on rapidly to outline her vision of how this new way of economic life should begin there in Brazil and then spread to all the other permanent Mariapoli and to wherever the Movement was present.

And as ever, her concern did not remain on a theoretical level. Before long she was going on to outline to the Araceli inhabitants what the next and immediate step was to be: they should study a project; they should set up a mini industrial zone on the Movement's estate, not right there in the little town but about four kilometres away; they should decide which entrepreneurs should be approached to participate; they should look for the right person to be the over-all manager of the scheme...Just listening to her speak with such rapidity and enthusiasm and attention to every detail left her audience breathless!

And she made it quite clear that many people from far and wide would come to study this new economic model: 'And we, for our part, obedient to the command to "Tell it from the rooftops", will use all the means at our disposal to spread this message, starting with our own media, the Movement's magazines and videos.'

She was proved right. The idea has taken off on every continent. Economists have come from all over the world to study it. One British student wrote her final dissertation on the effects of the little town of Araceli on the surrounding *favelas*. Of course, she had to mention the Economy of Communion. After it was assessed, she was immediately invited by her own and other universities to submit a doctoral thesis specifically on the theme of the Economy of Communion.

In 1995 a Brazilian sociologist, Vera Arujo, was invited to address a conference of 40 experts at Lublin University at the third international conference on 'Changes of mentality and perspectives of social integration in Europe'. She spoke on the Economy of Communion.

The following year, Lublin University awarded Chiara Lubich an honorary doctorate in Social Sciences. In her acceptance speech she was able to report that after just five years of operation, there were now some 600 enterprises participating in the Economy of Communion.

As the Senate Procession entered the Aula Magna of Lublin University on 19 June 1996, the crowded hall strained to see the guest of honour. At first no one recognized her. As one Polish journalist wrote, 'We expected to see this elegantly dressed lady whom we had come to know from photographs and on television.' It was only when the Senate had all taken position on the stage and Chiara had taken her place at a table set aside with her sponsor, the Dean of the Social Sciences Faculty, that people recognized her beneath the academic gown and cap. She had asked to sit to deliver her acceptance speech because, as she told friends, she was so nervous that she was afraid that her legs would give way if she stood at the lectern! It was only when she began to relax and smile that the people in the hall could really believe that it was Chiara Lubich.

The Dean of Faculty, Professor Adam Biela, gave a 20-minute speech outlining the reasons why Chiara was being given this award. She was the first woman ever to receive it. He said:

> In order for a candidate to be recognized for this particular title, it is customary to take into consideration their literary patrimony and their contribution to the development of a particular discipline. When the motion is being studied by the Faculty of Social Sciences, the contribution that the candidate has made to social sciences has to be demonstrated.
>
> The history of science shows that the contribution to the development of a particular scientific discipline cannot be measured by the formal culture of the given discipline, even less can it be measured by the number of books that have been written. What counts in the development of the science is above all the proposals of a new vision of problems, of new paradigms of research and of new suggestions for application.
>
> According to the contemporary philosopher Thomas S. Kuhn, the most famous of such turnabouts is the so-called Copernican revolution brought about by our great astronomer.
>
> The Faculty of Social Sciences at the Catholic University of Lublin includes in its sphere psychology, sociology, pedagogy and economy. The classifications of the sciences always link social sciences with normative sciences such as law and ethics. Up until now social sciences have not worked out a paradigm on the model of natural sciences, and they are still far removed from a Copernican revolution, which would allow them not only to describe and clarify social phenomena, but also to apply scientific models for building up in the economic and political life relationships which are more positive and constructive.
>
> Social sciences are looking at all costs for a paradigm which would allow them on the threshold of the twenty-first century to conquer the culture of the growth of individual ambitions, of an excess of autonomy on the part of individuals and elitist groups which do not take into account the good of other people; of chronic rivalry which is often the reason for aggressive behaviour; of a growing disproportion

between groups of people who grow rich in an unjust way and people who are marginalized to the misery of unemployment and homelessness. This kind of behaviour inevitably leads to a social pathology or to clear conflicts in local societies, whilst on a regional and international scale it leads to wars which bring with them death and new examples of genocide. This happens in Europe too.

Social sciences, therefore, are looking for a paradigm which would help to make the social reality more civilized, which could transform extensive areas of disintegration, conflict, wars and senseless deaths, which persons inflict on each other, into integration, concord and reciprocal goodwill among people.

The only alternative to social disintegration is integration; the only alternative to rivalry and egocentricity is human solidarity...

The phenomenon of the Focolare Movement, whose charismatic leader is Chiara Lubich, shows through practical applications that it is possible to build unity and social integration on new and deeper principles. The work of this Movement constitutes a living and real example of the application in social relationships of the *paradigm of unity*, which is so necessary to social sciences in order that they might acquire a new 'strength of application'...

Chiara Lubich is the author of many books recognized at the international level. But this is not the main motive for which the Council of the Faculty of Social Sciences has proposed this title of honorary doctorate. In the work of universities, researchers are valued because of the books they have written. We realize that Chiara Lubich has written her books above all as a means of announcing and promoting true social integration. Her social activity, which is intrinsic to the charisma of announcing an evangelical unity, constitutes a living inspiration and example of social sciences which are being pushed into creating *an interdisciplinary paradigm of unity*, as a methodological foundation for the building of theoretical models, of strategies of empirical research and of schemes of application...And so it is the values of inspiration and of application of this social phenomenon which consists in building up social, economic and religious infrastructures which make up the main reasons for conferring this title of honorary doctorate in Social Sciences.

The Dean went on to outline the four complementary dimensions of the Focolare Movement: social, economic, moral and religious. He particularly pointed out and explained the Economy of Communion:

> This idea of an economic system according to new economic princi-
> ples which presuppose the acquiring and the three-way sharing of
> profits for the edification of social and economic integration consti-
> tutes an example of how the paradigm of unity and solidarity of peo-
> ple – who should be sharing the fruits of their work and the
> responsibility for risk which economic activity brings – is being incar-
> nated. These proposals are not abstract theories, but they show that
> such a system is possible in every country, and also in Poland.

Professor Biela concluded by saying that he saw the essential contribution of Chiara Lubich as being the message of unity which the
Movement under her guidance brings about, and which demon-
strates that a new paradigm in social sciences is not only possible but
necessary – 'a paradigm of unity'.

The hall erupted into applause. One graduate of Lublin University, Patrycja Mikulska, who now lives and works in the town, said she
had never seen such a joyful degree ceremony.

The next day Chiara was back in the Aula Magna. As Patrycja
Mikulska, the editor of a magazine for small businesses reported, this
time she was 'no longer "in disguise", but appearing as her elegant
and graceful self, smartly dressed in bright colours.'

The new honorary Doctor fielded questions from the packed
hall. The topics ranged from what might follow from the newest
discoveries in cosmology to retaining old values in the new
economic and social climate of Poland. Patrycja Mikulska noted
that one question and its answer stood out for her. There was a
marked difference in attitude between the questioner and the re-
spondent. The question, 'How to cope with so much evil?' was
asked by a young graduate of the university. The voice betrayed a
feeling of disenchantment and weariness. Chiara responded that although we should use the available democratic means where necessary, we should not choose a direct confrontation with evil, but
rather we should fill the world and the situation in which we find
ourselves with positive values. The young questioner seemed tired

and pessimistic, but the elegantly dressed and dynamic 76-year-old was full of life, hope and positive solutions.

Once again, her message had captivated her audience. The next day she inaugurated and laid the foundation stone for her Movement's nineteenth little town, near Warsaw. Several Polish businesses had already signed up to participate in the Economy of Communion.

NINETEEN

FROM LONDON'S GUILDHALL
TO A TOKYO TEMPLE

The list of awards granted to Chiara Lubich, from literary prizes to the freedom of cities, from religious recognitions to academic awards, is already a long one. Every month, offers and requests to accept awards come into the Centre of the Work at Rocca di Papa. She replies graciously to all, but accepts only some of them.

One reason is that she doesn't have the time it would take to go around collecting them. She *is* the President of an international and multi-faceted organization. Apart from this, she has no interest in picking up titles or honours for herself. As with everything, since the beginning, she submits such decisions to her colleagues and to her superiors. When I asked her who her superiors were, she told me, 'the Council for the Laity and the Pope'.

The Pope is her superior, although she does not consult him over every offer of an award that drops through her letterbox. Rather, she will consult with the Pontifical Council for the Laity. When she is advised that it would be good for the Ideal or the Movement, she submits and graciously accepts the award. Thus, while I was once visiting her, an offer of an honorary degree in Sacred Theology arrived from the University of St Thomas in Manila. It was recommended to her that she accept, and a date was set for January 1997.

The President of the Council for the Laity is Cardinal Eduardo Pironio. His praise of Chiara expressed to me in July 1996 could not have been higher. He said, 'Chiara is a woman who radiates Jesus. What she says is the fruit of deep contemplation. She loves the Church and wants to live the essence of the Church as a mystery of communion. She has made the Church's passion for unity her own – this is the root of her genuine ecumenical activity – and has espoused the cause of world peace. She is a woman who has taken on the suffering of humanity; she has lived out Christ's passion which extends through time.'

In 1977, Chiara was awarded the prestigious Templeton Prize for Progress in Religion. Other winners have been Mother Teresa, Brother Roger, Dr Billy Graham and Alexander Solzhenitsyn.

The Jury for the Prize had been headed by Her Majesty Fabiola, Queen of the Belgians – she and Chiara later became firm friends – and included eminent Christians, Jews, Buddhists and Sikhs. Chiara remembers how she was reluctant to put herself in the limelight:

'The Gospel has taught me that the right hand must not know what the left hand is doing. The idea of all that publicity troubled me deeply. But the Gospel itself reassured me: "Let men see your good works and give glory to the Father." I am very conscious that the Focolare Movement is not my business but God's... Then I said to myself: "If the Templeton Prize serves to glorify God, let them give it to me." Having said that, I felt a little personal surge of joy, the joy of a schoolgirl who has been given a good mark and is pleased not only for herself but for her mother. They could have chosen a person from another religion, but that year they chose a Catholic. That made me happy for the Catholic Church, my mother.'

And on the day of the presentation itself, at the end of her acceptance speech, in which she outlined her own religious experience and the growth of the Movement, she announced that part of her prize money would be given to the Bishop of Rome for the 'House of Charity' which that diocese was setting up for people with various disabilities and handicaps. A hand-written letter from Paul VI of 19 April 1977 thanks his 'dearest daughter in Christ' for her letter of 15 April and 'the generous gift you sent in favour of the "House of Charity", being part of your Templeton Prize'.

Chiara told the 1,000 people jammed into the Guildhall that the rest of the prize money would be used 'to enlarge the maternity wing of the hospital in the little town of Fontem in Cameroon; to build two houses for those who are living in the *mocambos* shanty town in Recife [Brazil]; and to build the last stage of a religious and social training centre for Asians at Tagaytay in the Philippines.'

Her parting thought was: 'I would like to leave you with the words of the great Spanish mystic, John of the Cross: "Where you do not find love, put love and you will find love." '

After the ceremony, at which Chiara says she experienced a special presence of God, 'perhaps because we all believed in God', the first person to come up and congratulate her was a Tibetan monk. He said that he was going to write to the Dalai Lama, suggesting that he should contact Chiara. Members of other religions also pressed around her to offer their congratulations. But it was contact with Buddhists that would be a particular highlight of the next few years for Chiara.

To trace how she came to address 12,000 Buddhist leaders in 1981, we have to go back to the Second Session of the Second Vatican Council. While the Council Fathers were gathered in Rome from 29 September to 4 December 1963, there were some people who, in light of the great success of the Secretariat for Promoting Christian Unity, asked if it wouldn't now be appropriate to set up a secretariat for the major non-Christian religions in the world. Much discussion followed on the fringes of the Council on the advisability and utility of inviting non-Christian representatives as guests to the Council in the way that Canon Pawley and others represented the Christian denominations.

Finally, Pope Paul decided to do so. The first and only non-Christian Guest was invited to attend the Third Session of the Council held between 14 September and 21 November. He was Mr Nikkyo Niwano from Japan. He had founded the Buddhist movement Rissho Kosei-kai in 1938 after a sacred Buddhist text had become the cornerstone of his life in a similar way that Jesus' last prayer and testament had become for Chiara. The inspirational sentence was: 'The compassion of Buddha is like lotus flowers which grow in the mud; so must we make the mercy and truth of Buddha flower in society.'

Like Chiara's, his message would reach millions of people and, like the Focolare, what distinguishes Niwano's movement from other Buddhist groups is its lay nature. It is not essentially made up of monks but of lay Buddhists and is marked by a great international and inter-religious openness.

What Chiara only learned much later, after she had got to know him well, was how much Niwano's being received by Pope Paul VI when he attended the Third Session of the Vatican Council in 1964 had affected him. Chiara says: 'He spoke of that meeting with awe, because it was then that he had understood that he had to dedicate his whole life to a greater understanding between the religions of the East and the West. Just a few years later, his efforts led to the founding of the World Conference for Religion and Peace [the WCRP], of which he became honorary president. This conference made him well known in international circles.' In 1995 Chiara became Honorary President when the WCRP held its Sixth World Assembly.

A highlight of any trip to the West for members of Rissho Kosei-kai is to attend the weekly public audience of the Pope. Already in the 1970s some of the young people of Niwano's movement had met their Focolare counterparts in Japan, the United States and Italy. But it was not until Nikkyo Niwano was nominated for the Templeton Prize in 1979 that the two leaders met. He had read Chiara's Templeton speech and travelled to Italy to meet her.

They took to each other right away. Chiara says, 'When I met Niwano, my immediate reaction was that we were made to work together, because his organization and the Focolare Movement had so much in common.' The president of Rissho Kosei-kai evidently felt the same way, and there and then, at that first meeting, invited Chiara to visit Japan to share her religious experience with the leaders of his movement.

Chiara points out that, in her contacts and experience, what has fascinated so many members of Eastern religions is the suffering of Jesus, and more precisely, 'the suffering which he experienced and which led to his complete annihilation in the suffering of abandonment. Some Buddhist philosophers have told us that the Christian's renunciation of self in imitation of Jesus' kenosis on the Cross, as the Movement presents it, is very close to the perfection of the "void" in Buddhism.'

Two years after her first meeting with Niwano, Chiara travelled to the Far East. Arriving in Tokyo, her first calls were to see the local Archbishop and the Papal Nuncio. The Archbishop of Tokyo told her that Nikkyo Niwano was a 'pure of heart, sincere' person and a 'great personality who was esteemed and listened to, even in China'.

Chiara arrived for a visit to the Buddhist movement's headquarters at three o'clock on 21 December 1981. She noted in her diary that night that it reminded her of 1960, when she had first encountered Protestants. It was a new step.

On her arrival, he had all his staff lined up to greet her and presented them to her. After a warm welcome and short speeches, there was a meal and a private meeting between Niwano and Chiara, with Giulia Folonari present. Chiara was then given a tour of the movement's headquarters, and noted in her diary that everywhere there was 'Buddha, Buddha, Buddha!'

The first Focolare centre had been opened in Japan in 1976, and today there are some 3,000 Focolare members in that country. The first Focolare household opened in Manila in 1966, and there are now over 200,000 members in the whole of Asia. Apart from the usual meetings with the Movement and its various branches, the highlight of the visit to Japan was Chiara's address to 12,000 leaders of Niwano's Rissho Kosei-kai movement.

The Great Sacred Hall of the movement's temple was full and an overspill followed the proceedings from television link-ups in the foyer and the surrounding corridors. Chiara, standing at a lectern in front of a giant golden statute of the Buddha, told them:

Dear brothers and sisters in God,

Our meeting is not just one of chance. For some years already Providence has been drawing the Focolare and the Rissho Kosei-kai closer together...

Today I have the honour of presenting my spiritual experience. Take it as a gift of love offered by your sister.

As you certainly know, I am Christian and belong to the Catholic Church. The Catholic Church, which has been living in the world for 20 centuries, has as its principle aim the sanctification of people. It does this by means of the grace which Jesus brought on earth and which confers on men the dignity of Sons of God.

While the Church does this, following its founder, Jesus, it does not deny the earthly dimension of man, and works in every way to build peace, to care for the poor, to teach the ignorant, to feed the hungry, to clothe the naked, to relieve suffering in all sorts of ways which its love for humanity suggests to it. What the Church has given the world in these centuries, only God could measure.

The Catholic Church is one, is holy, is universal and is founded on the apostles chosen by Jesus. But if the Church is one and holy, the people who make it up, who live in the midst of the world, can sometimes be affected by the confusion and the negative influences which from time to time exist in humanity. It follows, then, that Christians can become tepid, that this love which Christ has brought from Heaven onto earth, their characteristic, can diminish in their hearts.

And so this is how the Spirit of God intervenes in the Church, in sometimes quite extraordinary ways by sending particular gifts, which are like a spiritual medicine. Hearts, which accept these graces, come together in spiritual Movements, which strengthen the Christian community.

And as in springtime the delicate buds which appear on the most fragile of stems reveal the life which flows in the trunk and the branches, so these gifts which serve to make the 'foliage' of the Church throughout the world become green again, are even purely by their existence a sign of the Church's vitality.

My experience, which goes hand in hand with the Focolare Movement, is linked to one of these springtimes in the Church of Christ today.

She then went on to tell her own story, from her commitment in 1943, to the experience of that group of first companions discovering the 'words' of Scripture: 'God is Love' (1 John 4:16); 'No greater love...than to lay down your life for your friends' (John 15:13); 'By this shall all men know you are my disciples, if you love one another' (John 13:35); 'Give and it will be given to you' (Luke 6:38); and so on until she came to the word, 'unless a grain of wheat dies...' Then she explained:

The members of the Movement know all this. They have experienced suffering, but also its beneficial effects. That much suffering has been loved is one of the causes of this rapid spread of the Movement throughout the world...

By way of purification by God, one can in fact enter little by little into contemplation of the things of God. Then we can understand something of His mysteries. And if the Christian in fact remains faithful to the message of love and suffering contained in the Gospel, he is led by the Spirit of God into a deeper unity with Christ, until he can say: 'It is no longer I who live but Christ who lives in me' (Galatians 2:20). So he becomes another Christ, in Christ, participating with Him in His filial relationship with the Father.

Chiara then, in a brief and concise manner, explained what the Holy Trinity is and how the Holy Spirit is the mutual love of the Father and the Son and how the Christian understands something of these mysteries by drawing on his own religious experience: 'He understands then how God is Love…The heart of my experience is this: the more we love the other, the more we find God. The more we find God, the more we love others.'

She told the 12,000 Buddhist leaders – all wearing a white sash over their shoulders, signifying their personal consecration to live the teachings of their sacred book, *The Lotus Sutra* – that after 40 years of existence the Movement now existed among Catholics in almost every nation in the world, and for the last 20 years also among Christians of other denominations. She told them what a marvellous experience it was for her when she met members of other religions:

> Every person, made in the image of God, has the possibility of a certain personal relationship with Him. Moreover, the very nature of man brings him to this communion. This is the affinity we find in various ways between our religion and others.
>
> It is this affinity with you, dearest brothers and sisters, which enables us to walk together side by side on this Holy Journey of Life, towards the goal which awaits us, and to work together for the good of humanity.

In her diary that night she remarked on the 'complete silence and absolute attention' that prevailed while she spoke. She was pleased that the youth of Niwano's movement expressed the desire to collaborate with the Focolare youth on a particular project, such as aid to the Third World. Chiara told them that they were to consider all the Focolare centres as their own. But what probably made her happiest of all was that one of the Buddhist leaders present told her that he now understood that God was Love.

Her overriding impression of the experience was expressed in her diary as follows: 'What a unique experience to tell these people, who didn't know them, the words of Jesus: "Every hair on your head is counted" (Matthew 10:30); "Give and it will be given to you" (Luke 6:38); "Ask and you shall receive" (Matthew 7:7). They didn't know they were so loved; now they know.'

From Japan, Chiara went on to visit the Focolare present in South Korea and Hong Kong before landing at Manila in the Philippines, where she stayed in the permanent Mariapolis of the Movement at Tagaytay for two weeks. While there, she inaugurated a study centre for members of the Movement in Asia, dedicated to the study of Eastern religions. The courses organized there would have three elements: (1) a comprehensive exploration of the religion to be studied, with an update on its current situation; (2) on-going reference to the truths of Christianity, given the familiarization with the other religion; (3) study of the guidelines for dialogue and evaluation contained in the relevant 'Directory' and documents of the Vatican Secretariat for Interreligious Dialogue.

The lessons are video-recorded and distributed to a network of study groups in other Asiatic countries. The same year, Chiara founded a school on similar lines for ecumenical dialogue between different Christian denominations at the Movement's permanent Mariapolis in Germany.

While in the Philippines, Chiara also addressed a meeting of the region's bishops, coming from the Philippines, Korea, Malaysia and Macau, as well as large gatherings of the Movement. A characteristic of every visit she makes to the Movement in other countries is a question session where members of the Movement submit questions for Chiara to answer directly. It comes back to her knack for communications and her desire that all the members of the Movement, in every part of the world, should always have direct contact and know what is going on at the centre of the Movement.

Just as Radio Vatican reports the voyages of John Paul II, so on every stage of her tour, it reported on Chiara's speeches and activities. The Italian press also charted her progress.

From the Philippines she went on to spend three days with the Movement in Australia and then two days in Thailand, before returning to Rome. The trip had lasted almost two months.

Contacts remain close between the Rissho Kosei-kai and Focolare. Niwano invited Chiara to Japan again in 1985 for his eightieth birthday celebrations – his *sanju* – on 15 November. Chiara was the honoured guest and read a speech in Niwano's honour. Thirty thousand members of the Buddhist movement listened with rapt attention to her talk while another 200,000 followed via video link-up.

She was also to have taken part in a question-and-answer session with youth members of the Rissho Kosei-kai on 24 November. But she had to cut her visit short as Pope John Paul II called her to be present at the extraordinary Synod of Bishops being held in Rome to mark the end of the Second Vatican Council. She prepared written answers to the questions that had already been submitted in advance, and she left Natalia Dallapiccola and Enzo Fondi to read these out in her place. Before leaving Tokyo, Chiara also gave an interview to Rissho Kosei-kai's daily newspaper, *Kosei Shinbun*, which has a print-run of 1.6 million copies.

In fact, following a suggestion from Pope Paul VI that Chiara and the Focolare expand their dialogue from being only with Christians of other denominations to dialogue also with members of other religious faiths, Chiara had recalled Natalia from Leipzig in 1976. Natalia and Fr Enzo Fondi were to head up the Focolare's Secretariat for Dialogue with Other Religions, a responsibility which they still held 20 years later.

Cardinal Francis Arinze is President of the Vatican's Council for Interreligious Dialogue. He appreciates greatly Chiara's charism and sums her up as someone who 'has deep spirituality, great faith in God, deep love for Christ, loyalty to the Church of Christ, zeal to share the love of Christ with others, openness of heart to other human beings and a great desire to build spiritual bridges between people. She is also a person of strong character, great discipline and quiet asceticism. She has tremendous energy for work. She speaks from the abundance of her inner spiritual treasure.'

Cardinal Arinze represents the Pope in all matters concerning dialogue with other religions. He says the Focolare often invite him or other members of his Council to speak at their gatherings. 'We reciprocate,' he says, 'and some Focolarini are among our official consultors. We get great help from the Focolarini when we organize a big gathering such as the 1986 Assisi World Day of Prayer for Peace.'

The Cardinal says he is happy to encourage the Focolare Movement, and he has regular dealings with Natalia Dallapiccola and Fr Enzo Fondi. They keep him informed of their activities and ask his advice on theological questions. Fr Fondi sometimes contributes papers to the Pontifical Council's review *Pro Dialogo*.

Cardinal Arinze told me the story of how a Buddhist monk from Thailand visited Loppiano and the Centre of the Work with his abbot in 1995. 'He had a long conversation with Chiara,' the Cardinal recalled, 'and said he regarded her as his spiritual mother. Then he asked Chiara to give him a new name. She gave him the name "Luce Ardente", which means "Burning Light".'

The Cardinal, who represents the Holy See and thus not only the Church but also the Vatican City State, must always be aware of protocol and correct diplomacy, as well as theological exactitude. He is all the more appreciative, therefore, that, 'The members of Focolare, because of their disarming love of others, can touch the hearts of other believers pretty quickly. The spirituality of unity which is central to the Focolare Movement, together with the willingness of the Focolarini for an exchange of religious experience with other believers, are a precious contribution to interreligious dialogue.'

This 'spirituality of unity', of course, was present right from the first days of the Movement. In notes in preparation for a talk in 1946 Chiara wrote:

This practice of 'making ourselves one' with others is not easy. It demands the complete emptiness of ourselves: the removal of ideas from our heads, of affections from our hearts, of everything from our wills in order to identify ourselves with others...

God wants us every day, every hour, to perfect this art which at times is exhausting and wearisome, but always marvellous, full of life and fruitful, this art of 'making ourselves one' with others: the art of loving...Every soul that wishes to achieve unity must have only one right: to serve everyone because in everyone it serves God.

There are also Jewish and Muslim Focolarini. In June 1996 the Mariapolis Centre at Castelgandolfo hosted the first international congress of Jewish Friends of the Focolare. Participants came from all around the world and, what was most striking, even for them, from every Jewish tradition.

Before leaving Castelgandolfo at the end of their encounter, the participants made a gift of an embroidered tapestry of the Hebrew word *Shalom*. They all signed a note accompanying it, which read:

Carissima Chiara

With an immense gratitude in our hearts, we offer you our gift – of *Shalom* – peace, wholeness, oneness. As you can see, this little tapestry, our gift to you, is made up of many diverse strands. But they come together to form a harmony of colour and beauty.

And this is how we, your Jewish children gathered at Castelgandolfo, feel now: though different in many ways, we all come together in your Ideal, to form one song, one voice, one note.

With you, we feel ready to go ahead to help build a better world for all humanity.

Natalia Dallapiccola and Enzo Fondi, who look after the aspect of interreligious dialogue in the Movement, point out that in the current climate it is not always prudent to say who and where are the Muslim men and women Focolarini. Suffice to say that they live mostly in Europe and North Africa. Chiara takes a great interest in her Muslim Focolarini friends, as she does with the Buddhist, Jewish and other Focolarini. She is pleased that they find a renewed interest in the Koran, for example. She believes that they rediscover the passages where Jesus is praised as a prophet and Mary is honoured. This makes her happy.

Before she left Tokyo in November 1985 to return to Rome for the Synod of Bishops at the Pope's request, Nikkyo Niwano gave Chiara a fan as a gift. On it, in Chinese characters, were written the words of a revered Buddhist monk of the ninth century. It read: 'If my heart is one with the will of God, it will see thousands of other hearts coming to life around it.'

TWENTY

A TREE WITH MANY BRANCHES
– A MANTLE TO COVER EVERY VOCATION

As the Focolare Movement grew in size and spread throughout the world, so also it has continued to develop and enlarge internally. After the discovery of the vocation of the married Focolarino with Igino Giordani, very quickly hundreds of couples responded to this vocation too. While living in their own 'family community', they share the same radical commitment as the single Focolarini. Whereas the consecrated celibates put everything they have, including their salaries, into a common pot – the 'communion of goods' – the married Focolarini contribute what they can afford after their family commitments have been met. They share too with the single Focolarini a complete availability to be moved within a regional zone of the Movement or even transferred to another country.

But from early on, Chiara had recognized that the vocation to be a totally consecrated Focolarino was a radical one, and there were many people who would want to share in the community and lifestyle of the Focolare without necessarily making the religious promises of poverty, chastity and obedience.

Following Pope Pius XII's appeal for Christians to meet the void of atheism by bringing 'God...God...God', she acted quickly and founded a branch of the Movement to be known as the Volunteers. They are full members of Focolare, either married or single, who have either not felt the vocation to the radical commitment of the consecrated Focolarini or who have been discerned by the leaders of the Movement as not having that vocation. They make the basic commitment common to all the branches of the Movement, which is to keep the presence of Jesus alive among them. The Volunteers are organized in local cells or nuclei in order to share a community life, according to their possibilities. They meet once a week and share in the communion of goods. In all this, the households of consecrated celibate men or women Focolarini, together with those of married Focolarini, form the hub or centre around which all the other activities naturally gravitate.

The 1960s and 1970s saw the birth and growth of several 'branches' within the Focolare Movement. Indeed, Pope Paul VI described the Focolare Movement as 'a tree which has become abundant with fruits'. That tree now has 16 branches, each counting many thousands of members and a whole range of social activities.

While the Focolare is primarily a lay movement within the Church(es), there are also now thousands of priests, monks and nuns, and even bishops, who are attached in one way or another. Chiara explains that this is just as it should be. The vocations may be different, but they all share the same aims: union with God and with one another, and as a result the creation of a united world. As in the Church itself, in the Focolare Movement there is room for every vocation.

Chiara came to understand this better when one day she was looking at a medieval statue of the Virgin Mary. She says: 'I saw this statue of the Virgin Mary wearing a great mantle which enfolded and protected castles and churches, craftsmen and monks, bishops and mothers of children, the rich and the poor – all the people that made up a city of those times. More than being an excessive expression of devotion, it was rather a way of depicting the relationship which the Mother of God has with the Church, with humanity. It's a way of representing her universal motherhood, which is one of the cardinal points of our Faith.

'It's much the same with us. The Movement is a bit like a living copy of that image, of what the image represents. In a way that resembles Mary, this Work of hers is like a mantle that gathers together whole sections of the Church and humanity, because God has given it the gift of creating a family out of them. It's a gift, a charism, that makes the Movement resemble Mary in her maternal and unifying role.'

In the Movement's administrative 'Centre of the Work' at Rocca di Papa a mosaic was commissioned to decorate the chapel when it was built in 1965. It represents 'Mary Mother of the Church', which title Pope Paul VI had officially accorded her on the closing day of the Third Session of the Second Vatican Council (21 November

1964). At the Movement's international meeting centre at Castelgan-dolfo, the chapel is decorated with a modern sculpture, almost like a latter-day representation of that medieval image which Chiara re-ferred to. It shows the Virgin Mary with mantle outstretched and covering the array of vocations within the Church. Igino Giordani, the first married Focolarino, is recognizable in it, as is John Paul II in a typical gesture, holding a child in his arms.

In 1966, in the era of the 'flower people' and shortly before the student revolts of the 'Summer of '68', Chiara founded a youth branch of the Focolare Movement. The new generation would come to be known in the Movement's shorthand as 'the Gen'. In the following years, this section would come to be further subdivi-ded so that the different age-groups could each have their own branch – right down to the 'Gen 5', the tiny tots.

As a young teacher in the mountain villages around Trent, Chiara had already found that if you made education fun, the children en-joyed it – and retained the lesson. She would spend hours devising games as a way of teaching her classes geography or maths or reli-gion. Even now, when there is a large gathering of one of the younger children's branches of the Movement, Chiara herself will think up games which somehow manage to occupy and captivate the several thousand children present in the grounds of the Centre of the Work – and always with a lesson involved: God's love for each one, for example, or how to 'create' Jesus in the midst.

Although there had been regional and local gatherings of young people from the beginning – and weren't the first summer Mariapoli simply groups of young people holidaying together? – the first large gathering of the Movement's youth, a Genfest, was held at the per-manent Mariapolis of Loppiano on 1 May 1973. In the atmosphere of the 'youth culture' and the rock bands of the 1970s, two music groups had been founded at Loppiano, a boys' band known as Gen Rosso and a girls' one known as Gen Verde. Renewed with each succeeding generation of 'trainee Focolarini' who pass through Lop-piano, today the two music groups are known world-wide. They have their own recording studio at Loppiano where they produce their records, cassettes and CDs, and they give concerts in many countries throughout the world. Of course, their music unasham-edly promotes a message – that of unity and a united world – which immediately appeals to youth. Gen Rosso are now under contract to the international record company EMI.

I was amused to learn that when Chiara goes for her daily run in the car with her devoted secretary Giulia Folonari, she prefers to listen to pop and rock music – anything with a lively beat or tempo! While I was there, she had just discovered, and taken to, rap music produced by the young people. It is her latest favourite listening material. The sight of this pint-sized, elegantly dressed-and-coiffured septuagenarian shaking her head and slapping her knee to the beat of rap as she is driven through the Italian countryside is a joy to behold! But then, she likes everything that is new, provided that it is harmonious, beautiful and decent. She encourages the hundreds of young people who do the school of formation at Loppiano and the other formation centres of the Movement every year to discover and use their talents. Each centre has art and craft workshops. As new paintings, sculptures and fabrics arrive at her offices as gifts from these young people, so Chiara constantly changes the items decorating her office suite and the corridor alongside. No time for staleness: always something new – new beauty, new talent, new ideas. Even in her own focolare house where she lives with three companions, she will often start rearranging the furniture at ten o'clock at night. Nothing stands still when she is around. Perhaps that's one reason why the young people identify with her so much – and enthusiastically welcome her uncompromising message.

Following the success of the first Genfest attended by 10,000 young people at Loppiano, the 1975 gathering was held in Rome. This was a Holy Year, when millions of Christians made a pilgrimage to the Eternal City. The Focolare youth were no exception: 20,000 of them gathered in a sports stadium after visiting the catacombs and the sites of the deaths of the early martyrs on the preceding days. The next day, a Sunday, they gathered for Mass, which was celebrated by Pope Paul VI in St Peter's Basilica.

Apart from her reverence for the successor of Peter, no doubt Chiara, ever the teacher, had in mind the importance of example, the power of the dramatic gesture, when she went down on her knees in front of Paul VI to present the youth to him.

In the midst of the Universal Holy Year, when Rome was thronged with pilgrims and the Pope was stretched to his limits, receiving

groups of pilgrims and leading special Holy Year events on top of all
his normal duties, he took the time to write out in his own hand the
speech he would give to Chiara's young people who had come to St
Peter's Basilica that day. In a photocopy of his hand-written speech,
the Pope's enthusiasm in welcoming the Focolare youth is evident:

> Young 'Gen',
> We greet you.
> We greet you with all our heart! With a great joy!
> You are welcome in the name of Christ as children!
> As brothers and sisters!
> As friends!
> We are now at St Peter's tomb, the apostle chosen by the Lord Jesus
> as the foundation on which to build his Church, the unique and uni-
> versal gathering of the new humanity.
> For 'Gen' this is a point of arrival; it is a point of departure!
> Listen to the voice of a friend for a few moments.

And then, in a 20-minute address, the ageing Pope revealed that he
completely understood the 'Gen spirit' as he taught and encouraged
them. He recognized that they had made a fundamental choice.
While most of the world's youth around them were searching for
answers and had made a negative and rebellious choice in the rejec-
tion of the mores of society and their parents' generation, the Gen
had made a conscious choice of Christ. 'You have made another
choice, and because of this we call you Gen, a new Generation.'
Further exploring this choice with them, he continued:

> Two oceans: the divinity of Jesus Christ and Jesus Christ's mission in
> the world. Try to imagine in some way this first essential aspect of His
> Divine person, living in the infinite and transcendent nature of the
> eternal Word of God and living in the man-Jesus born of the Virgin
> Mary through the work of the Holy Spirit. Then do the same with
> the second aspect: His insertion into the cosmos, our history, our des-
> tiny, our life, our intimate conversation [Baruch 3:38].
>
> You will experience an explosion of the reasoning capacity of your
> mind, breaking into an ecstasy of wisdom, truth and mystery which
> tries to expand more and more but without reaching all the possible

dimensions in order, then, to break into love which surpasses all aspects of knowledge [Ephesians 3:18–19].

It seems to us that you Focolarini have tackled this twofold problem! Who is Christ? Who is Christ for us? And hence, the fire of light, enthusiasm, action, love, the gift of self and joy have come alive within you and, in a new fulness within, you have understood everything: God, yourself, your life, people, the times we live in, the central direction to give to the whole of your existence...

You will have to suffer with Him, like Him, for Him! But do not be afraid, Gen, be certain! You will have brought about your own salvation and that of the modern world. And like today, you will always be...good and happy.

The next large international Genfest was held in 1980 at the Flaminio sports stadium in Rome. The young people chose John Paul II as their leader and were greeted by him in St Peter's Square the next day.

In 1985 a new youth initiative was founded: Youth for a United World. It is under this arm that young people in the Focolare can co-operate with young people of the Rissho Kossei-kai movement and other groups. In October 1985, 350,000 of them signed a message for peace addressed to Ronald Reagan and Mikhail Gorbachev at the time of the Summit Meeting for Disarmament at Geneva. When the war in Lebanon reached crisis-point in 1989, Youth for a United World not only delivered appeals to the embassies around the world of countries which could intervene, but organized aid from all over the world which was distributed within the Lebanon by local members of Youth for a United World. Since the fall of the Berlin Wall in December 1989, YUW members in Western Europe have been organizing the delivery of medical and other supplies to Eastern European countries. They raise funds to set up small businesses in Eastern Europe which will create jobs, and they arrange cultural and educational exchange trips between young people from East and West.

During the world-wide television transmission of the 1995 Genfest, which was being held in Rome, the United World Fund was launched. Its aim was to establish a network uniting youth from the northern and southern hemispheres, through a sharing of goods.

The Fund was to be used particularly to provide scholarships to youth in underdeveloped countries and to form local leaders who will share a 'global mentality of unity in their own countries'. A year later, youth from around the world had already started to contribute to the United World Fund, and 40 projects were being financed in 30 countries.

The New Families Movement was founded in 1967. Among their recent projects is 'Adoption at a distance' (launched in 1990), where families undertake to support financially a child's education and development in a Third World country. These 'adoption' projects are organized by Focolarini 'on the ground' in the country concerned. As of May 1996 there were 60 such projects running in 31 different countries, involving nearly 10,000 'adoptions at a distance'. In 1996, for example, members of Focolare in Bujumbura, Burundi, reported as follows:

> In these times of terrible crisis, the 'adoption at a distance' project is like manna from heaven for many of the orphans and refugee families who fled the civil war, leaving everything behind. They had nothing left but prayer, and every night got together with their children and asked God to let them survive for another day. That's why, when they speak of the 'adoption at a distance' project they say, 'God has answered our prayers. He has come to help us.'

When possible, the organizing 'agents' on the ground travel into the interior of the country to the villages and refugee camps to meet personally all the children who have been 'adopted at a distance'. One little girl wrote from Burundi: 'Next time you have a gift for me, try to find a child who is poorer than I am, and give it to him or her...'

The New Families Movement is registered as a United Nations Non-Governmental Organization (NGO). Their second international Familyfest was held in 1993 to help launch the UN Year of the Family. The European Space Agency and other satellite bodies collaborated to link up gatherings of New Families throughout the world with each other and with the central gathering in Rome. Millions of others were able to follow the proceedings on television, thanks to the world satellite broadcast, picked up by national, regional and cable channels world-wide.

Archbishop John Foley, an American in charge of the Pontifical Council for Social Communications, told me that he considered Chiara and the Focolare to be 'truly a model for the use of the various media in and by the Church'.

Perhaps, though, Chiara could still have something to learn! Archbishop Foley has picked up one 'fault'. Whether speaking to individuals, to a group or on television, the Focolare foundress more often than not becomes quite animated in her eagerness to communicate or elaborate on her ideas. The Archbishop, who is also a 'media man', says of her: 'Technically, I would have only one complaint – that Chiara speaks too fast, although she speaks clearly.' As a non-native Italian speaker he says he sometimes has to strain to follow her every word, 'when the words literally cascade from her!'

That criticism is balanced out, though, by the Archbishop's overall impression of Chiara as 'a woman truly blessed by God with a depth, simplicity and clarity of thought and of presentation that are, in their own way, spell-binding without being in any way demagogic. There is a warmth about her presentations that is contagious, and it is evident that what she says is completely consistent with what she believes. She is authentic – and that communicates itself.'

Another branch of the Focolare Movement is for priests. From the earliest days and the vocation of Pasquale Foresi to the priesthood, there have been consecrated Focolarini who have gone on to become priests within the Movement. Their first vocation is to be a Focolarino, living a community life with their fellow Focolarini, and then to be a priest. Then there are priests already ordained in their own dioceses and working in parishes who meet the Focolare Ideal and wish to share in it. Some of them live in priests' focolares. And so with priests and brothers in religious orders. All can share in the Ideal and participate in the Movement according to their circumstances in life. Chiara clearly says that while we are in this life we need the priesthood and the sacraments, but these things will not last. In the life of Heaven all that will endure from this life will be unity and charity. Everything else will pass away. One result of her insistence on this is that there is no unhealthy clericalism in the Focolare. The priest or the minister is another Focolarino first, a minister second. The Movement produces a bi-monthly review for ministers and seminarians.

In 1982 Pope John Paul II concelebrated Mass with 7,000 priests of the Focolare Movement in the Paul VI audience hall in the Vatican. It was the largest ever such concelebration, and the Vatican newspaper reported that 'history had been made'.

Today there are over 50,000 religious sisters attached to the Movement. Again, from the very earliest days, it was often communities of religious who welcomed the message of Chiara and her first companions. It was through religious orders and congregations that the Movement was invited to other continents outside Europe.

The international secretariat at Rocca di Papa, which co-ordinates all the national and regional secretariats for Sisters from various Orders and Congregations, is led by Sister Loreto. A member of the Sisters of the Precious Blood, she has been 'lent' by her Congregation to do this work.

In April 1995 Chiara addressed a meeting of the national and regional secretariats of women religious who had gathered at the Castelgandolfo conference centre on the occasion of the twenty-fifth anniversary of the Church's recognition of their branch of the Focolare. She spoke on the theme of 'Women Religious and collective spirituality'. First of all she assured the 1,000 sisters present that apart from whatever apostolate they and their congregations were involved in – nursing or education, for example – they were valuable to the Church first of all as religious sisters. 'You are always useful because the holiness of a Sister strengthens the whole Mystical Body.'

In what Chiara said next, she reveals that half a century and more after those first companions gathered around her, she is completely sure that she is the guardian of a charism which is meant for the service of the whole Church. She said she understood that all those women present were religious sisters because they had encountered a charism – that of the founder or foundress of their Order or Congregation. They had left everything to follow that. She continued:

> But let's say that during her life a religious sister meets another charism, considered by the Church to be good, indeed excellent, to the point that she feels it is in harmony with the spiritual life she is already living.
>
> What should this sister do?

It is clear. She must adhere to this new calling with the same love with which she responded to the first.

It was clear because 'the adherence to this new spirituality, as provided for by the Movement's Statutes, has been approved by the Church Herself.'

Quoting from a talk that Pope John Paul II had given just two months previously to a group of Bishops linked with Focolare, Chiara affirmed that a spirituality of communion was a constitutive element belonging to the very nature of the Christian vocation. The Pope had said: 'A renewed proclamation of the Gospel cannot be consistent and cannot be effective if it is not accompanied by a sound spirituality of communion.'

Perhaps herein lies the answer to a worry that Archbishop John Foley, head of the Pontifical Council for the Media, raised with me when discussing Chiara and her spirituality. Often in relation to Focolare the term 'collective spirituality' is used. The Archbishop said he found Chiara's spirituality inspiring and edifying, but 'I wish it could be expressed not as "collective spirituality" but as a "spirituality of communion" or "of community".'

With the instincts of a pastor, Archbishop Foley pointed out that his objection to 'collective spirituality' was for two reasons. First, 'Each one of us is ultimately responsible individually before God for how we have used His gifts and responded to His mandates – one of which, of course, is to love others as He has loved us.' Secondly, the Archbishop pointed out that 'the Communist experience has made me, and I believe many people, suspicious of the term "collective". Also for some it could become an excuse to evade or undervalue a sense of personal responsibility.'

Chiara seems to have answered that in her address to the sisters, by stressing the Pope's insistence on a 'sound' spirituality of communion. She would be the first to emphasize that nothing can take the place of a personal prayer-relationship with God. All the community life and activities must flow from that. From her earliest talks and letters she insisted that 'time is short; soon you will have to come before your Creator to be judged.' The implication is that God will not ask you what Focolare did, but 'What did you do?'

Not for the first time in her life, Chiara drew on St Teresa of Avila to provide an example. Teresa had spoken of an 'interior castle', Chiara told the sisters. 'But the moment has come, at least it seems to us, to discover, illuminate and build, besides the "interior castle" of our own soul, also the "exterior castle".' This exterior castle she saw as the whole Movement, including the sisters of the national secretariats and in their convents.

Then, revealing her own understanding that the Movement is not an end in itself, but that it is the charism which is important, for the whole Church, she said:

This spirituality has gone beyond the structures of the Movement. Right up to persons in positions of responsibility in the Church, like the Bishops or the superiors of Religious Orders, who want to turn their Orders into an exterior castle. We can see then that this charism [of keeping Jesus in the Midst] not only makes our Movement an exterior castle, but also tends to make the entire ecclesial body an exterior castle. Thus, this spirituality can also embrace the vast world of men and women religious who, through it, make the Church more one and more holy.

I thought I had finally detected an area where Chiara was not completely in union with the thought of the Pope, when someone told me that she had spoken to the sisters about 'removing the veil'. In fact, when I read her talk through, it was clear that at one point she had spoken about the development of spiritualities – and in reference to a spirituality which stressed solitude and flight from the world, she said that the cloister and the veil had been used to reinforce this.

She did not, however, say anything about religious sisters casting off their veils. She told them that Focolarine do not wear any distinguishing habits: 'But sisters, for example, are special persons and so they must be faithful to their own way of dressing in order to do the Will of God. The Will of God is a fundamental cornerstone of the collective spirituality.' She then quoted at length a speech by John Paul II in which he spoke of the importance of the religious habit for sisters both as a reminder to themselves and the rest of the Church, and a sign to others, of their consecration. The quote was greeted by loud applause from the sisters assembled around Chiara at Rocca di Papa.

In 1976 three bishops who all knew the Focolare Movement well decided to spend some time together and help one another grow in the spirituality of unity. They spent a summer holiday together. One of them was Bishop Klaus Hemmerle of Aachen in Germany. A noted theologian, he was already a Focolare priest. After the three bishops had experienced the joy of simply living the Gospel together in the same spirit, Hemmerle asked Chiara how this experience of the Movement could be shared with other bishops. Chiara said that perhaps his question was a prompting from the Holy Spirit. She had often said that Focolare never felt as much Church as when there was a bishop or bishops present.

Chiara, Hemmerle and the Co-ordinating Council of the Movement decided to organize an encounter for bishops who were interested in the Focolare spirituality for themselves, as opposed to for their dioceses. In February 1977 twelve bishops came to Rocca di Papa. As well as the local Bishop of Frascati, the others came from Europe, Thailand, Hong Kong, Chile, Columbia and Brazil. As they wanted to do everything in unity with the successor of Peter, they informed Pope Paul VI of their meeting. He invited them into Rome and at the general audience he introduced each of them to the thousands of people present in the Nervi Audience Hall. To their surprise he told them to explain to the people what they were trying to do. The visiting bishops told the equally surprised audience that they were simply trying to live the Gospel together as bishops. Paul VI gave them a strong encouragement and blessing.

In January 1978, 23 bishops came together. They didn't see Pope Paul on that occasion but he sent them his blessing. He died later that year, on 6 August.

In an audience after the election of John Paul II, the new Pope introduced a similar group of bishops to the faithful as 'Bishops, Friends of Focolare.' Since then, the number of bishops openly associating with the Movement has grown dramatically. As the role of the bishop is to be the centre and guardian of unity for his diocese or 'local church', it is not surprising that so many of them should find help in this spirituality of unity proposed by Chiara Lubich.

There is now also a secretariat at the Centre of the Work to co-ordinate meetings of the Bishop-Friends of the Movement. The bishops, too, share in the communion of goods from their private resources, and in this way bishops from poorer regions are enabled to attend the gatherings. Every time they meet as a group, or spend a few days together, they let the Pope know and assure him of their communion with him. In 1982, Pope John Paul told a group of these bishops whom he had invited to visit him at Castelgandolfo that they should share this experience with bishops of other denominations. Chiara had expressed the same idea earlier that year. Thus, apart from the usual gathering of Catholic bishops by 'zone', region, or occasionally world-wide, there are now also annual meetings of bishops from the Catholic, Anglican, Orthodox, Armenian, Coptic, Lutheran and other churches. They have met at Istanbul, at Ottmaring and at Trent, and in November 1996 their meeting was held at the Movement's 'Centre for Unity' at Welwyn Garden City in England.

I asked Chiara why it is that these, the authorized teachers, the chief pastors in their respective churches, are eager to learn from her. She shrugged and replied, 'It's the charism.'

'What, precisely, do you mean?' I pressed.

'Well, it's the Holy Spirit, isn't it?' she said.

Following Cardinal Basil Hume and then Cardinal Martini of Milan as President of the European Bishops' Conferences of the Catholic Church, a bishop from Central and Eastern Europe was elected to that post for the first time in 1993. He is the Archbishop of Prague, Cardinal Miloslav Vlk.

Forcibly laicized by the Communist state in Czechoslovakia (even as a seminarian he had refused to join the Communist Youth Organization), he was forced to work as any other labourer. He was assigned a job as a window-cleaner in Prague – that was hard work in the cold Czech winters! But Vlk secretly continued his ministry as a priest. He was strengthened in that by the fact that he shared with many other Czech friends this Ideal proposed by Chiara Lubich, which he had first encountered in 1964.

He was forced to live in a lodging house, and the police monitored his activities. A fighter and extremely intelligent, he found ways to outwit them, and his clandestine ministry touched and strengthened thousands living in bleak times under the heavy hand of enforced Communism. He says that the simple living of the Focolare spirituality naturally allowed him to witness to the people he met.

With the 'Velvet Revolution' in the air and the Communists knowing that their days in power were numbered, Vlk was once more allowed to function as a priest. After a few months in a parish in Prague, Pope John Paul named him, in March 1991, bishop of a diocese in Bohemia. A year later he was appointed auxiliary bishop to the aged hero of the Revolution, Cardinal Tomasek of Prague. During the 'Gentle Revolution', when the Czechs had stood night after night in Wenceslas Square and rattled their keys to signify the bells tolling for the dying Communist regime, they had chanted for Vaclev Havel and Cardinal Tomasek.

After the death of Bishop Hemmerle in 1994, Cardinal Vlk, who had been appointed Archbishop of Prague, took on the role of chairing the meetings of the Bishop Friends of the Focolare Movement.

In February of 1995 a group of about 80 Bishop Friends of the Movement were meeting together at the Movement's Mariapolis Centre at Castelgandolfo, when the Pope asked them to come into Rome to visit him – accompanied by Chiara Lubich. A photograph appeared in the next day's *Osservatore Romano* (17 February 1995) of Chiara standing next to the Pope, both of them surrounded by bishops of all ages and nationalities.

At the start of the encounter, Cardinal Vlk, as spokesman for the Bishop Friends, reminded the Pope how the group of bishops associated with the Movement had begun with Bishop Klaus Hemmerle, who had died two years before. The Cardinal said that they had all experienced how the spirituality of the Focolare, with its central theme of Jesus' testament 'that they all may be one', was in complete harmony with their own episcopal charism.

The Pope first of all welcomed especially Chiara Lubich and then the 'Eminent Lord Cardinals and brothers in the Episcopate'. He went on to speak about a 'spirituality of communion' and 'the Church as icon of the Holy Trinity being a mystery of communion and sacrament of unity'.

He told them (as Chiara later quoted to the religious sisters in the Movement) that 'A renewed proclamation of the Gospel will not be coherent and effective if it is not accompanied by a strong spirituality of communion, cultivated by prayer, asceticism, and that in the context of everyday relationships.'

The Pope had once asked Vlk what it is like when the bishops are gathered to listen to Chiara. Vlk said, 'She really confirms our charism as bishops.'

'And Chiara?' asked the Pope. 'How is she with you bishops?'

'Ah, well. When she speaks to us of unity she is like our teacher, but the rest of the time it is as if she is a disciple of ours.'

On 26 May 1996, Cardinal Vlk, while on a visit to Rome, called down to Rocca di Papa to see Chiara. They were chatting things over, and Chiara wondered how this branch of 'Bishop Friends' of the Movement could be formally incorporated into the structures and statutes which have to be approved by the Church, as Bishop Hemmerle had previously requested.

Following this, the Pope invited Cardinal Vlk, Chiara and Giulia Folonari to lunch, and they were able to discuss this subject with him. At the end of lunch the Pope said that he would give his approval for the branch of Bishop Friends of the Movement. Presently the competent dicasteries of the Holy See are studying how to formulate this.

At that time there were 780 Bishop Friends of the Focolare. Since 1996, a bishop, too, can now become, like every other vocation in the Church, a part of the Focolare.

TWENTY-ONE

NEW HUMANITY – 'WHERE THERE IS NO LOVE, BRING LOVE...'

There is still another 'arm' of Focolare. Like so many of the others, it would take a book to describe fully all that it does. This one in a way embraces and interlaps with all the social initiatives by and within the Focolare Movement.

In 1959 Chiara gathered her friends who were Members of Parliament. While Giordani, De Gasperi, Montini and others were Christian Democrats, it must be remembered that her own brother, the family member she was closest to, was an ardent Communist. Chiara has never been involved in party politics but, like her brother Gino, like De Gasperi, sees politics merely as a way of serving one's people.

This meeting of politicians whom she knew gave rise to the St Catherine Centre. Its aim was to unite people involved in politics, of whatever party and whatever level. Chiara believed then, as she does now, that if people in the same line of work could put Jesus in their midst, that was the first and most important thing. All their activities born of that meeting of heart and mind would be fruitful.

The following year, a similar scheme was launched for those working in the world of health and medicine with the creation of the St Luke Centre.

And so, quite spontaneously, members of the Movement sought to bring their ideal of unity and harmony into the world of work. Those involved in trade unions sought unity between their colleagues, whether Christian Democrat or Communist, and tried to bring an atmosphere of co-operation into dealings with management and unions. (Incidentally, it was a group of Communist trade unionists in a factory in Genoa who donated the money required to lay piping to bring fresh water to the Focolare Permanent Mariapolis at Fontem in Cameroon.)

In 1968 Chiara sought to formalize this area of the Work by creating a mass movement called New Humanity. By this means people could find others in similar fields of work. Thus the world of health and medicine could see doctors, nurses, porters, cleaners and receptionists all meeting together once in a while in their own work-place to see how they could better serve their patients and colleagues.

Those in the world of the arts can be in touch and collaborate with one another, exploring and sharing ways of putting their spirituality of unity into practice. One consecrated Focolarina, Lilliana Cosi, is a professional ballet dancer who has danced with Nureyev. She was for many years a prima ballerina of the Scala at Milan and also danced for years as prima ballerina with the Bolshoi Ballet, the first Italian to do so after a gap of some 70 years. Lilliana sees her work as an extension of her prayer.

Anne Devine, an artist from Glasgow in Scotland, says that through the experience of mutual love encountered in the Focolare spirituality and in New Humanity, she has 'rediscovered the role of an artist. I no longer see it as an indulgence but as a service to the wider community.' On a more direct level she says that her paintings are influenced not only by her own life experience and journeys through different lands, but even by writings of Igino Giordani and Chiara Lubich. Of her paintings with a religious theme, she says, 'My painting, *Pieta*, and all the images of Mary which have come into my work, are directly influenced by the writings of Chiara on Mary Desolate.'

Michel Pochet, a writer and artist, put his love of art to one side to concentrate on being responsible for the Focolare Movement in Belgium. After doing this for 20 years, he is now based at the Centre of the Work in Rocca di Papa and devotes his time to keeping in touch with the many people associated with the Movement in one way or another who are also professional artists. Chiara's vision of a 'new art' is already seen in the work coming out of the various studios and workshops of the Movement's little town of Loppiano.

At the first international congress of New Humanity in 1983, held in a sports stadium in Rome, Chiara told the Pope, who had come to it, that the lay people who formed New Humanity wanted to give a Christian soul to the world of work.

Reviewing that event on video, it is remarkable how relaxed and at ease the Pope is at this international gathering. While Chiara made her presentation, he did not sit on a throne or place of honour, but simply in the front row of the audience. Chiara assured him of how happy they were to welcome him and of how they could have no better confirmation than having Jesus among them in the person of his Vicar the Pope.

John Paul II only mounted the stage when it was his turn to speak. His teaching was met with the usual enthusiasm and applause, and at the end Chiara stepped forward to the front of the stage to say something to him. Rather than have her craning up to him from the floor of the auditorium, he jumped off the front of the stage and stood with Chiara on the same level. The photographers went wild, and as their flash-guns went off all around, the Pope was happy to pose for photographs with Chiara.

The international New Humanity was recognized as an NGO by the United Nations in 1987 and in Italy as an NGO by the Italian Government in 1988.

An example of how New Humanity works on a practical everyday level is provided by some English members. They are all involved in the world of health. One, a nurse, remarked to a colleague also involved in health-care and with whom she met once a week, that she was saddened by the waste she saw in her hospital. The hospital was being refurbished and old beds and equipment were being thrown out. They decided that there was nothing to be lost by approaching the authorities. These same were happy to give permission to the two women to collect equipment that was destined for the scrapheap and send it to hospitals in Eastern Europe and Africa.

In early 1996 it was announced that the United Nations would declare 1999 the 'Year of the Elderly' and would organize a world conference on 'A Society for Every Age'. New Humanity decided that they would hold their own international conference in 1997 on 'A role for the elderly in a United World'. Its findings would form their submission to the later UN conference.

Vera Arujo, the Brazilian sociologist who has worked closely with Chiara in developing the Economy of Communion, says: 'Today we have to deal with a new form of poverty – structural, organized poverty. The answer is solidarity.' That could be taken as a concise summary of what New Humanity is all about: the application of the charism given to Chiara Lubich to change hearts and through the promotion of unity-solidarity, to change structures.

On 6 August 1978, the Supreme Pontiff, Paul VI, died at his summer residence of Castlegandolfo. A great friend of Focolare had passed from this life. He was the one who as Monsignor Montini of the Secretariat of State had welcomed Giulia Folonari into his office to hear why she had left home and family to join this young movement. It was he who had reassured Chiara and her companions when the Church had to carry out its enquiries into Focolare that this would provide a protection and assurance for the Movement in the longer term. He was right.

As Pope, he had encouraged Chiara and worked with her on the enlargement of the Statutes. He had been served by her in his desire for ever-closer communion with the Orthodox East in the person of Patriarch Athenagoras. When Paul died, the Focolare published a book of all his talks and teachings given to the different branches of the Movement. Chiara had a place of honour among the Cardinals and Heads of State at his funeral in St Peter's Square.

His elected successor was the smiling and diminutive Archbishop of Venice, known as John Paul I. He had known and encouraged the Focolare in his own diocese. He was a friend. But his reign was so short that there had not been time for any direct contact with him as Pope.

The second Conclave of 1978 produced a shock for the Italians, most of whom had never heard of the Polish Cardinal Wojtyla. He was certainly not one whom the media had picked out as likely to be elected. Despite the shock, he soon won over the hearts of the people when he appeared on the balcony of St Peter's and told them he came from 'a far country'. Some Italians, though, knew all about him. They had even worked with him in his own diocese of Cracow in Poland.

This Pope was in no hurry to unlock the Conclave doors and send his electors back out into the streets of Rome. The Conclave structures stayed in place and first of all he arranged a dinner for the College of Cardinals. Gordon Thomas and Max Morgan-Witts in their book *Pontiff* describe how the new Polish Pope personally went around all the tables serving the Cardinals. He even led the sing-song, and was persuaded to give a couple of solos. Tears streamed

down the face of the ageing Primate of Poland, who had so gallant-
ly resisted both the Nazis and then the Communists. Cardinal
Wyszynski now saw his protégé elected to the See of Peter.

While the doors of the Apostolic Palace remained closed and
the Cardinals inside prepared to enthrone the new Pope, who
chose to be known as the 'Servant of the servants of God', his private secretary made a direct telephone call to Rocca di Papa. He
knew Anna Fratta was at the Centre of the Work, visiting from
Poland. He said: 'The Cardinal – er – His Holiness – would very
much like to meet Miss Lubich. Could you both be here at seven
o'clock tomorrow morning?'

The new Pope, before he had even been enthroned, had invited
Chiara and Anna Fratta to his private Mass in the chapel of the Papal
apartments. As she and Chiara made their way through all the temporary structures put in place to house the Conclave and locked
doors were opened for them, Anna remembered that it was only five
months since she had welcomed the Archbishop to the summer
Mariapolis she had organized outside Cracow.

After Mass, with a thousand duties awaiting him and dignitaries
from around the world arriving for his enthronement, Papa Wojtyla
stood and chatted to Anna and Chiara. He had long wanted to meet
Miss Lubich, he said, and was delighted to do so now. For one of the
first times in his reign, he conferred the Apostolic Blessing.

The two contemporaries have worked closely together ever since.
He no longer calls her 'Signorina Lubich' but 'Chiara', and in his letters from the Apostolic Palace the early formal style of address, 'To
Signorina Chiara Lubich, President of the Focolare Movement', has
given way to the respectful but informal 'Dear Signorina Chiara'.

When he looks at Chiara on occasions such as listening to her
speech at the New Humanity congress in 1983, his regard reveals
the great respect in which he so obviously holds her. Informally,
such as when she visits him in the Vatican or he visits a Focolare
Centre, his gentle embracing of her face with both hands – as he
does with Mother Teresa – betrays the paternal affection which he
feels for her.

Since it had been built in the early 1960s the Centre of the Work
at Rocca di Papa had been used for international meetings of the
Co-ordinating Council and branches of the Movement. For larger

congresses, the Movement had, and still does, hire a sports arena such as the Flaminio or Palaeur stadia in the suburbs of Rome.

Quite simply, the Centre of the Work was becoming too small to host the larger 'internal' meetings of the Movement. Already, on the administrative side alone, there is no longer enough office space there. Flats, apartments and houses are rented in and around Rocca di Papa just to house the secretariat for New Families, for instance, or the international secretariat for the religious sisters in the Movement. In the Centre itself there is an auditorium, but it only holds between 300 and 400 people. Already at the monthly telephone link-ups with Chiara, it is packed to bursting point with the collaborators who work in the Centre or the other secretariats round about. They just cannot all fit in.

The Pope, in his regular meetings with Chiara about the progress of the Movement, knew of this situation. On the Eve of the Feast of St Nicholas, 5 December 1982, Chiara received a phone call from the Vatican. The Audience Hall on the Papal Estate at Castelgandolfo was being put at the disposal of the Focolare.

Commissioned by Pope Pius XII to receive the increasing numbers of pilgrims who were making their way out even to Castelgandolfo when the Pope spent the summer there, the hall had become less and less suitable during the reign of John Paul II. First, the numbers trekking out to see him at Castelgandolfo were increasing, so that he would have to address them in the open air from a balcony of the Papal palace.

Rather than having summer pilgrims all bussing out to the lakeside village, he decided to take the helicopter back in to St Peter's when there were large audiences to be held in the summer. For his traditional Sunday recitation of the Angelus, he would meet with pilgrims in the courtyard at Castelgandolfo.

Chiara deputed Nunzi Cilento, a Roman herself, who had managed the Centre of the Work for 25 years, to take charge of the new Focolare centre at Castelgandolfo. It would become their international Mariapolis centre and would be used for meetings of up to just over 2,000 people. Nunzi oversaw the conversion of the single-storey audience hall into a three-storey complex including auditoria, meeting rooms, sleeping accommodation, cafeteria, chapel, shop and exhibition area.

All this conversion work cost millions of pounds. Chiara launched Operation Brick, and the members of the Movement 'taxed' themselves by contributing around five dollars per month. Within a couple of years everything was paid for, with no debts.

When the Pope is in residence 'next door' in the Papal palace, he often invites members of the Movement 'up to his house'. Sometimes there will be a concert being performed by a visiting orchestra or ensemble and, again, he will invite Focolarini from the international Mariapolis centre up to join him.

Or sometimes he will invite himself down to the Mariapolis centre. Nunzi explains that there is a 'hot line', a direct telephone link on the internal phone system with the Pope's office. Thus, for example, during the Christmas holidays in 1986, Nunzi received a call from the Pope's private secretary, Mgr Dziwisz, saying, 'We're coming down.' The Pope, wearing a comfortable cardigan over his usual immaculate white cassock, strolled through his garden and out through a door in the garden wall into the grounds of the Mariapolis centre.

Nunzi remembers that work was being done in the chapel at that time. The marble floor was about to be laid, so the floor was covered in rubble and plaster. The Pope wanted to visit the chapel. Spotless cassock or not, the presence of Jesus-Eucharist was there in the tabernacle, and the Pope immediately fell to his knees on the floor.

Before he left, John Paul told the delighted Focolarini who had received him that one could in fact consider the house of the Holy Family at Nazareth as the first Mariapolis. 'In that house,' he said, 'the principal mystery is certainly Christ, but he is given to us through an intermediary, the woman; this woman spoken of in Genesis and in the Apocalypse, a woman become a historical personality in the person of the Virgin Mary. I think that is part of the very nature of what you call Mariapolis: to make Mary present, to put her presence in relief as God Himself did in the night of Bethlehem and during 30 years spent in Nazareth.'

On 19 August 1984 the Pope spent an afternoon at the Centre of the Work of Mary. He certainly appeared to feel quite at home. As he and Mgr Dziwisz met with members of the Movement's Central Co-ordinating Council, the mood was respectful but certainly informal. The Holy Father sat on a slightly raised dais, the Council in semi-circular rows around him, with Chiara to the Holy Father's right, her own and the Pope's private secretaries just behind her. It was noticeable that the Focolare priests on the Council wore clerical dress for the occasion, something most of them normally don't do, with special permission, except at official Church functions.

After an overview of the Movement with Chiara and the Central Co-ordinating Council, a wider meeting took place with the hundreds of other people who are based at the Centre of the Work and others who had come to Italy from various countries for the occasion. Finally a short concert was laid on for the Pope.

Before taking his leave, Pope John Paul gave a short impromptu talk, which was recorded and then published in *L'Osservatore Romano* three days later. He said:

> During the different parts of our meeting, I've made many reflections. I will now try to sum up everything in a statement and in a wish. The statement touches on the central nucleus of your Movement, which is love. Definitely love is the start, the beginning of many institutions and structures of all the apostolate, of all the religious families. Love is rich. It bears in itself different potentialities, and it spreads in human hearts the different charisms. With this meeting I've been able to get a little closer to what forms the charism proper of your Movement; or I could say in a different way, I've been able to get closer to understanding better how love – which is the gift of the Holy Spirit and which He has poured into hearts, His greatest virtue – how love constitutes the most excellent way, the principal animation of your Movement. It is good that you have found such a way, this vocation of love…
>
> There have been in the history of the Church many radicalisms of love, almost all contained in the supreme radicalism of Christ Jesus. There's been the radicalism of St Francis, of St Ignatius of Loyola, of Charles de Foucauld and many others up to our days. There's also your radicalism of love, the radicalism of love of Chiara of the Focolarini: a radicalism which discovers the depth of love, and its simplicity, and discovers all the demands of love in different situations, and seeks to make this love always conquer in every circumstance…

A little later, the Pope expressed this wish for the Focolare:

> I wish that you continue along this same road. You already have a very clear direction, a profoundly marked characteristic, a charism in the richness of love which has its source in God Himself, in the Holy Spirit. You have already found your field, your dwelling. My wish for you is that you should develop always more and more this reality, which is proper to your vocation, and bring to the world today, which has great need of it, love, and through love, to bring God. This is my wish.

Having stated his wish, it wasn't enough. It seems the Holy Father, Pope John Paul II, wanted to express as much as he could his appreciation for, and blessing of, the Focolare way. He went on, as is completely natural to him in all his dealings, to commend the Work to the intercession of Mary. That in turn led him to speak of Focolare's role both in the Church and in the world. He continued:

> I entrust you in a special way to the Most Holy Virgin, to the Mother of Christ and of the Church, our Mother, the Mother of the Apostles, the Mother of every Mariapolis in the world. I entrust you to her, because she more than all men, knew how to live love, the radicalism of love, in the most simple, marvellous and absolutely original way. You have been fascinated by the Virgin, by her holiness, by that love that pulsates in her heart and you want to imitate her.
>
> My wish for you is that you obtain this always more and more. Indeed my wish for you is that you draw closer through Mary to Jesus, who has shown us that God is love, and to the Holy Spirit who is the operator of love in our hearts, thanks to the cross and resurrection of Jesus.
>
> I thank you once again for having received me in your home, in your family. I want to extend these wishes to all the Focolarini of the world, because you are very closely bound together and you try to form a big Christian, evangelical, family in all the world.
>
> I want to commend myself to this family and I must thank you for your apostolate, because I am here as the successor of Peter concerned about the apostolate of the Church. I am convinced, indeed I see, I experience what aspect of the apostolate of the contemporary Church is properly yours. I wish you to be a leaven in the mass of mankind,

and of the people of God. I wish that you may be an evangelical leaven in the Church, which has recognized its dimension with the Second Vatican Council in the Constitution *Lumen Gentium* and in the pastoral constitution *Gaudiem et Spes*. I see that you mean to follow authentically that vision of the Church, that self-definition that the Church gave of itself in the Second Vatican Council.

This is how I see your contacts, which are very fruitful in the ecumenical dimension; with our brothers who are not Christians, who possess their religious riches – as I have been able to appreciate, for example, during my short visit to Korea and in Thailand – and then the contacts with the secularized world, with non-believers, with atheists and agnostics.

Everywhere it is the Church, and as St John of the Cross said: 'Where there is not love, bring love, and there you will find love.' I think that can be applied very well to your apostolate in all environments, not only in those of the Church, of its Catholic body, but also in its ecumenical dimensions, and in contacts of dialogue with non-Christians, with non-believers. Love opens the road. My wish is that this road, thanks to you, may always be more open for the Church.

After imparting his Apostolic Blessing, the Pope added a final word: 'So I say to you as God the Creator said on the day of the creation of man, of man and woman: "Increase and multiply." '

TWENTY-TWO

THE 'FEMININE GENIUS'
– THE WORK OF A WOMAN

Six years after that 1984 visit of Pope John Paul to the Centre of the Work of the Focolare, definitive statutes of the Work were approved by the Holy See on 29 June 1990, the Feast of Saints Peter and Paul. They were presented to Chiara in her role of Foundress and President by the President of the Pontifical Council for the Laity, Cardinal Pironio, who retired in 1996.

Just before that final approval was granted by John Paul II, Chiara was visiting him one day to discuss the final format. She somewhat hesitantly raised the proposition which had been put to her by many members of the Movement, including the 60-strong Central Co-ordinating Council – that the President of the Work of Mary should always be a woman.

She was bowled over by the Pope's response. 'It is not a question that the Work of Mary *may* always have a woman President, Chiara,' he told her, 'but that the President *must* always be a woman!'

The Holy Father went on to explain to her an idea often raised in recent times by one of the great theologians of this century, Hans Urs Von Balthasar. It was the 'Marian Profile' of the Church. He outlined to her how the Church has traditionally been seen to have a Petrine profile, a Pauline profile and a Johanine profile. He was convinced of the importance of the Marian profile.

In fact, Henri de Lubac (whom John Paul raised to the Cardinalate) had done much work on this aspect of ecclesiology and Von Balthasar had done a lot to bring all the research on the aspects of the Church's profiles together. He would claim that they were all eminently biblical and that the richness of each of the aspects or profiles of the Church were interdependent.

Briefly, the 'Petrine Profile' represents the Apostolic layer of the Church. There has been an historical transmission through the ages of the Faith and means of sanctification. This the Church passes on in her Creeds and Sacramental life. The Apostolic office of Peter and the apostles/pastors has responsiblities. They are to sanctify, to teach and to guide or govern. This task (which the Second Vatican Council defined as both 'gift' and 'task') represents also the priestly, prophetical and royal roles of Christ the great High Priest. The Petrine profile of the Church is an irreducible layer but not the only one. Because it was the very one most at issue in the Protestant Reformation, the Catholic counter-reformers laid great stress on defending it. This, perhaps, led to an overemphasis on the Petrine profile of the Church.

The *Pauline aspect* of the Church starts out, not surprisingly, in the Apostle Paul who highlights in his letters the *dynamic* layer of the Church. Paul's own conversion experience through a dramatic intervention from on high on his way to Damascus is the very key to understanding this layer of the Church. It illustrates that the Risen Lord may intervene at any time in His Church. The Church is His Body. ('Saul, Saul, why are you persecuting *me*?') Christians are therefore living members of His Body. He is its Head and from whom the Body draws its life. The Head of the Church blesses His Body with charisms, conversions and commission. Particular charisms are witnessed in such characters as Benedict in the fifth/sixth centuries, a Francis and a Dominic in the tenth and eleventh centuries or an Ignatius of Loyola in the sixteenth century. A charism is for the good of the whole Church, but there must be a recipient of it. Great and dramatic conversions are witnessed throughout the life of the Church from Paul himself to Augustine or Ignatius in the past, right up to such figures as Charles de Foucauld or Matt Talbot in our own day. Of course, apart from the dramatic and extraordinary, there are the daily conversions of a sincere Christian. The Church, too, lives with a commission which is constantly exercised both within and without its own Body – external evangelization as witnessed in a Paul or a Francis Xavier as well as within the Church as seen in a Thérèse of Lisieux or a Charles de Foucauld.

The Pauline aspect of the Church is in the care of the Petrine as seen already in St Paul's Second Letter to the Corinthians.

The *Johanine profile* represents the Church as Communion; Divine/human communion. The Life of communion of the Holy Trinity is brought to earth by one of the Persons of the Trinity – the Word of God. He communicates the life of His Homeland as seen, for example, in his great last priestly prayer in John 17: 'Father, may they all be one in me as I am in you...'

Under the Johanine aspect, the Church is understood as a Communion of Life. The supreme law of the Church is the New Commandment of Jesus. The opening verses of St John's First Letter (1 John 1:1–4) sum up this vision of the Church: 'What we have seen and heard we announce to you also, so that you will join with us in the fellowship that we have with the Father and with His Son Jesus Christ. We write this in order that our joy may be complete.' This represents the praying form of the Church which should be a community built on faith, hope and charity. In brief, the Johanine profile of the Church is seen to represent the Communion between God and humanity, and within all of humanity itself. The Second Vatican Council highlighted this aspect of the Church's own identity in the fourth chapter of its document, *Lumen Gentium*.

Now these three profiles are all seen to be contained in the Marian profile of the Church. This is a layer of the Church of which Mary the Mother of Jesus is the real symbol. The Church, according to Scripture, is the Bride of Christ and a bride that is fruitful; that is, is mother, mother of many children. So the Church is seen as, and is ever called to be, the faithful Bride of Christ the Bridegroom. This symbol represents closeness and fidelity to Christ – which leads to fruitfulness.

Mary, and the Marian profile of the Church, symbolize the body which must receive all *in order to give* all. Mary receives the Son of God in order to give that Son away to all Humanity. It is the same with the Church. She receives the means of grace, the Word of God, the Sacraments, etc., in order precisely to pass on or give them away.

Just as Mary was present at the birth of the Church at Pentecost, yet did not claim the priestly offices for herself, but nurtured them in the Apostles, so the other profiles of the Church are contained in the Marian profile of the Church herself. This is an irreducible aspect of the Church which was also highlighted by the Second Vatican Council.

In a talk to the Roman Curia in December 1987, the Pope had declared the Marian profile of the Church to be 'just as fundamental and characteristic as the apostolic and Petrine profile, if not more so'. Indeed, this Pope, who had broken all the conventions of heraldry with his insistence that the large initial 'M' for Mary should stand alongside the Cross on his blazen, and his chosen motto of *totus tuus* signifying his own dedication to the Virgin Mary, went further. He asserted to the assembled Curia that 'the Marian dimension of the Church precedes the Petrine, while being closely bound and complementary to it.'

Chiara says of him: 'The *totus tuus* which the Pope addresses to Mary is not a mere figure of speech for him, it's the code by which he lives. It explains his Marian personality, his greatness, his human sensitivity. It elevates him and at the same time brings him to the level of all, a man among many, a genuine "servant of the servants of God", with an awareness of his own Petrine charism and free of all trace of clericalism.'

On 15 August 1988 Pope John Paul published his encyclical letter *Mulieris Dignitatem* ('On the Dignity of Women'). Chiara later hailed it by saying, 'Apart from the Gospel, no other document throughout history has done as much to celebrate women's dignity.'

It was the Pope's letter on women which first made me interested in interviewing Chiara Lubich as the female head of the largest lay movement in the Church, and one which while being primarily lay, also included priests, nuns and religious. My initial approach was sympathetically heard, although granting an interview to me was not a priority in Chiara's schedule at that time! Her secretary, Giulia Folonari, told me to keep in touch, and when Chiara was going to be in one place for more than a few days, something would be arranged.

At the end of June 1992 a 'Supercongress' of Youth for a United World was held. More than 6,000 boys and girls of the Movement gathered in Rome were linked up by satellite to similar groups gathered in major cities throughout the world. Chiara dashed back from an overseas trip to be there.

The problem was that it took place immediately after an extremely gruelling extended tour of the Movement in Africa. Chiara's health collapsed. The extreme fatigue had a serious effect on her heart condition – like her father and her brother Gino, she has an irregular heartbeat. This did not usually occasion any problem for the fit and extremely active septuagenarian, but now the years of unstinting self-giving took their toll.

Chiara's doctor advised a long period of uninterrupted rest in the Swiss Alps to allow her to regain complete health. At the beginning of July, she left as usual for Switzerland. During her extended stay there she continued to follow the progress of the Movement.

The following year, on 4 September 1993, her beloved older brother Gino died. Her doctor did not give Chiara permission to interrupt her own convalescence, and so she was unable to attend the burial of her brother in the family plot where her parents are also buried. Luigia Lubich had died on the Feast of the Motherhood of Mary, 11 October 1983.

Chiara was back in Rome, however, in time to celebrate the fiftieth 'birthday' of the Focolare on 7 December 1993. On the occasion of the fiftieth anniversary of her spiritual experience in the 'little house' at Loreto, in 1989, she had made a pilgrimage of thanksgiving with a whole group of her first companions.

The period of Chiara's extended stay in Switzerland was a trying time for members of the Movement who, naturally, were worried about her. She prefers not to speak about her health, partly because she never wants the focus on herself. As far as the well-being of the Movement was concerned, she had no worry, being reassured since the Statutes approved by the Church had made provision for a Central Co-ordinating Council on which were represented all the branches and aspects of the Work, including the permanent Mariapoli. Elections are held to this Council every six years.

While Chiara has a great admiration for Pope John Paul II not only as Vicar of Christ but as a priest and as a person (she admires his 'Marian personality'), it is obvious that the Pope in turn appreciates the contribution to the Church in the twentieth century which this working-class woman from Trent has made.

When she was convalescing in Switzerland, the Pope once received a large group of Focolarini in audience in the courtyard at the Papal residence at Castelgandolfo. 'Where's Chiara?' he asked publicly. 'Let's pray she'll be here the next time I meet you,' he added.

And it was only years later, when she had fully recovered and was back in full swing at the helm of the Movement, that Chiara learned from some of her closest collaborators that Sister Lucia of Fatima had also been kept aware of her condition. She had sent a message saying that Chiara needed to take this time to rest and get completely well again, because her work was important and there was a lot more for her to do! Her schedule since she took up the reins again proves the truth of Sister Lucia's observation.

When I once asked Chiara about holidays and even retiring, she found the idea hilarious. I asked her if she were not concerned about her first companions, who are still in harness and travelling around the world visiting and encouraging the Movement in the different continents. Didn't they at least deserve to retire and live a quiet life? Further laughter from her and Giulia!

'No,' said Chiara. 'This is what keeps them so young! With us, it's a bit like the Pope – the concept of retirement doesn't exist!'

Quizzing Giulia separately one time, I asked her if she had annual holidays. Did she get away and spend time with her family in her native North Italy? She looked at me as if I were a man who had lost his reason. 'What? Are you crazy?' her eyes seemed to say. 'Why should I want to miss out on a single day spent in the Focolare and with Chiara?'

What is it about this woman that inspired, and still inspires, countless young people to give up home and family to follow Christ in this way, within this Work of Mary? How is it that hundreds of thousands of men are happy to be part of a work led by a woman?

Gorgio Marchetti is head of the section of men Focolarini. He is trained as a medical doctor, a psychiatrist and a Catholic priest. He says that the men more than the women cherish this privilege of always having a woman as head of the Movement. 'Precisely because we are the Work of Mary,' he explains. 'The most important thing for us is that we all be and live as Christians. This is the first and most fundamental thing. It comes before the question of hierarchy and organization. Von Balthasar's idea of the emerging Marian profile of the Church is confirmed for us men by life in the Work of Mary. Our Statutes say we are, and are always to be, "a presence of Mary in the Church".'

Von Balthasar, confidant and biographer of the Swiss mystic Adrienne von Speyr, recognized some similarity between Chiara's spirituality of Jesus Forsaken and some of the writings of von Speyr. Before he died he had on several occasions asked to meet Chiara to explore this. They never managed to meet. He, who had once said that among the greatest needs of our time was for 'theology on its knees', would surely have appreciated an exchange with the woman who as a girl literally studied philosophy on her knees and whose 'Abba School' aims to reconcile the disciplines of philosophy and theology.

Von Balthasar, one of the great Mariologists of our times, also took a keen interest in the 'ecclesial movements'. In his book *A First Glance at Adrienne von Speyr*, he wrote: 'Charisms are not distributed at random but are dispensed by God to supply what is needful and lacking in His Church at each historical moment. If they are from God they usually do not flow with the latest fashionable trend, but much more likely contain an antidote and remedy for perils of the time.'

Reading this reminded me of Chiara's response when I once questioned her unfailing loyalty to the Pope and the bishops in the light of her understanding of 'He who hears you, hears me.' 'It may not be fashionable,' she said, 'but it is the truth.'

Going even further, she attributes the growth and spread of the Focolare to their obedience to the Bishops. 'The first reason is our unity with the Church's hierarchy,' she says. 'The second reason is unity among ourselves in Christ's name.'

While it is becoming fashionable in some quarters to campaign for a female priesthood in the Catholic Church, in the way that women have recently been admitted to the ministry of the Church of England, Chiara will have none of it. Any attempt to get her to see such a claim as legitimate is a non-starter.

'For a start,' she says, 'we know that even were the presbyterate conferred on women, it would not be valid. Such a grace of ordination just does not adhere to a woman. Christ himself chose a male priesthood.

'It's true that Jesus did not speak on this subject, but He gave an incomparable model to female humanity, the one to whom all the great Christian women in history have looked, and that person is Mary, His Mother. Every woman who truly wants to serve the Church can recognize her calling by looking at Mary.'

And recognizing this calling is fundamental to Chiara's thought. What is important is to be a Christian, a follower of Christ, to live his commands, including the law of love and His last prayer for unity. This is the common vocation to be discovered and lived by all Christians. Priesthood, hierarchy, is a further calling to service for the sake of the Church within that basic calling. Thus the Focolare insists that the first vocation of its members is to be Focolarini. Those men who feel a call to priesthood have that discerned in the context of their first vocation as Focolarini. In short, priesthood is not somehow a 'highest vocation' to which one should aspire.

'The most important thing is love,' says Chiara. 'We know it well. You do not go to Heaven because you are a priest or a bishop. You go there because you have loved. While priests and bishops are the pillars on which Christ has placed his Church, they can also find themselves in Hell. In that place you will not find either women or men who have loved.'

With this 'Marian Pope' and with his encyclical 'On the Dignity of Women', Chiara believes the Church has come a long way in its understanding of the role of women. In early 1996 she said:

I believe this is a privileged moment for women in the Church. To be honest, though, it was Jesus Himself who gave women back their dignity and their specific role in the plan of redemption that He had fulfilled. Going against the customs of His time, He had a unique and original relationship with women. The Pope stresses this fact in certain passages of *Mulieris Dignitatem* which form the most beautiful and fascinating pages of that encyclical.

In the Early Church, then, Mary and women are present in the Cenacle together with the disciples awaiting the Holy Spirit. Throughout the whole life of the Church, women have worked often in a silent yet effective way.

Today we need to understand all over again the specific talent of women in light of the times we are living in. In the Church, according to our Faith, women are not called to the ministerial priesthood. It is exactly because they are not called to the ministerial priesthood that women can ensure that the royal priesthood shines forth in the Church and in the world, actualizing the gift of the Holy Spirit received at Baptism.

At an Angelus address on 3 September 1995, John Paul II said, 'Who can imagine the new beauty that the countenance of the

Church will assume when the feminine genius will be involved in the various areas of its life?'

'The feminine genius': it would appear that it is in this sense that John Paul has recognized the Work of Mary and the charism of Chiara Lubich. As Von Balthasar wrote, charisms distributed by God usually contain an antidote and remedy for the ills of our time. Perhaps one of the greatest signs of the twentieth century has been the struggle or yearning for women to redefine their role in society as well as in the Church. For Chiara it is quite clear:

> Christ alone fulfils the needs and hopes of women living today and the women of the future. Only at 'his school' will they be able to learn that love that gives fulness to their being. It will be Christ, therefore, who will open new avenues to women, not only through His Church but through the thousands and thousands of ways that He alone knows.
>
> The promotion of the dignity of women will then be beneficial to men, too. If women are not given the right place, men are not given it either. It is in the harmony of their respective tasks and roles that the secret to a development of history in the sense willed by God lies.

While Christ alone is seen as the fulfilment of the needs and hopes of people today and in every age, Chiara has never had any doubt that the model for women is Mary the mother of Jesus:

> Mary is *the* answer to woman. The reason is simple, yet unfathomable. Love is Mary's greatness. If God clothed her with extraordinary gifts, as the mother of His Son, she responded to this predilection with a total 'yes' which is a complete expression of her love. She thus welcomed in her womb Love made flesh, she then became the first disciple of Jesus, the perfect Christian, because she did not live her own life. She let God's Word live in her.
>
> Mary is the Word of God put into practice. Nobody can say like Mary: 'It is no longer I, but Christ that lives in me' [Galatians 2:20].

And as the Focolare has been a lay Movement right from the very start, Chiara of the Focolarini is quite clear that Mary is a model for all lay people in the Church. She says:

> The sanctity of Mary is the sanctity of the laity. We don't say of Mary that she practised certain forms of penance, or had particular attitudes. Her life unfolded first in the privacy of her home and of her village, and then she followed Jesus, participating actively in the proclamation and fulfilment of redemption. It is said in the Gospel that she was docile to the plans and to the will of God. In this lies her sanctity, a way to sanctity which is good for all.

'When the Tongues of Flame Are In-folded'
– New Heavens and New Earths

'A way of sanctity which is good for all...' Perhaps in those words which Chiara used to describe taking Mary as model there is an apt description of how she would see her own Movement. From her earliest days, as witnessed in her letters, she was anxious to prepare her friends for the moment when they, as well as she herself, would come face to face with God.

While she does not like anybody considering her as a mother – as she sees herself as a sister of all – it is clear that Chiara has maternal feelings towards at least the younger generations of the Movement. After participating in one of the Movement's monthly world-wide telephone link-ups, I asked Chiara how she felt as President when on such occasions thousands of members of the Movement are all linked up to the Centre of the Work and she is there in the centre, the focus for everyone.

She said what she felt in those moments was just what she felt when she was with me or with anyone else. And you believe her. Because she does honestly accept and love each individual she meets. But I persisted. Surely she must feel a bit like a mother?

'Oh, of course,' she confessed. 'But that's something different.'

Was this the gift she had once said she had received from her perpetual consecration to virginity?

'Yes, that's it. It's a consequence of a *true* virginity. Because virginity has no value in itself if it is not for the Kingdom of Heaven, if it's not for this maternity. This is being like Mary. Mary had virginity in order to be mother.'

This maternal instinct is betrayed in her concern not only for the well-being of all the members of the Movement in all the practical details, but above all – as she learned from her own mother's example of teaching her children to pray – for the things that ultimately matter for all eternity. She wants sanctity for all the Focolarini, for all members of the Movement, and ultimately for all people.

When speaking about Igino Giordani one day, whom she refers to as a 'co-founder', I was aware that she really considers him as one of the great lay personalities of the Church in our time. I asked if she expected him to be made a saint one day. She said she hoped so. Was there a Cause for Beatification under way, then?

No, she said, they hadn't started on that path yet. But the study centre on Igino Giordani continues to collate material about and by him, all with a view to preparing an eventual definitive biography, which is an essential part of the process leading to Beatification.

In many organizations, both religious and lay, in the Church, there is almost a race to promote Causes. Did the Focolare not have any Causes at all under way, then?

'No, we don't have any yet,' said Chiara. 'We will have many. There will be many people who are already dead, who died in a state of holiness because this spirituality makes little saints. But we've never done anything about promoting Causes. In the future, when they've nothing else to do, they can think about making saints.'

And what does it mean to be a saint?

Without hesitation Chiara replies, 'To be Jesus, to be another Jesus, another Mary.'

We have consistently seen how Chiara does not like the limelight being shone on her. When it is unavoidable as part of her work for the Movement and in obedience to her superiors, she overcomes her natural inclinations and graciously accepts being the centre of attention. But she will never lose an opportunity either. In such moments she will take the occasion to speak about the things of God and encourage her listeners.

Despite the Movement being over 50 years old now, or perhaps only 50 years young, interest in Chiara in both religious and secular media has not diminished. Quite the contrary. While I was with her in August 1996 a fax arrived from the United Nations Educational, Scientific and Cultural Organization (UNESCO) stating that the Organization's international jury had decided to award her its 1996 UNESCO Education for Peace Prize. It cited her work as Foundress and President of the Focolare Movement, 'in building peace and unity between persons, generations, social categories and peoples, thanks to the personal participation of all these categories: children, young people and adults, rich and poor, believers of all religions as well as atheists.'

Whereas in Britain this news received only a couple of paragraphs in the Catholic press, in many countries throughout the world it was headline news, both in print and broadcast media.

In 1995 a renowned Italian theologian and Mariologist, Stefano De Fiores, published a book in the *Christian Spirituality* series entitled *La 'Nuova' Spiritualita (The 'New' Spirituality)*. A Doctor in Spiritual Theology lecturing in Systematic Mariology and Marian Spirituality at the Pontifical Gregorian University, he outlined a 'Spirituality of Vatican II' and post-conciliar developments in spirituality. Among the texts reproduced as examples in his book were some by Adrienne von Speyr, Hans-Urs Von Balthasar, Martin Luther King, Pope John XXIII, Karl Rahner, Olivier Clement and Pope John Paul II. There among those twentieth-century 'greats' he cited Chiara Lubich. And to boot, he used two of her texts alongside one from everyone else!

In March 1996 another book was launched amidst much publicity in Rome. Written by two respected Italian authors, *When the Church is Woman: Feminine Stories of Faith* recounted the faith stories of 13 well-known Italian women, from famous nuns to Angela Buttiglione, the television journalist. Each chapter heading was accompanied by a revealing statement by the personality involved. One read: 'If the Pope and the Church do not take account of our opinion, if they don't accept our terms, the Church will be the loser.'

Heading up this list of 13 famous Italian women was Chiara Lubich. The chosen statement for her chapter was: 'We are just a little hand helping the Church to realize the programme which Jesus indicated: "That they may all be one."' The authors described Chiara as 'the Catherine of Siena of the twentieth century, a great reformer of the Church'. Much publicity surrounded the launch of the book, attended even by a Cardinal from the Vatican. Chiara did not attend.

Every month there are new articles about her and/or some aspect of her Movement appearing in magazines and newspapers in different countries. As I left her after a visit in Switzerland in the summer of 1996, I came across a French magazine in the railway station whose cover story was about Chiara Lubich and the Focolare.

It is true that as 'her' Work has continued to expand over more than half a century, more people than ever are intrigued as to who this personality is. It is difficult within the space of a single book, let alone a magazine article, to illustrate the depth and the many facets of an organization whose work covers so many areas of human activity.

Perhaps also for this very reason, Chiara very rarely grants interviews outside Focolare's own media. Where does one begin to explain the range of the Movement's activities? Besides, every moment of her day is accounted for. She is anxious to ensure that every act she makes is in conformity with the Will of God for her at that moment. (And she understands the Will of God as not being something static, to be confused with a nice comfortable routine, but something dynamic and constantly challenging.) For her, besides her own sanctification, her first duties are as President of the Focolare and the faithful use of the charism entrusted to her.

She has a fondness for one particular title given to the Virgin Mary by the Catholic Church in the Litany of Loreto; Mystical Rose. If the focolare is to be in some way 'a presence of Mary in the Church' it must also be a 'mystical rose'; each and every part of it, every petal, every individusl, must be pleasing to God. As a rose grows from a bud which encloses all its being, and then opens out to reveal so many petals, each petal being a work in itself, so too with the Movement.

Someone once asked Chiara how she managed to feel responsible for so many people. She replied, 'It's not so much that I feel responsible for people; I try to follow God.'

When asked what she thought she had achieved in her life, she replied, 'I think I can say that I have tried to follow God throughout my life. Obviously, there have been mistakes and weaknesses, and I have had to begin again, leaving all that went wrong in God's mercy. My intention has always been to follow God. I have been helped in this by the community, by Jesus in our midst, who has always straightened me out and got me on my feet again.

'What sort of assessment can I make? I think Jesus will be the one to do that. Has He been pleased with what I have done? I would like to hope so, because the Church, His representative, has approved the Movement. But even if He were to say that no, He wasn't pleased, it would be fine with me. In my heart there is only immense gratitude towards Him.'

Of course, it is a teaching of the Catholic Church that there is such a state, or place, known as Purgatory.

'Yes. And who knows how necessary that will be for all of us? But we go towards death not with an attitude of fear: we are going towards Love. And not with the idea of losing anything but with the idea of acquiring things.'

So what is Purgatory, then?

'I think it is a certainty that we are on the way to God, a certainty that we will arrive there. But we will indeed feel the absence of God. But with the certainty that we will reach it. But it *is worth it*. It's worth Purgatory in order to go to Paradise. But in Purgatory there won't be time, it won't be long, the wait won't be long, it will be happening all at the same time, simultaneously.'

And what of evil spirits and the Devil? Do they exist?

'Oh yes, the Devil exists. I remember in the incident when I was once tempted to stop loving Natalia. At that time I was undergoing a lot of trials and spiritual upheavals. Natalia was near me one time and I felt as if there were somebody right next to me telling me, "Don't love her, don't love her, don't love her." You see, charity was and is my very Ideal and if you love, then you'll understand, you'll have light. Because love brings you light. But at that moment I had the impression that it was the Devil right there beside me, telling me not to love, that to love was a waste of time.

'I said to myself, "But Natalia is such a good person that I'll continue to love her anyway", and that's how I got out of it. And I think the Devil went to Hell.'

So, I wondered, what does Chiara Lubich think Heaven will be like?

She threw up her hands and laughed: 'Ah! If I could tell you what Heaven is like!' – as if to say, 'Is that all?' And then, immediately serious, she began to share her understanding of Heaven:

'It seems to me that Heaven is participation, through Christ, in the life of the Holy Trinity, and to find ourselves in the Heart of the Father. And there to participate, as St John of the Cross says, in the life of these three Persons of the Trinity. And in the life of Jesus – a repeating of the mysteries of the life of Jesus. That, it seems to me, is what Paradise will be.

'We'll always see new things, always new things. As I understand it, we will be introduced into the Trinity, and into the dynamics of the Trinity. And it will be always new, always new, always new.

'Because, as the Fathers of the Church say, if we live as Christians we are divinized. And even though we are adopted we will be *truly* children of God. So, as I see it, we will be truly God; not like God, because God is God Himself, but through participation we'll always be truly God.

'And we will have all the inheritance of Jesus, which is the whole of Paradise – in all of its evolution, because it won't be a static, fixed thing. It's dynamic. And it seems to me that it will be a continual renewal of our union with God, the Persons of the Trinity, and among ourselves. Each one of us will be the Paradise of the other. But first the Trinity will be our Paradise. Then there will be Jesus in the Trinity, Mary, each one of us; we will be Paradise for the other person, because each one of us will be God, each with his own personality. So, each one will have something different from us, even though we'll all be God.

'And everything which makes up the inheritance of Heaven will belong to us. As St Paul says, "We are children but also co-heirs with Christ." So if here on earth we already have a wonderful life, a marvellous life, even as the saints have maybe at the end of their lives, Paradise is infinitely more than this.

'So, it is not that death will bring us something sad, it will bring us a door which is opened for us towards something which is extraordinary. And there will be new things; new heavens and new earths. It seems to me that everything will be full of colour. And just as we see the fields and the stars, there will be things because there is a new heaven and a new earth.

'There will be a union of souls. As I envision it, we will feel nature, which will be all one with us. Because in our humanity, even nature will find, in a certain way, its own redemption. Heaven is something altogether wonderful.'

Provincial girl, political instability, the Great Depression, a World War, a bombed city. A consecrated soul, a host of companions, just an ordinary person, the Work of Mary. An Ideal. Home and hearth, Focolare. Fire bearers, Focolarini.

'Behold, I come to make all things new!'
REVELATION 21:5

Quick now, here, now, always —
A condition of complete simplicity
(Costing not less than everything)
and all shall be well and
All manner of things shall be well
When the tongues of flame are in-folded
Into the crowned knot of fire
And the fire and the rose are one.

T. S. ELIOT, *FOUR QUARTETS*

Permanent Mariapoli Around the World as at 1996

Country	City	Name of Mariapolis
Europe		
Italy	Loppiano (Florence)	Renata
Switzerland	Montet	Foco
Switzerland	Baar	Pietra Angolare
Germany	Ottmaring	Nuova Legge
Belgium	Rotselaar	Vita
Spain	Castel d'Aro	Loreto
Croatia	Krizevci	Faro
Poland	Warsaw	Fiore
Americas		
Argentina	O'Higgins	Andrea
Brazil	Vargem Grande Paolo (San Paolo)	Araceli
Brazil	Recife	Santa Maria
Brazil	Belem	Gloria
Mexico	Acatzingo	Il Diamante
USA	Hyde Park, New York	Luminosa
Africa		
Cameroon	Fontem	Maria Mai
Kenya	Nairobi	Piero
Ivory Coast	Man	Vittoria
Asia		
Philippines	Tagaytay (Manila)	Pace
Oceania		
Australia	Melbourne	Marilen

Original Title of Books by Chiara Lubich

Title	First Published	Translated into Languages
Meditazioni	1959	26
Pensieri	1961	5
Frammenti	1963	8
Fermenti di Unità	1963	4
Diario 64/65	1967	3
Tutti Siano Uno	1968	24
Saper Perdere	1969	12
Ai Gen 3	1970	4
La Carità come Ideale	1971	16
Sí, Sí. No, No	1973	12
Colloqui con i Gen	1974	4
Parola di Vita	1975	16
L'Eucaristia	1977	14
L'Attrativa del Tempo Moderno	1978	14
L'Essenziale Oggi	1978	2
Uomini al Servizio di Tutti	1978	14
Gesù nel Fratello	1979	15
Tutti Uno	1979	3
Essere la Tua Parola/1	1980	7
Dio è Vicino	1981	1
Il Sí dell'Uomo a Dio	1981	18
Essere la Tua Parola/2	1982	4
Costruire sulla Roccia	1983	0
La Vita, un Viaggio	1984	8
L'unità e Gesù Abbandonato	1984	16
Incontri con l'Oriente	1986	2

In Cammino col Risorto	1987	5
Parola che Si Fa Vita	1989	11
Cercando le Cose di Lassù	1992	1
Santi Insieme	1994	0
Cristo Dispiegato nei Secoli	1994	0
Scrivere il Vangelo con la Vita	1995	0

Books by Chiara Lubich
published in English translation★

Diary 1964/65
The Eucharist
Fragments of Wisdom
From Scripture to Life
Jesus in Our Midst
Jesus the Heart of His Message: Unity and Jesus Forsaken
Journey
Journey to Heaven
Knowing How to Lose
The Love That Comes From God: Reflections on the Family
May They All Be One
On the Holy Journey
Our Yes to God
Servants of All
Spiritual Writings Volume 1: A Call to Love
Spiritual Writings Volume 2: When Our Love Is Charity
When Did We See You Lord?
When Our Love Is Charity
The Word of Life
Yes Yes, No No

★*All published by New City, New York/London/Manila*

BIBLIOGRAPHY

De Fiores, Stefano, *La 'Nuova' Spiritualita*, Rome, Edizioni
    Studium, 1995
Flannery, Austin, General Editor, *Vatican Council II: The Conciliar
    and Post-Conciliar Documents*, Ireland, Dominican
    Publications, 1975
The Focolare Movement, *Unity: Our Adventure*, New York,
    New City Press, 1987
— *Paolo VI al Movimento dei Focolari*, Rome, Citta Nuova
    Editrice, 1978
Foresi, Pasquale, *God Among Men*, London, New City, 1974
Giordani, Igino, *Diary of Fire*, London, New City, 1981
Lorit, Sergius C. and Grimaldi, Nuzzo M., *Focolare After Thirty
    Years*, New York, New City Press, 1976
Lubich, Chiara, *Diary 1964–65*, New York, New City
    Press, 1987
— *From Scripture to Life*, New York, New City Press, 1991
— *Incontri Con L'Oriente*, Rome, Citta Nuova Editrice, 1986
— *Knowing How to Lose*, London, New City, 1981
— *Man's Yes to God*, London, New City, 1982
— *May They All Be One*, London, New City, 1977
— *Meditations*, London, New City, 1989
— *Servants Of All*, London, New City, 1979
— *The Eucharist*, London, New City, 1979
— *The Word of Life*, London, New City, 1981
— *Where Two or Three*, London, New City, 1977
— *Yes Yes, No No*, London, New City, 1977
McGregor, Bede and Norris, Thomas (Editors), *The Beauty of
    Christ: An Introduction to the Theology of Hans Urs Van Balthasar*,
    Edinburgh, T. & T. Clark, 1994

Mitchell, Donald W., *Spirituality and Emptiness: The Dynamics of Spiritual Life in Buddhism and Christianity*, New York, Paulist Press, 1991

Pochet, Michel, *Stars & Tears: A Conversation With Chiara Lubich*, London, New City, 1985

Renfrew, Charles, *The Litany of Loreto*, London, Catholic Truth Society, 1985

Robertson, Edwin, *Chiara*, Christian Journals (Ireland), 1978

— *The Fire of Love: A Life of Igino Giordani 'Foco'*, London, New City, 1989

— *Catching Fire: The Spiritual Ideal of the Focolare Movement*, Guildford, Eagle, 1993

Rynne, Xavier, *The Second Session*, London, Faber and Faber, 1964

Von Balthasar, Hans-Urs, *A First Glance at Adrienne von Speyer*, San Francisco, Ignatius Press, 1981

— *Mary For Today*, Slough, St Paul Publications, 1987

— *Test everything. Hold fast to what is good*, interview with Von Balthasar by Angelo Scola, San Francisco, Ignatius Press, 1989

Wiltgen, Ralph M., *The Rhine Flows Into the Tiber: A History of Vatican II*, Rockford, Illinois, Tan Books, 1978

Zambonini, Franca, *Chiara Lubich: L'Aventure De L'Unité*, Paris, Nouvelle Cité, 1991

The following reviews were consulted by the author:

Citta Nuova, Rome, Citta Nuova Editrice

L'Osservatore Romano, Rome, Italian and English editions

New City, London, Focolare Movement

Nuova Umanita: Rivista Bimestrale di Cultura, Rome, Citta Nuova Editrice della PAMOM

Pro Dialogo, Rome, Pontificium Consilium Pro Dialogo Inter Religiones

INDEX